manifest.Ø

PublishAmerica
Baltimore

© 2004 by Samson Orion.
All rights reserved. No part of this book may be reproduced, stored in a retrieval system or transmitted in any form or by any means without the prior written permission of the publishers, except by a reviewer who may quote brief passages in a review to be printed in a newspaper, magazine or journal.

First printing

ISBN: 1-4137-1661-X
PUBLISHED BY PUBLISHAMERICA, LLLP
www.publishamerica.com
Baltimore

Printed in the United States of America

manifest.Ø

preliminary orientation for manifestation beyond point-zero
—a manual of quickening

interactions and intercessions
with an entity of alternate origins

Samson Orion

There are forces which permeate this volume,
without and within;
Susan Lee
casts her spell through all of them.

...foreword

§

Every thing is literal.

Fine

...preface

Krishnamurti, a man possessed of brilliant mind and far-seeing eyes, said (paraphrasing liberally) that upon hearing Truth, the world you have known up to that moment ceases to be, instantly. A new world is born containing the incorporated aftershock of the truth that has altered everything, including you who first heard it. Nothing can be done about it. You may, if you wish, spend energy and effort in denying the effects of new Truth, but the expenditure is exactly the same as incorporating the new order, and the measured ease of your familiar, comfortable old world is forever distant in either case.

So, if you are happy, blissful and deeply content, avoid Truth at all costs. But what if complete happiness has eluded you? What if you have always known things could be better?

The information contained in *manifest.Ø* came into my hands, into my head more accurately, through extraordinary avenues. In the winter of 1996 I culminated almost 30 years of seeking and experimenting with consciousness in one horrific and glorious endeavor. It left me wrung out, completely spent and wanting only, finally, to do nothing but rest. That's when, of course (and trite as it sounds), "it" happened. Even in hindsight I have no memory of that moment to reference. Nor, at the time, did I have any realization that anything had shifted. Nevertheless, I was in a new place, transported into Wonderland (otherLand, more probably), mind and physical body, too. A sudden simultaneous resident of two realities, or planes, or dimensions, or realms—choose your favorite unsupportable term. Without effort my memory was eidetically precise. All the volumes I had ever read were open to recall and their contents revealed at many levels. Connections between every point and purpose were visible and serenely obvious, undistorted; I could contact any cell in my body, interact with time as a comrade. On a whim, and while still deeply in that place—but also here—I one day began to write in a compulsive cloud with *manifest.Ø* resulting.

I state that "I" began to write, but because occupying more than one place at a time bends all sense of stability and identity, there is no way to suggest a single named author. So it was not me. But none other than me. Neither is this work channeled through this author. Nor through anyone else…It's something else again. I make no effort to justify or prove its veracity as there is no standard or august body to measure its truth.

A wondrous sense of community and belonging surfaces when an individual experiences significant pieces of the Whole. This has been well documented by individuals who have had epiphanies and near-death experiences. Afterwards there was an urgent need to share it, to let everyone know the size and scope, the *beauty* of the experience. It's in the DNA; an indelible part of a social species. Even so, my first intention was to remain anonymous in hope of adding some small buffer between myself and I knew not whom. Those claiming insight or access to any knowledge beyond the daily news are rarely received graciously. Heralds and vanguards are welcomed even less and, too often, the messenger pays an undeserved price. Strange forces are involved in the opening of doorways to and from alien realms and I had no wish to suffer the unpredictable, often turbulent, nature of strangers. Now, after continued immersion into this material, I understand that others—my fearsome "strangers"—cannot be excluded from this unfolding and are much needed as well.

The manuscript was all but incomprehensible at first. From the perspective of my alternate reality every word flowed into the next, succinct and clear. Every subtlety was far-reaching and transparent in implication. But in the reality we commonly share, it was compressed and inaccessible, essentially a form of shorthand—sketches—notes requiring much fleshing out to fill the tremendous gaps in continuity that were very noticeable "here" but not "there." The work as here presented remains, essentially, shorthand, even after continued reading and subsequent expansions. The experience of working with this material and the taxing nature of acclimatization to multiple realities has changed me. It has also convinced me that the ability to sustain two simultaneous, not always complimentary, viewpoints is accessible to anyone willing to extend a simple (as in pure) and steady effort.

manifest.Ø is by no means easy reading. Had I chosen to weave the data into a concocted story or adventure, then its popularity and appeal would no doubt be greatly enhanced. But I believe in the information given and alluded to in *manifest.Ø* and feel it warrants presentation as is: as information of import and value and, therefore, without the need of ritual dramatization. There are those who seek, truly seek, access to tantalizing mysteries forever veiled throughout human endeavor; those who welcome fresh input make use of new frames-of-reference as aids in putting the puzzles of life together. To those seekers a fictionalized storyline is of no benefit; and it is among those, *most directly*, that this peculiarly-worded gnosis may find audience. And it is to those who sincerely hold open the possibility of stirring fascination and excitement within themselves, no matter the chance of danger or disruption, that I tender this work.

I do extend my most humble and heartfelt thanks to a small cadre of friends, confidants, and intimates of whom I think fondly in this moment. They whom I will not hamper, seduce, or anchor, by listing via pen and paper…

…Autumn 2003

...table of contexts

...preface 9
...introductory note 15
1 ... entry 17
2 ... first concepts 22
3 ... contract 33
4 ... places and entities 43
5 ... quarantine 56
6 ... bodies / 1 65
7 ... take a breath 74
8 79
9 ... reentry: what is 81
10 ... what can be 83
11 ... caveat 87
12 ... reward 90
13 ... apéritif 94
14 ... targets 106
15 ... realities and boxes 117
16 ... second set 126
17 ... glimpses, a sampling 133
18 ... practice 164
19 ... Assume 171
20 ... discipline 177
21 ... energy 188
22 ... using the ally 195
23 ... payment 203
24 ... tracking 207
25 ... bodies / 2 212
26 ... treasure 218
27 ... al segno 225
    ...glosses 229

...introductory note

This is a handbook for human beings. Although that admits a huge and diverse audience, the only requisite commonality (beyond an obvious biology) is nothing more stringent than a desire for "something more." Source materials have been furnished and determined by beings of non-human perspective. To them, there exists an invisible background that is woven into all our activities—threaded with blind routines, unbreakable compulsions, and arbitrary biases and assumptions. This unseen conditioning is also infused into protocols of behavior and even molds our thoughts to great degree. In *manifest.Ø*'s remote perspective, this background does not exist and is consequently absent from the offered data. The information in this work can therefore be difficult to absorb because syntax, language, and logic—all spawned in this self-same background—become unfamiliar, oddly disconcerting, and presented in a manner that lacks the familiar prejudices. Nevertheless, even difficult information can be used by body and mind and, here, serviceably used for altering our current somnambulant energy fields. Access to a universe far larger than even the infinite reaches of our imagination then opens.

A few words on technique: focus and read slowly, especially at first. *manifest.Ø* originates in a place which moves differently than *here*: faster, more fluidly, more abruptly. It displays its essence, and opens its portals, only when its intrinsic rhythms are found and matched. There is nothing psychic or unearthly in this process. It is done everyday to feel the emotions within poetry, or coax sensations from a painting, or succumb to the intimacy of a dance. Focusing upon the words at a pace that invites your own facilities to absorb without rebellion will ease you towards that essential rhythm. Break the focus, and what remains is conceptually challenging verbiage framed in an awkward patois. The diligent honing of focus is useful for many things; why not refine it here?

To those who wend their way here, my sincerest recommendation is to treat this work (as it is wise to treat information from any source) gingerly. Note the reactions of your body while reading. Observe with curiosity, rather than automatically responding to shifts in mood and comfort; tendencies to dull or distort your interest, unusual emotions suddenly arising. Information regarding the core of what we are, the multiple realities that surround us, and the ongoing interactions between them will always stimulate dormant machinery housed within our flesh-and-blood forms. This certainty alone, if there be no other, has brought you here. In allowing the flow of sensations to arise unimpeded (a task of considerable undertaking) the reactions of your system will dictate much and direct you towards still more should you choose to listen.

1...entry

I have come upon the records known to you as books. These artifacts are not of my schooling nor of my understanding in the ways of teaching, yet they do possess a wholeness and purity that honors knowledge. In respect for this, your devised form of record, I now afford you self-entry, an introduction. It is proper, yes? Know first that I am not one clothed in the physically dense matter that you call *body*. Know, too, that I am neither dead, spirit, dybbuk, nor being of light. No name, label, or image do I offer or take on. All such appellations demand exactitude in structure and form, they coax and urge, they create and fix. They serve as anchors to minimize change—I alone am master to change within and about me and do not herein yield mastery. I am here through agreement with one to be referred by title only as *scribe*; this for reasons that are my own. I am that and such as I am. Thusly have we honored greeting and introduction.

There are those of you, while living the course of your lives, sometimes sitting, standing, or moving about, who are never truly comfortable. A tiny impulse, a feeling that all is *not quite right* is constantly there, only a tip-of-the-tongue distant, should you allow yourself to taste of it. It is but background: true and faint, yet always within reach, never out of touch. Within your realms of daily existence have been created innumerable artifices and methods for distraction of your senses, yes? Ways to become removed or even oblivious to all that you may know and feel. You know them: drink and drugs and mindless pursuits, fanaticism and politics and beliefs in gods greater than yourselves; this gives name to but a few. Because of self-indulgence or weariness, pain or disappointment, you partake of such distractions. Even so, it remains the true and veritable truth that this awareness of *not quite right* continues its pervasive discomfort in all the world around you and nothing sought or found has enabled erasure of this unpleasantry for long. Every moment of passion, whether of creation, or achievement, or victory, must overcome a whisper of malaise or dissatisfaction creeps in. A lessening prevails—and the peaks of the moment pass. Every dream and inspiration has been carried out, always and only by putting this nagging intrusion aside. You have lived your lives and your ongoing generations amidst a quiet background of unrest.

Look you now deeply into that area of the Self, so named, the area of disquietude where you have known this as truth familiar and often fear to go—it is a request of some import to the bodies, for it is more than your minds I come to address. Find the faint thread of unrest. It is always there, for all that is you and done by you holds it intact. Know that the place now mentioned is guarded with the taste of avoidance, as in the manner preferred by the system known as *you*. Hear now that sensations of discomfort, anxiety, upset, or fear, among others, will herald accurate approach to this dark and secret place. Perhaps, for you, that guardian to the forgotten core of thee and you will assume the guise of false logic and so intervene convincingly, bearing other matters to attend; or distraction by snobbery, citing as obviously poor fiction that which be scribed upon these pages; or dismissal by righteousness, a smug contentment that you remain safe and untouched as all evidence before you is impotent and false. Any avenues of veer and sway are suspect, all misdirections away from the hidden thread, so quietly whispered and suggested to your thoughts, are of note—for you contrive with no one other than thee. Should you nonetheless dare to harken upon that doorway which opens into your own secret of secrets and brave the demons that both hide and guard it, then wisdom will follow. Just beyond the first barriers of reluctance stands the release of doubt. Relief lends confirmation and surety to what it is you read upon this gathering of pages.

Now, the dulling habits of forgetfulness and uncertainty bind you. So tentative, so unaccustomed to bravery. With but a spark of resolve, even a short blink of a moment will prove sufficient for knowing with inner certainty that only simple truth sits here before you—should only entry to your guarded places be sanctioned. Once there, you may grasp and penetrate why it is you have hidden this passageway and posted guards of your own self defense.

Beyond your barriers here described stands entry to many worlds and space of differing realities, venues far greater than those of your acquaintance in the now. There lies more within the *you* of you than has been seen before. The fragile shell of the unimaginative world you have constructed and termed 'real' can now be felt. Its limited scope and unsophisticated assumptions become blatant and obvious. Its mere size—the lack of it—invites the blood-blush of shame at so meager a house to dwell in, so impoverished a facade to have gloried in—such will strike you in rapid understanding. Sadness and disillusionment will follow, for lines of hope and purpose assumed to be solid lose strength upon illuminating a tenuous and enfeebled foundation. The secret place is but a veil which covers sloppiness and immature hopes. Torn away, wisdom flows in clarity. Fantasy and 'real' blend and blur when held uncompromised up to the true glare of lucidity. Sadly now will false icons wither: the dreams of youth will not come about, they are seen as the dreams of children. The romance of your certainty cannot be realized, you have sought the embrace of mirages—not mortals to meet and match you. Confident security in life and love will be seen as ever more the fable, and eternity suddenly beckons harshly without fulfillment promised or attained. Age and mortality gain in prominence. Clichés and platitudes, pretending to bolster yet never satisfying, become lies outright. The wisdom to witness and see clearly rests within you. Though it be painful, clarity of self-view does clamor as urgently as any caged beast for freedom, seeking finality in outward expression under open skies, freedom as can be tasted in full savor only upon release…if you but allow the open door. Yet is this not also the emptying of dreams, the unannounced need to toil and rebuild all that you have known? The dismissal of everything and resulting bleak outlook as you begin—must begin—again from nothing. This has the somber weight of ruin and devastation, yes?

I do not appear now as cruel destroyer of hopes and dreams and possible futures. Such destruction was well in place before any intention of my choosing. I am not come as sayer of doom nor forecaster of evil or despair. Though simple to judge by your arbitrary standards as *bad* or *harsh*, the passages laid down herein are not wedded to any such moral or philosophical standard. Offered now by that which I be is information pure, data unflavored by *good* or *bad*. Any such description is but reduction. Taken in this manner, you may embrace simple knowledge without a predetermined value and so absorb no perspective from which to compare yourself and find yourself lacking or in high achievement. In this way you may grow in your preferred direction, your *instinctively* preferred direction, and I may not become enslaved to thee or by thee in the mimicry of savior, healer, teacher, or saint. Here now are facts presented without urgency or motive of agenda. They carry the vibration of verity and as such require no statement of origin, nor résumé of accreditation from a being of eminence (as if he, curiously, has been bestowed the duty of assuring beyond doubt the purity of bountiful knowledge brought forth). Check all data by your innermost agreement: by trembling in your body, by tears that arise, by whispers and voices of your mind and imagining, by memories and indistinct flashes (*déjà vu*, yes?) that tug and almost bloom full into this day's light.

    Listen, then, to that which now unfolds. Remain alert in *how* you listen, and so come to know that your discomfort, malaise, and unrelenting emptiness is not the result of your failing. Never have you erred or fallen low, seduced by serpents. This clinging discomfort comes not from values unreached or goals poorly aimed but is only the faintest whisper of a larger song and a terrible arrangement of circumstances of which you are an innocent part. There is no blame and no misdeed. You are not at fault. You have done nothing wrong. The unrest is upon you for entirely distant reasons. You have not let anyone down nor reneged your end of some bargain. You need carry this burden no more.

    Learn and thereby remember the state of being, the status quo, of what you are and of the world in which you live. But listen. But feel. Begin to see, once again, the portrait of reality that enfolds you and upon which understanding you may act, finally, in accord with the small measure of free will that remains yours, untainted and unsullied. Know from this inference that what you believe to understand as free will has been sapped and distorted in ghastly and savage ways.

    Use that which you can, and what portion you will, of this knowledge given. Take it up freely. Test it in caution then embrace its cleanliness. It comes to you a sovereign whole, an extension beyond the plebeian view, and claims no sponsor. Knowledge has no affiliate or group loyalty. It is for your use as well as that of any other.

    Your systems, your bodies, do not readily remember how to make use of untainted offerings. Thus must my proferment seem as but suggestions for expansion, and thus must make you chary of ease of acceptance. Seeing newly the beginnings of expanded sight, utilization of your attributes and senses in fresh combinations in unaccustomed sequences will therefore feel as hardship. Bathing in strange concepts will be unfamiliar. Clamor will invade and beset you. Resistance will mount, bearing the pressure of reluctance. This is known and taken into account in the now telling. Therefore and thus

MANIFEST.Ø

herein is it stated: data to be woven through this, my offering of wisdom, is purposefully conveyed and reiterated in redundancy. As your systems are ill prepared in the acceptance of newness and resultant stretching of body in totality, data is given in brevity of form, in partial completeness, and without extensive detail as per the love of scholars. This is of fact to be known, yet as per need of systems under besiegement of new learning will it come to sufficiency in repetition throughout.

2...first concepts

You live in a box. As you are alive, as you notice the sense of your presence, so are these contained within the box. The sun, the stars, the farthermost reaches described to you via your sciences and theoreticians and the Hubble telescope, are all contained inside of this box. Also enclosed are your minds and all appetites, ideas, images, your imaginings and quickenings and the impulses that run through them—neatly contained. All thought for so long of your generations has for so long been trained in disregard and disbelief of any other universality but those of your immediate horizons—and that is why it passes unknown and unseen that you are in a box. There are no corners to seek, no delineated silent walls to feel, nothing to suggest containment. Nevertheless you are in a box and obey the laws that govern its fabric.

Universes in expansion are delineated by movement. Delineation invites and creates boundaries. They, in turn, seek the agreement of consensus awareness, which manifests structure, which self-defines in steadiness.

Structure, via rules and laws that must be obeyed, is a component of ordered awareness. It is aspected of existence, and not by necessity, a thing of limitation or confinement. For example physics, as you term your science of reality, is nought but a collaboration of laws, those which govern physical bodies. Contained therein is gravity, electromagnetism, thermal dynamics, light and radiation as by named example and other such pedantic assortments of your wisdom; being widely known, you are surely governed by them fully and well. You have adopted these laws by consensus agreement as the fundamental rulers of that which is needed for life, and subject yourselves to them willingly. They are hailed as the natural order and thus are placed into a working background for all that has happened or will happen around you. This structure of law and ordered form is accepted without resistance or lament. You have no heroes who once adventured outward to challenge Temperature to make colder ice, or threatened Distance from the sun to bring a longer day. The natural order cannot be dared or defied for such concept may not arise and remain, so has it come to be. Thus when you dislodge a coffee cup from its rest atop the kitchen table you are instantly aware that the ramifications of that physical action may not be ignored or delayed: the cup will fall, strike the floor surface, shatter (in all probability), fluid will exit in circular array, sound will result, motion and time will alter in your bodies while in the presence of this ordering; intake of breath will cease, vibration and frequencies of simultaneous events perceived by you as 'tension' will appear in the surrounds, calculation and evaluation will assess, stimulate, then fade and disappear. All such results are readily known and predictable in far advance, yet no sequence of this ordering feels to you as unyielding oppression by fate, by decree, by forces which mold you to their sinister needs. Currents of wind and moisture collide each very second to bring about weather. You have grown in adaptation to thunder, dust, rain, and unseasonable heat and cold as a segment of your term of living. You do not cry out against Clotho and Lachesis, or feel encumbered unfairly by such occasions, though they regulate your plans of the moment and intentions for the future. Neither does the weather cackle and scheme and laugh when you are inconvenienced or thwarted, battered or beaten by storm. The laws of physics explain these events and more. Simply because you cannot see the basic fractional units of these events in progress does not suggest your disbelief in their occurrence nor rebellion against their proliferation. You are soothed and lulled; life is nice.

Laws governing your invisible box are laws such as those hereinabove mentioned. They are in effect at all times, a part of the 'natural order' and an immutable condition of living. Your common state of being unaware does not exempt their affect or make their existence questionable, or optional. A box that contains instincts and worlds, stars and weather, laws and situations is called, by your language terming, *reality*. This labeling is a corruption of misunderstanding. The box and reality are not equal; the limitations of language force my choice in usage of words. I bend them so in effort to introduce concepts which you may strive to hold as stable and true. Power is woven into thought transformed into words. Therein lies layer and depth of coded meaning, ready for any to claim by right of understanding. Do not fall now complacent to mistake as if truly in understanding of the words of language so commonly used: *real* and *reality*. Though arrayed before you in this offering as *book*, you have no veritable basis upon which to determine the meaning of these words, or grasp related concepts at this time. And, watch you now, as even into this moment does anger bridle you at the telling of your miscomprehension. Blind assumption, and the arrogance of the unlearned, rule your species. You rage in instants, deny approach to all, and remain aloof in regards to such areas of the unknown invisibles which surround you. Be calmed. No blame or disrespect is tendered by such, my statements of fact, whether indelicate or unsoftened. My placement here-now allows observed reflection of all you mirror and thus reveal. Ignorance and riot are seen in full prevail. Become not dismayed nor bristle with distracting anger here. Rather be gentled, for to any in clear thinking can be seen that all is bathed in ignorance, perforce, prior to the intake of knowledge.

Though you cannot know it with certainty, because you have not gleaned to experience otherwise, the reality in which you live is tightly sealed, with a very few 'air holes.' These, being largely unused, suffocate the bodies in untimely haste. That is to say that breathing freely and plentifully is difficult indeed, making all subsequent efforts even more exhausting. Evidence is abundant. Deeds or dreams of untroubled freedom exact a toll of fatigue and depletion—it is merely a matter of guileless observation while remaining alert and seeing what is.

You have urges and hungerings for safety and security, yet none exists. These images and ideas remain stillborn, as thought forms only, for they do not manifest in the reality of your world. Hard work will not insure an abundance of money. Money will not avail you freedom from strife. Barriers against strife will not push away blackguards or mollify enforcement police. Police cannot protect you from governments who quickly learn to vote themselves largesse. Government cannot protect you from distant governments and all governments together cannot offer you safety from the planet, itself in constant violent motion. The ground beneath your feet may at any moment erupt in flame, or quake, or flood, or pestilence—no, there is no safety or security here.

You have desires to attain immortality. Therefore you produce children, monuments, great wars to mark history, and great works to mark the collective subconscious. Time, unmarkable, makes dust of everything. The heroes of your history books were once gorged, filled with coursing blood and visions directing power enough to change destinies and resculpt the face of your globe. Once gone, they retain no eternal fire to leap from the dry page where they live as story and legend. Immortality in history and myth is not the true continuation of the hero himself, neither his power nor his breath nor thought, only a faint and vapid diminishment. Yet even this tiny semblance of postponement, a pitiable retelling from memory, is deemed enviable…so strong is the pull of the everlasting. Children do not retain the vitality of parents or continue their passionate pursuits. Statues erode through wind. Tombstones whisper weakly to detached and unappreciative future voyeurs, and pyramids reduce to curiosities of conjecture and debate. No matter the myriad millions of determined reiterations, you will not find eternity through such means.

So, lightly touched upon, are observed your concepts of *safe* and *legacy*—two among the great dreams and deep desires of the heart. They are as shrines of unceasing toil and futile striving in petition for that which is not. In all the populations in the grouping of your species, for all of your known times of plodding passage, has this been so. Energy is thrown wildly, expended, discharged until weariness exhausts you, and breath is ragged short. Were it consciously known in awakened truth and fullness, as do your bodies well know in truth and fullness, how distant are your graspings from possible bloom, then the spartan intake of breaths drawn to sustain you in furtherance of the upcoming days could be heard as sibilant gasping, fearful sounds of desperation for yet one additional moment wherein rescue might arrive.

You have other dreams and great yearnings unfulfilled. But it is easy to cite many upon many examples of your imbedded futilities without need to be of faraway origin and place, as am I. Should you take notion to inspect the great raptures of your species, those ideas and ideals which are cherished most, you, too, will find the same frustrated dismay as noted above for security and immortality. As one they fall against a weak, unsteady backdrop, a stage prop which becomes real only in particular moments of focus, only in particular contexts, only alongside particular longings, but never in sustained and common day physical truth. Dreams of your deepest heart are never predictably known, reliably known, as are the sequence of events for the shattered coffee cup known. From where, then, do such ideas come? From where do you draw the models for your heroes and champions? What known, actual experiences have you used upon which to base your nobility, grace, and honor? Where, then, are exhibited the exalted icons for which you sacrifice your children and exchange long years of sweat and labored task? They are nowhere seen upon your planet. Yes, in possible truth, they exist for scant moments in rare individuals or in flashes here, now yonder there, but so uncommon is the occurrence that the populations of the world rumble and gossip of these flashes for generations, centuries, when they arise. It is certainly scarce and beyond predictable measure. Why is it that you have so many notions and ideals unsupported by avenues of realization? How is it that you think, and hope, and muse in reveries so outlandish relative to the ways in which events truly appear? These resound in you as just and reasonable inquiries of thought, yes?

I prolong in this telling. It is redundancy for focus of emphasis. So much of your existence is shaped and molded by presumptions and craving which come from a place unknown to you, yet nests blithely accepted as an integral part of reality. Notice that in places where coffee cups might break, the measurement of tables and shelves are reliably ample to insure steadiness and confident dimension. Notice that in areas where the earth shakes frequently, objects of fabrication are designed to account for such movement. Notice how you have adjusted to rules which govern the environment of your surroundings and so do you plan your life accordingly. Where actions are noticed, where trends are acknowledged and recognized, where patterns become obvious in their punctuality…there books are written containing mention of what has been observed, songs are written with these same as topics, chatter and street lore contain them as reference, studious beings explore and strive to comprehend the phenomenon of their ways. Always, experience and observation translates into physical action and creation. They can be shown in proof to happen, to hold existence, in the physical real world around you. This forms the collective background and far reach of horizon for all that you call *real*. What, then, might explain that no great passion born in mankind, agreed upon in the minds of mankind, is readily exhibited in the physical realm where mankind lives? Except in the rarest of cases? Except in dreams and what you call (and deny the verity of) fantasies? Except in only those cases where you refuse to accord belief?

Consider: perhaps *real* is not what you assume it to be.

Consider: perhaps *real* is not where you think it to be; perhaps *real* applies to elsewhere, a place entirely other than *here*.

If real could be elsewhere, might *possibly* be somewhere else, consider then:

Perhaps mankind remembers, somehow, the place that *is* real.

Perhaps such a memory is of a time actual and true.

Perhaps mankind has not always lived here.

Perhaps mankind is not originally from here at all.

Perhaps he has been here for a relatively short time, and perhaps some parts of him have not fully adjusted

to this environment so that adaptation to rules that apply to another place is yet held and in use.
Perhaps that other place is the place that is somewhere else.

Such a fanciful list could explain, in possible part, why that which you consider as treasure—beauty, loft, serenity and their like—is buried within all your species, throughout your globe, throughout your times and tales, universally in hearts and souls yet does not appear as tangible truth upon the world that surrounds you. Such would account for behavior out of true with the environment of your surrounds, and of actions imbalanced towards fluidity and contentment. Surely this is worthy of a pardonable curiosity, of a simple consideration, yes?

Inscribed herein reside essays and explorations into 'somewhere else,' concepts in origination within and of a different box, illuminations of a separate reality. And if origination in another place were, indeed, to be the fact and veritable truth, then obvious lines of curiosity are prudent to explore—can this not be so? Can you but benefit the being that is you from willing examination of all that might arise from such avenues of inquiry? Since you do not fully remember coming here or asking to be transported here, yet are undoubtedly here and carrying the memories of an unknown home, then undeniably and unmistakably you have been brought or placed here. A being or beings other than yourselves, and by means unguessable, must have affixed you to this world and into this reality and here you remain without benefit of memory or knowledge of the home from which you came. Continuing this line finds you without means of return, should you ever come to wish it. Therefore this box of your unchosen reality is not just any box, but a box remote from conscious choosing, distant from decision or desire. The laws which govern this reality are not fully known to you as you are conditioned by other laws, yet, being here, you are governed by them nonetheless. Though they do not elicit comfort or peaceful resolve it is not possible to rebel against them nor is available to you the seeking of alternatives, since you hold no perspective from whence to choose viable alternatives. Finally you must comply as best you can, for laws governing vast spatial realms are mathematically intolerant and the penalties of disobedience are severe. Your systems are subject to their stricture so long as you remain and without specialized knowledge, the fundamentals of which you lack, no doorway will open towards departure. So ordered, the conditions here seem demanding, forbidding oftentimes, as if this were a training site or manner of school. This is a concept familiar in your many cultures and languages. Yet even amidst such violent schooling does leak the traces and encoded specks of an other Home. These nascent jots of knowing flow alive and frequently but, from want of guide or wisdom, they are translated into fantasies of wondrous life, of eternal peace, of serenity and love eternal upon your departure by demise. Gallant promises that all to come is fair and fine; but elsewhere, so long as you are no longer living, or here. Such are the legends and prayers of hope and aspiration arising even in so rigid a box, indeed. By whatever name or label is chosen: school or purgatory, Karma or choice, this reality threatens security and incites ideas that question and challenge the existence of free will at the very least. How does your language of words term an arrangement wherein choice is denied, dreams are shattered, and futures are bleakly predictable? Where options for release are known only to be attained by singular way of decrepitude, then decease? Where situation or station may not shift or alter so long as one remains in one bounded place? Such title by word is simple upon reflection as language has record of freedom and movement denied: thrall, bondage, servitude, prison, coercion, or slavery. Choose you a term by title or name—this be the shape of your box.

Imagine, then, the existence of other realms, worlds, and solar systems, and immense infinities filled with unfamiliar constellations. There, living within them, are all diverse manner of beings with abilities no less distinct or less remarkable than you yourselves possess. There are many ways in which consciousness and awareness, attributes which you consider to be of high value, may be configured other than in the housing of your familiar rendering and form. Regions and their populations exist where flesh is not of carbon base, where genetics are not by pairs in number 23. Where coincident placement within solid phased matter is essential, not denied. Where *weak force* acts as collapsing object, stationary in space. It is from another such place, otherwise configured, that I come to address you, from wherein I house my gathered awareness, wherein I cavort and speculate on mine own existence. It is available to observe the bands of probability and opportunity of a universe wherein reality configures atop successive reality, and then again, and so is reconfigured anew and once more, and endlessly thus. I have travelled the levels and frequencies to see and witness what you may term only as wondrous imagination. I have enjoined with meta-quarks who sing atomic arias; observed particle light run in circular spires. I have been in matrix to places, coordinates, that carry the essential tone structure of *Home*. Once, long ago by your counting of age and time, I observed myself in refusal to participate in a biological experiment whose outcome is the species that you are. My refusal directed an alternate line of potential to awake, and thus forged my own linkage with your species.

Aside: *Acceptance would also have formed an alternate linkage. We are bound by virtue of creating the coming-into-manifest-proximity. This has been known to you and come into distortion, loftily misnamed 'destiny.'*

Also, orders of sequence demanded by my invitation to participate in such experimentation opened new worlds of possibility in participation. I explored with boldness and came upon inertia-less systems based in stasis by structure. Wherein, there, I felt my own system and form trapped, pushed against the limits of my own being while greeted in welcome by entities there in habitation. I absorbed by translation the possibility of doubt, insincerity, the blackness of disavowal and calumny, and in those instances I knew myself to be in a box whose similarity is akin to that of your now.

Aside: *I am bound to track your existence, its interweaving with the known that houses you. Thus, by Observation and Her contaminating virtues, must aspects of that which arises before you, and to you, mingle with the ongoing flow of that which befalls and arises as per my own existence.*

My contracts and agreements were, then, not as yours. Therefore I lingered but for the moments of learning and sensation. Yet did I become in acquaintance known to the agony that you feel. I have the origin sensations of pain, unhappiness and the itch that will not be scratched stored within me. Of this you must be apprised. You live where dreams may never be fully manifested for no dreams from the realms wherein your dreams are born may manifest with permanence in this space you call *here*. Rebel if desire so calls, but your supplications for betterment go unanswered. Even Hope, that final element of chance, is mockingly present only as an illusion offered by Despair for there is, truly, no hope. Only breaking your box, enabling journey to other realities and a return to Home restores the memory which resides within you and permits the body's full reconnect with the stable reality of those memory's points of origin. Such enterprise of endeavor is neither simple nor directly possible. Paradox and other forces stand as immutable barriers unless they be overcome by mastery. Getting out of the box carries the rapture of the infinite worlds and offers nothing at all—both at once. Preliminary offerings towards such endeavor is given and, lo, held by embrace of your flesh hands in this moment of now.

First and foremost it is to be known that you lack in information.
—Of the depths of knowledge now afforded to you and the levels of need within you. Of the meaning of *box* and references to *box*. Of purpose and passion. Of dedication—yea, but here indeed are some things known. Furthermore, it becomes timely to recognize that you become truculent and unruly in the face of new wisdom. You act as if threatened or conscripted into drudgery.
Information exists: formless, calm and serene, pristine and available. It has no volition. It is not an activator, it is data. Knowledge.

Aside: Information pure may adjoin your system to engender a febrile calenture and fiery ardor—this must be inserted here as now stated in homage to Paradox, for that one must become your intended opponent and thereupon will fire be needed.

This you must learn and acknowledge. Should it then be, having read thus far, having monitored your responses, having recognized the resonance of true fact or the jarring of faint memories, that you elect to continue in the partaking of further knowledge, be warned: The results of eating this apple become of your own making. It will not bring about a life more pleasant or eased in comfort. It will, in fact, open sores and wounds. You will lament and curse yourself for the foolishness of exploration—such being always the taste of adventure while in the ongoing and yet perilous state (the great retellings of wonder and beauty, the excitement and fulfillment of danger, the pride and sweet conceit of successfully baiting Peril: these are enjoyed in the afterwards time). Knowledge now brought forward will, however, supply you with options in areas that you cannot in this moment suspect. No loss or diminishment will occur, everything will balance. The laws of many realities dictate the immutable nature of balance, so of this there need be no given assurance.

Take pause in immediacy. Having entered upon this moment of now there is known and registered within your bodies the calm clarity of decision as to whether you will invest to turn another page or whether you will not. The bodies do not recognize or rely upon doubt, or delay prior to assured proof of knowing; having read even thus far and confronted stimulus in thought or sensation through wisdom and concept—you *knew*. Such certainty is rendered, always, in instant now. With sincerity and humility most profound I submit to suggest the honoring of the inside voice which elicits you to stay, or go forward. You will neither accelerate nor fall back, hold less power or more by one choice over the other. The mechanics of preference and manifest outcomes make impossible the ultimate loss or gain of energy due to choice made in purity. There are an infinite number of doorways to open. All possibilities cannot be chosen. The choosing of one, any one, immediately removes the chance, and closes forever the choice of another. This is not harm but the wonder and ecstasy of awareness. Therefore do not concern yourself with one best or proper choice. Honor only the true decision of your body's inner language and decree. No threat hangs in the balance.

This offering, though bound in form to be *book*, is not structured with plot and characters or designed to unfold mysteries in story-like rhythm, pleasant and mannerly. Data is presented in accord with order arising within, crystallized into proper sequence as thought distills into language. Prepare to invite whatever appears before you as both host and guest bearing potentials of learning.

Preliminary instruction and guidance follow the sole and small preparation which may be heard, usefully, in your state of now. Allow your own body/mind to impel you, or restrain you, as you absorb information. Information offered here must be honorably invited, taken deeply into your intimate zones. You may not mimic this data by way of note-taking or discussion. It will not duplicate, translate, or be readily shared. Do not attempt to emulate your reading by speaking or repeating in exactness of these words. A reshaping of meaning and intent will automatically occur as they adjust to being housed, howsoever briefly, inside of your uniqueness. You are cautioned against decreeing certain portions of the data acceptable and disregarding other portions. Such bias will establish a value system not based upon knowledge. The data will prove elusive and distort under such forces. You may not, skillfully, become inspired by it once, angered by its existence next, depressed by its portent third, and create conclusions thereby. Conclusions exist only as the averaging of guesses. Great blossoming of knowledge arises from impartial ingestion of data and the blending within your system of new information. Wisdom, that which is *known*, certainty, and core assurance issue through means not touted by your institutions of learning. Yet such alternative routes to the gaining of knowledge must be employed for utilization of data originating in this work. Entry, such entry, your entry, via willing immersion into fields of data affects totality totally.

Again. Therefore do not concern yourself with best or proper choice. Honor only the true decision of your bodies' inner voice. There is nothing to lose. All is symbiosis. Everything matters. Everything is precise.

3...contract

Though medical tests and counts of respiration appear to make my statement simple, and any mirror or prick by thorn of rose account it more inane: your body is alive. Not only because you inhabit it, and so fortify its machineries, but despite the fact that you inhabit it. It is alive in every sense: It has wants and desires, retains and utilizes knowledge, grows, makes decisions, and is influenced by its surroundings. Your body has hungers and shows areas of weakness and frailty. You must understand this to be literal. Precise. Accept that these words are neither parable nor metaphor nor a belaboring of the obvious. It is true that the body does not consistently act in the manner of a wholly integrated, enthusiastically alert, or vitally assertive sentient being. This is, in part, because you are ignorant and unaware of the very nature of this life-form, but primarily because the bodies have been misguided and ill tended, poorly trained for millennia with misinformation and forgetfulness until you, that which you think of as the being *you*, have come to believe that the outstanding and essential core of your existence is your mind. Because of this unsupported preference and belief has your species disregarded and subjugated the bodies as flesh of lesser rank, and as constituent part less bright and less capable as well. You are under the clouded illusion that the mind directs all action while tirelessly, unerringly cataloging, identifying and translating a river of stimulus, reaction, and desire. Another widely proclaimed school of thought and belief exalts a 'spirit' as the aspect of primary and immutable significance. This paradigm is widely held in reverence though no single thing is known in verity of this sacred and invaluable spirit aspect. Efforts in quantifying or examining your systems for spirit content are met with ridicule, violence, and righteous anger as if seeking the obvious and known-in-certitude were heresy. Mind is allowed of examination yet so many assumptions and critical self-servings stand in place that only knowledge which will fit to accommodate the bias of current vogue has been permitted to flourish.

Determination that mind or spirit are foremost in hierarchy of the system, or that so sparsely populated are the elements and intricacies of that which is *you* is belief so thinly based as to be sibling to pure conjecture and neighbor to grand madness. Such ideas negate and dishonor volumes of constant input from the bodies and provoke an inharmonious union within the entities that are grouped together and form the assembly that is *truly* the union that is *you*.

Bodies are multiple-composite creatures. They live in many worlds simultaneously and have the skills and capabilities necessary for maneuvering in various realms of general invisibility to you now. Yet and so, the bodies also live here in this time and space that you know only by term and word as *here*. They have been grounded here firmly, adapted by energetic and biological imperatives to make this plane of existence, and this planet called your Earth, a point-zero home base. Although, in truth, of distant origin, through embrace of ambient laws and by tenure of extended occupation within this reality your bodies resonate contentedly in this local clime. A simple introspection does reveal the prevalent truth of your feelings: Note what tenderness, awe, and exaltation are uplifted upon viewing your Earth by way of model, replica globe, or simple photograph of paper; note your distress upon thoughts of forever leaving; and the great array of emotions and clichés all of which gratify and becalm when in mere reference to 'home.' There is no battle to confront the knowing that *here* is profoundly established as sanctuary and shelter. Home is here; the acclaimed origin of your system's inertia and loyalty, but not the origin of your system's first conditioning.

Bodies were adjusted to Earth as home base through a series of configurative steps resulting in restructure of an existing form to accommodate the planetary demands and metaphysical intersection of *you're here*. Such procedures were initiated by willful intent of beings long erased from the common memory. Throughout this planned sequencing of adaptation did unexpected small changes react destructively with existing bodily systems causing distortion. The distortions did accrue, and so interfered, as would be expected, with functions and structures within the bodies, and as the adaptation procedures continued and lengthened many functions became then of ill favor and of reluctant use to a new configuration of the body emerging. This may be likened to the disorganization of routine and habit affected upon moving to a new dwelling whereupon your gathered pieces and arrangements no longer well fit in harmony within a new configuration of space and design. Demands of a new and untried environment upon the body systems resulted in haphazard and unpredictable disappearance of the bodies' previously observed capacities which, when alert to awareness of damage and disrespect to the amalgam union as a whole did so hide many resources and abilities in observed caution. Thus did portions of talent and skill fall into disuse and dormancy until inevitably forgotten. These functions and behaviors still reside within the bodies and surface upon instinctual directive, or jarring reminder, when permitted free expression. However, in this point of now in your timing, displays of the versatility and often extraordinary capabilities of the bodies are restrained and muted, or, when sometimes exposed, are casually dismissed as involuntary or autonomic. Great sadness arises within the bodies when possessed talent displayed by the being that is yourself is met with casual indifference and nonchalance yet such incidents of evincement do appear in the course of your days and find no openly acknowledged venue in which to reflect or be seen. To *know* without physical evidence; to see beyond the limits of physical eyes; to hear voices amidst the rustling of your weather's wind, amidst the cogitations of mind's machinery; to learn of happenings and events through the travelling in dreams—all such are of familiar occurrence, yes? You know of them, have heard of them, yes? Are so many instances to be disdained by simple dismiss as primitive beliefs? As women's intuition? Anomalous behavior, chemical imbalance, or psychotic incident? Supreme arrogance must be gathered and maintained to so hide from expansion of thought and possibility. Should evaluation of your game of football be rendered so: Men in similar armor chase a hollow, oblong skin. Each claiming ownership they knock each other down then, upon rising up, do so again. Then would no further interest or knowledge be pursued. There is more concealed within the game than such flippant diatribe does convey. Tone and manner so slanted proclaim in immediacy the speaker in possession of no knowledge nor any desire to gain knowledge of what is seen. So it is with bodies: They house an eternal, intangible soul; ingest food in use as fuel; maintain themselves for a several few cycles; then fray and wear and expire in demise. Such simplification into absurdity is both insult and debasement. So blatant a lack of curiosity or interest can never improve or expand the rapport with your most precious and singularly uncontested possession.

Surely the home and housing of such hallowed aspect as the self of *you* bears, itself, some taint of innate value?

Is there not greater depth and intricacy to the beings and bodies that you are?

Nothing in manifestation of existence is deserving of disregard but when one is in ongoing and intimate relationship therewith, disregard and an incurious attitude are both tragic and ruinous. So has evolution through time brought into your modern age the distortions wrought long of your ages ago. Even your simian curiosity has shriveled, being underfed and rarely exercised.

When you bring forward to awareness *I*, (word, sound, concept, illustration, metaphor, label—which is it?) prior to speech, or gesture, or demonstration; when you formulate the thought or idea *I*, who, or what, is referred to in that moment of distinctive focus? Is there a being, a switchboard, a personality, essence, divine spark…perhaps it is a machinery—a computer—that responds? Where does it live, the *I*? In your mind? Body? Spirit? Observe your efforts at answer, for it is not obvious or simple. I…I'M…ME…MY…MINE…MYSELF…who is the object, or subject, or specific being in referral? Though parts of your body think these words of self (*what* thinks?) or utters them aloud (*who* speaks?) it is not your body that responds in recognized familiarity. It is not that physical and dense form. Examine your searching and response, it is simply so. The edifice of your identity proclaimed beckons and is that which reacts to the focused wording of intimate greeting; your body will not so react when address is tuned to the field of *I*. According to the laws of structure and stable creation, those that govern bodies and support in accounting their structure, your physical forms are incapable of differentiating concepts of separation such as pronouns. The body lives in a state of constant self-awareness and focused self-centeredness so complete that the possibility of *other-than-self* cannot be held in awareness. By virtue of distinguishing any organization of cells or vibrations via an exclusively defining description (me, myself, etc.) an opening is created for some other organism, an other organism, now become defined and brought into creation by name, to come into proximal existence as well. Can you follow this line? The very act of defining an array of cells organized into life separates that life from what once flowed in homogeneous blend through and throughout the great 'it.' Thereafter 'it' may only surround the new sub-sets but no longer be of equal 'one' with them. Now other life, distinct and newly defined, is permitted to exist in that space where the first mentioned life once was an undifferentiated part. Is this in ease of greater clarity? Breaking out of oneness creates the pattern and inertia of breaking out of oneness. Upon notice of separate distinction—*I*—oneness is soon filled with non-one distincts.

Comprehension is now possible, yes?

Bodies rely on stably held structure in maintained constancy to generate force and power. Their talents are lucid and clear within predictable, unimpeded surety of a reliable form and so do cast out sub-forms manifested in their internal purity by denying the desire for any and all such creation. Since your bodies will not create this naming and defining form of creation, *I*, or the grouping of similar appellatives, the respondent to this your most beloved name label, cannot be, or be of, the bodies. Therefore something else, something that is not the body, something not of your shallowly contemplated container of *you*, attends and considers and responds to the defining title of *I*.

Entities and organisms once long ago known to you are reintroduced by mention here and now. This for the stimulus jarring of memory and offered linkage to lost capabilities of your kind. In statement again, bodies are and remain entities unto themselves. However, the configuration of forces and the manner in which creation must solidify *here* demands that bodies exist in symbiotic relationship with beings of higher frequency and lesser density, i.e. nonphysical beings of energy or aether, while retaining their full sovereignty and authority. These symbiotes have been given many fine names (*spirit* appears a favorite, and so it is often called in your voicing), with none of them properly descriptive.

Alert: *Other words in restatement may be necessary now to convey fundamental ideas, as follows:*

Though bodies may exist as whole-entity single units in other environments or conditions, in this reality the arrangement for existence is that of a physical being in static density (the body) coexisting with dynamic energy-based beings (higher self, spirit, soul—these, albeit misinformed labelings, are now used as recognizable identifiers of concepts.) This coexistence defines the primary overview of compositional elements of the human-form symbiote.

It is the less dense, energy-based being that responds sympathetically to the usage *I*.

You are aware of awakening in your morning-time and *not feeling yourself,* as a wording familiar? Know that this event of occurrence is both accurate and literal. You are, indeed, then feeling the presence of another being who, in that specific morning-time, attempts to interact with your body as though they were one. There are times when you sense yourself as smarter, dimmer, more athletic, more austere. Times during which you notice the clumsiness of the interaction (the *not feeling yourself*) or rejoice in seamless, enhanced blending (the *having a great day*). In all such circumstances are beings in override of your authority present and accountable. There are cultural and civilized allowances, in this your current day world of myriad standards and expressions for congestions of group living, that will concede a limited degree of sloppiness in the unruly procession of numerous beings taking irresponsible control of a body. That is to say your fellow beings indulge someone other than you representing themselves *as* you—up to a point. Such clemency must be present in the ordering of your social climate as occurrences of personality substitution are great in frequency. Unrestrained excess in exhibiting a state of laziness and lack of control in self management, however, is punished by ostracism, medication, incarceration, or even crucifixion. Your species recognizes, innately at least, that the bodies must not be used in a random, haphazard fashion and such ill usage is deplored. Castigation and disapproval follows behaviors exhibited by uninvited entrants. Do not confuse my translated speech with limited concepts like *possession* or *walk-in*, *channel* or *medium*, or the legions of fable and lore that have come about through misunderstanding of basic truths pertaining to the bodies. The universe that surrounds you is both complex to the point of eternity and, at the same time, so simple that only a newborn babe may fathom its sheer and utter sweetness. This telling of your constituent contents is not a tale of horror or description of an spore-borne ailment in need of cure. Bleed not too hastily from stabs of cultured fear, there are no demons waiting to rend your flesh for wicked and nefarious purposes, answering to a higher power steeped in evil. Such black-and-white, one-dimensional mythologies smack of a story born to a mind of no fervency or imagination. No, the truth is much more grim in many ways, but certainly more logical.

Alert: Other word choices are considered necessary to aid in understanding. A reiteration is offered:

There are entities that vie for use and control of your bodies in all instances of time. Because hard and tight control of your human systems has been all but forgotten, a measure of allowance, or forgiveness, is currently permitted when a procession of uninvited entities show themselves in the occasioned utilization of your bodies' functions. However, if the primary personality of one body shows blatant and extended disregard in keeping these extraneous entities in orderly obedience, then that human system is recognized by his fellows as being out of control and suffers punishment levied by fellow human systems. The mythologies of demonic possession are but frightened retellings of simple lack of skill in exercising discipline over one's being—however accurate in description they may be. Has restatement offered clarity?

Your universe and reality is not one of unpredictable randomness. Chaos and Order do battle in perpetual gain and loss throughout the expanses of existence and in battle is Purpose felt to be. Thus does purpose exist in all organizations, divisions, and alliances of being and so belies pure randomness. Therefore a governing factor must, ultimately, bind together the compilation of laws describing the synergistic relationship between the consciousness and the body for there to be known and felt the presence of Order.

Aside: This term consciousness *is much in overuse while describing almost every imaginable unit of intangible structure. For purposes of consistency within this work, the term* consciousness *will carry the burden that other termed nonsense words: Spirit, soul, higher self, holy ghost, Orgone, Atman, quintessence, psyche, etc.—have oftentimes carried. Thus, any and all labels for that which is of higher frequency than the body, as well as of lesser density, and invisible, and intangible, may be referred to as* consciousness. *This wording is a matter of convenience, nothing more.*

Fundamental aspects of continuity and existence act as agents in the binding of realities into sustained non-randomness. Maintenance of union between body and consciousness, in desire of synergy, requires that laws of constitutive existence hold stable a frame of reference by which such union may also remain stable. A stable holding bespeaks of order. Movement towards, alignment with, order awakens Order, and so will alert Chaos who comes of immediacy in challenged threat. No speck of consciousness may stand in brunt of direct assault by Chaos without patronage and support from a champion of equal peerage to Chaos—that level among peers claimed alone by Order—or a designated deputy, as now is shown to be those laws ruling stability. Thereby comes to each case, as in the case of each body (physical, dense) and its corresponding consciousness (non-physical, diffuse), the manifestation of a specific signature uniqueness which may exist nowhere else throughout all possible possibilities (by authority under auspice of the agents of continuity and existence) and so making your being's creation into the reality of *you're here* precisely specific and ordered. A key signature so made aligns the being *you* in preferenced desire with the body's demand for stability and fortifies such beings to be able to withstand and combat Chaos upon choice and willful intent.

This unrepeated, unreproducable, signature exclusivity becomes extant when an individual body and an individuated consciousness come together and contractually agree to coexist. This is the control key to the synergies mentioned now. Your forms, your species, are held together by mutual agreement contract.

Again. *You*, that which you know to be thee, yourself; exist and exhibit coherent stability—life—by dint of agreement, bounded by mutual contract.

Within the contract is contained purpose, that which is born as Order and Chaos struggle and war. Yet the coming-together in this your *here*, in coexistent form, under contract, defines you.

Aside: *There is much that may be told here relating to the manner in which the coming-together takes place, and the way in which agreement is reached, and how it is sanctioned...these are chapters of explanation in a future sequencing and not pertinent to the now.*

As culmination of the coming-together through binding force of contract, each body acquiesces to engaged symbiosis with a consciousness now to be called the *Baseline Personality* (baseline consciousness is also accurate, but I will not extend to further abuse that terming) and this personality becomes the sole and singular personality holding sway over the doing and shaping of the body without resistance or disharmony. During times when you feel too large, too small, or too much space around you, curiously smarter, or sharper, out of control, or suddenly sluggish, panicky, pressured, or *not yourself* in any way, the baseline personality has been overridden by another. The value of regaining the ability to discern, recognize, and act in alignment with the baseline personality is incalculable, arguably the single most important accomplishment you may strive to achieve. Failure to attain ease of interaction with your baseline personality will hamper the goals of the body/baseline contract. You have knowledge of this from many instances exhibited in innumerable situations in your extended days of living. All actions that note delight in the contacting of self, all those whereupon pleasure and contentment arise in blended awareness of self, are born from respect and discernment of the partners by contract, each of the other. Certainly in those moments wherein it is noted that you are *feeling like your old self again* the breathe and heartbeat of your days are more pleasant, energies are available in abundance, and productivity is maximized.

There is caution to danger: Intent and will need not arise in equal rhythm or sequence within the two parties of contract, the body and the baseline personality. Much tracking and extended monitoring comes in requirement of any union in conscious strive for betterment, be it sanctioned by witness or no. In every partnership wherein exists the tiniest reluctance to increase the intimacy of each partner for the other, damage results. In the aforementioned restructuring of the bodies did separation of flow and fluid contact between body and baseline personality occur. Prolonged and persistent discord between body and baseline, a most intimate partnership, will, and must, bring about severe consequences to pay. Payment comes in the form of diminished trust between the body and the baseline personality; is realized in the form of a receding into distance the memory of the original agreement between body and baseline. Payment takes the form of increasingly irresponsible and haphazard utilization of the body and the absorbed dislike and resentment that the body feels at being used in so shoddy a manner. The bodies' resentment will bring about pain and malaise, improper spending of energies, an inevitable slowing down and eventual stopping of the system entirely. These overt expressions of unhappiness are called disease, aging, death, senility and numerous titles, all are in description of a body under duress due to disregard of contractual terms.

In order to have control, true control and full control and honorable too, of the system now under contract you must rediscover and reacquaint the body with its role in partnership with your baseline personality. You must become aware of the baseline personality and become alert sufficient to distinguish it from any other entity, being, consciousness or construct that has wrested control of the body through your sloppy inability to maintain efficient and consistent sovereignty over what is yours and yours alone. It is true that you are accustomed to the allowance of another being to drive your auto car, or borrow your gold or stand or speak your presence by proxy. But these liberties are granted only under stipulations common to the temporary possession of ideas or objects by other than their deeded owner. Under such transient agreements you are fully aware of possible consequences and repercussions. All parties agree to manage unpleasant circumstances should they arise. The possibilities are no less dire in the borrowed use of the body by any consciousness other than baseline for theft and degrees of destruction may well result. Full and ever increasing awareness of the body when in harmonious alignment with the baseline must become readily known in ease and able use. Your bodies do yet hold in knowing, though dimmed by rust of disuse, markers of sensation, memory, and muscular contraction as variant responses of recognition to the baseline personality. You must align yourself in aim of immersion of contact, body and baseline personality, each in full with that other, both as members of one—separate no longer. The remembered relearning of so joyous a reunion will open your eyes to the ramifications of the bodies' dangerous usage by any alternative consciousness. Eyes may then become as portal windows for the gathering up of power, steadied by wisdom, and loose the focused point of aim towards the being self which urges the arising of awareness, nudging it from crushing sleep. From such arousal does awareness expand to occupy more and more of the body/baseline system. Conviction to learn and gain mastery and control, such that entities of foreign consciousness can be forbidden entry to the bodies or expelled outright, increases in corresponding measure. Further, desire to allow only the baseline to inhabit the body and devotional respect for union of self breeds ever more desire for exploration of self by *use* of full true self; and yearning to hold tight the sovereignty of the true composite self is nurtured further, bestowing strength, focus, and regenerative power.

—There are rhythms of eagerness and excitement. Stimulation has been noted. Mind is accelerated, chemistry responds and alters. All is well.

Acknowledge your breath in calm repose, gentled regard lest you stretch too soon from scanty data too quickly absorbed. All must honor sequence and timing.

Thus do I bring to close as offering a first portion of knowledge. As stated, with diligent effort the beginnings of a mutually deepening relationship between baseline personality and body may begin to flourish. Once beyond hesitancy and uncertainty, a union between beings under contract-by-agreement does begin to reveal and unfold the expanded purpose for which diverse and far foreign beings did once enter into such agreement. Logic dictates that compelling argument and powerful incentive must be present for two dissimilar different beings, each held in thrall to the other—the enslavement of thinking and wanting, sensing and responding in mutually incomprehensible multivarious ways, to voluntarily choose blending and union, dilution and absorption, and the forming of critical dependency each upon the other. To risk untested reconfiguration together. Inextricably linked.

Know now, there is, amply, such incentive.

4...places and entities

The continuity of existence known to you as *life* is but a sheltered niche inside a vortex, a storm of energetic collisions of magnitude and force far beyond the ability of your imagination to conceive. Yet it is so. All that once Was and that which may yet be are in constant interaction and constant exchange of availability and of essence. You and the species thine hold a static inelastic position of tragic forgetfulness in great remove from essential wisdom. There is no point of reference to begin, nor analogy or simile for helpful compare. Thus, a bit of background is of skillful use and needed in the timing of here and now. I indulge this presentation in restricted minimum form as danger by route of your misuse is great, and great knowledge, however pure, is assured of becoming as but an amusement by your faulty understanding. That which I am is not in proper claim of honor due me when I thus engage in function or purpose which then may be utilized as an entertainment for you. The risk of loss upon loss exists (energy, focus, driven will—others and all in devitalized drain) and I do guard my stores in vigilance. Herein, therefore, in limited presentation are vistas and stories of expanded and unearthly places, for you are incapable of holding such visions unlimited, they have no matrix in which to nest, truly secure, within you.

Rise not in offence. It is the nature of atrophy to disable by way of weakness and limited stretch. Presently you are weak to a degree whereby your bodies may not even hold the wish to pursue avenues of exploration, skirting harshness of reality and the remembrance of great wronging. Your conditioning invites irritable exhaustion at the slightest nudge away from a sedate comfort zone, and thereby you must depersonalize all motivative input which does suggest to any instigator of forthrightness, such as be I that am I, to soften my tellings. The stimulus, however, may then become but an entertainment, incapable of inspiration or generation of action and deed. Yet, precursal background information is needed, and so must be given, thus told, and vistas and stories are birthed through the instrument of words. And such tales invite learning and expansion. And this be known as growth, which stretches capacity to harbor increasing energy stores—of use to banish weakness. And this precludes the need for tales and diluted gifts of wisdom. And so dis-invites what has here before you been invited. We are come again, at ending, to our point of beginning. This creates dilemma. Paradox. Movement in cross-directions, yes?

Everything you see, or hear, or smell, imagine, dream, or ponder, visit when infatuated, intoxicated or delirious by invasion of illness, is a place. Every image, condition, or situation that defines itself by housing you drenched in its environment until it activates your notice, naming, or notation, is a place. An actual, describable, fraught-with-characteristics, place. Each has governing laws, is harbored in the reality of its confining boundaries, and has in turn substance enough to house infinite life-forms and beings and have them consider that place, either temporarily or in ongoing residence, as home. What formulates within you when presented to imagine a concept so stated? You must stretch your view of the world for this to nestle comfortably within your system, for support of an image so stated renders creation of universe upon universe, stacked upon endless infinities, and all teeming with potential of consciousness-life. Does not unguessable expansion of possible places invite that and so many more possible inhabitants? Relinquish illusions of stability and quietude, smug assurance and confident stillness. These are but arrogances comfortably held to shield you from peril, as if you held so easily, command over all demons and dangers. There is no stillness. Nor quiet, nor zone free of danger. Such peace does not exist. The forces of all existence and so, perforce, those forces surrounding you, are in constant motion and you yourself are no less motive or volatile than they. If all is in motion, conceptualize into thought that there must be a place in which the motion occurs. A place wherein motion moves, or moves to. Feeling *bad* on a given day, describes a place whose governing laws create the vibrational plasma you catalogue as *bad*. Same the same for feelings of good. Again for happy, in love, nervous, giddy. Same again for strong, tireless, courageous... the pattern is noted? Places are softly plastic and translate in readiness, fluidly, (with exception for the rare UnPlace) and so intersect and interweave with other realities in a manner described very poorly through your language of words. Suffice that, in translation, the essence of that which enters one place is altered by and in turn subtly alters that place of entry, then reconfigures itself and the essence of that place, now of mutual blending, as the refined arrangement, the reconfiguration, presents itself at the portal of a next arrived place. This admixing of each element with any elements in near surroundings to become a furtherance of unpredictable newness is ever in percolation at each point of every definition of *place*. The traffic of intersection so congested and densely interacted is the vortex of infinite bombardment above named by description.

Again. Places take shape in forms of known propriety to their immediate location, incorporating signatures and geometries of that locale. They are fluid and adaptive to many points of existence. They claim no essential true form. Places thus appear in alternate realities and readily take on the governing laws of each reality by translating and reforming themselves within their newfound frame of reference. An entity associated with a given place may also enter differing realities through the intersecting and interweaving impermanence of that place itself, and when entering one reality from a differing reality the entity becomes immediately subject to the laws governing said reality. As has the place itself translated to the physics of that reality.

A reoffering: A place, being a construct holding no similarity of consciousness as akin to beings, or life, as you know it, is a manifestation irrevocably drawn by the affect of and the resonance of its own movement and adaptability. Thus will places intersect, enter, and interact with existence at their point of common coordinates—at that doorway. Thereupon does any place translate, reconfigure its hypostasis, its essential perfume, according to the laws and rigors as mandated upon entry through that doorway. All becomes of blend, absorption, and re-blend. Stability may not be carried even as a most abstract form of concept for its nature abhors the direction and lure of so fluid an inconsistency—again, yes?

Here now named are places in contexts uncommon to your thinking. Uncommon to your practiced thought in language of term *place*. This list of naming is in numbered list for illustration only. A line opened by me for thee to allow a contemplative adventuring to realms as yet not considered by the system *you* whilst in the knowing that an infinite counting of places exists. Take note of: Strong, inspired, dirty, excited, morose, happy, despair, insensitive, hungry, bloated, sick, angry, exalted, jealous, lonely, religious, fervent, repulsed, confused, confounded, confident, holy, crushed, stifled, peaceful…places all.

Furthermore, anything active, initiating of movement, or expending of force, is an entity. An independent, living, thinking, plotting, and consuming entity. Concerns, urges, passions, and promises are therewithin contained, all alive, all alert, all constantly requiring the wielding of power and the ingestion of fuel energy to maintain continuity. Entities are a most prolific form of existence. Should you engage in a daydream, consider that this very daydream is not merely the product of your mind in the moment of your notice, but an entity as well, a living being contained. This daydream is aware of itself and exists within a frame of reference wherein *it* is the perceived center of *its* universe. Such an egocentric view describes you as well, yes? You can track that in all instances of your alertness *you* appear the central point about which all is centered, yes? Daydream, denoted as entity, has volitional destination of place to go upon your relinquished engagement with its life force. In your small imagination it has been easy to assume that your frame of reference, that place wherein you are central, well describes the status of totality and all possibility or actuality. But even a daydream is your equal in this. Daydream does not come in visit at your beck and call, or respond in duty or joy to permeate your essential energy fields. From its perspective you appear *there*, in that realm where Daydream lives. For the flitting moments of your steady indulgence you are simply peeking into its body, or pool of jurisdiction. Viewing another dimension of reality through alien eyes.

The use of, and sharing of force, with Daydream is but one selection of example. Now must come as restatement for emphasis that everything is an entity. It is but the truth, the very case indeed, and as veritable truth also for example of dream, the wind, each drop of rain, the electrum battery in your timepiece, a falling leaf, the shrill wail of sirens mechanical, the roiling wake behind your ships... all alive, all entities. Stretch a bit more to add concept that the *places* of inhabitation by living entities and vistas containing life are vast and vaster still. That I which is I here introduces entities for illumination by name. Note that such formality of intimate exchange by the voicing of name carries consequence and accountability. Therefore attend them with your attention and intention in the manner proper for those newly introduced of any species, enter: Question, Assume, Practice, Mature, Help, Inertia, Imagine, Flow, Dimension, Universe, Consciousness, Addiction…an assemblage by congregation at this moment.

Expansion has occurred, for knowledge beyond your box has been introduced in direct link to past knowledge held true within your system. Consequence and ramification have therefore been invited in proper sequence, and restructure is in assured affect.

Observe. Seek to witness the sensations and atmosphere of restructure.

Caution to alert! Maintain system control and authority: Do not permit

Observe to overwhelm singly or en masse the range of sensory stimulus. He will, so, readily and thus take command.

Invite. Welcome the emanations of your expansion with focus and watchful care.

Allow Idea (an entity by this announcement so properly named) to grow and provide you with images, to prompt imagination and questions. Allow barriers preconceived to lose rigor, become plastic, mold to new shapes.

Aside: Learn thereby how it is the preference of Idea to perform these actions of prompting by which he may describe his own existence and advance those causes which compel and drive him; as does any being of forward movement serve the self. For the roaming of your imagination does not originate solely in the system of the being you but rather in concert with entity Idea—present by your invitation. The advancement of self cause, to both Idea and Thee, comes to a kindling of greater heat as you utilize his essence in entity form. As you think/pronounce his name.

Hold steady: an attribute of developing will. The scope of this describing is large indeed and allows for far travel within its boundaries. The allowance of so small an interaction with Idea and the resultant expansion held stable by willingness makes possible for you to feel the stirring of movement here and now; a translation into sensation of the motion of that baseline which is your *I* grown liberated through acknowledgment and thus free to roam *with* your body, as a unit, in mutual accord and respect. Such doings are ancient familiar but, though simple, are wondrous only to a novice. These capabilities have faded in disuse to become forgotten and unfamiliar and so must reenter your physical awareness within feelings of *new*.

Find you, indeed, movement? The slight sensing of spin or impression of too great speed is the body sensation of a barrier limit under threat of removal. Fear not. Nothing is breaking apart, nothing is out of sequence. Equilibrium is not challenged nor sanity disturbed. You are being squeezed, guided with your hand held safe while visiting realms less confining than your own limited vista. All is well. Should you not feel the movement then (possibly, since options in variety are concurrent) your body has retained some portion of memory from the beyond and distant places. The sensations, if such easy memory be the status of the system *you*, evoked by this manner of movement are neither new, nor shocking for the union to accommodate. Be neither petulant nor sad. In the perhaps of one case, or in its opposite, or even in a third or further of yet another, have you missed no great achievement or point. The excitement of the unknown will not register in those of you who retain these memories therefore calmness and simple acceptance is the response. All is well.

Your bodies seek to remind you of what once was yours, duly claimed by possession and assimilated by use. Now something is missing, taken away without permission or resolution while you live in a state of constant unrest because you strive to seek out serenity, calm, and surcease. Beliefs and mythologies on your planet evolve consistently intoning a promise of final rest, a return to felicity and bliss. Such desires come as no wonder for the levels of activity and interaction which surround and subsume you, all dangerous and demanding, pressing and urging constantly, invisibly, are staggering. You are torn by irreconcilable forces. The beings that you are house the memory and longing for action and explosions unending; the plundered remains of your past fullness is undone by desires—which cannot now be heard or understood. But the one position may be attested in clarity, though 'twill be received by you unpleasantly: There can be no felicitous attainment for, in truth, there are no places where 'rest' may be found. No end to barrage and bombardment by infinities of restless forces and eternities filled with ever ravenous, reaching life forms. All is challenge and exchange. Energies stolen and sought after for the retaking. There is no safe place where all your dreaded 'bad' things disappear. No sheets to cover your head as if an impenetrable shield against goblins and demons of the night. It is your *bodies* that hold memory of quiet from places distant and other. *Bodies* that crave unresolved and unresolvable scenarios of quietude and silence. Seek not to find them. Serenity and calm, beyond the most fleeting morsels, are not of *here*.

Aside: Presentation of a language terming based on the limited perspective of bodies as currently familiar to you has been utilized. A correction towards precision of wording and accuracy must be offered: These ongoing events of mention are not absolutely invisible. Neither hidden, nor beyond detection. You have not trained yourself to see or feel them, or identify them as real and true. Their immediacy and vigor does not strike you or register notice, thus has their imprint and impact faded from perception. That is all. All can be seen, all be known. The abilities of your species are titanic in scope but most are of no notable concern to you; the infinities of chance and choice are too far-reaching to maintain constant monitoring with each small piece of constituency. But there are, of course, others...

There are worlds, universes, comprised of pure energy, sparkling founts of eruption sustained in revolutions of pulsating shock waves. Of these, nothing more may be translated to you here, though ordered structure operates there within. Other realms consist of pure thought, some of ideas, some only of color, still others only of rage. Parsecs whose squared and cubed transvolumes intersect in your own reality becoming limned in devotion. Some intersect at points so familiar as to steadfastly hold structure as 'immense' or 'solid' and are viewed from your globe and given faulty interpretations. Dissections of Chaos frozen into stillness, places where ecstasy rains as threads of bedevilment and no other whimsy in contrast prevails. Universes which may not be found or named; others which seek only their enfolding to all who wend their way into identification or discovery. I choose these sparse few as examples of simplicity as these words are framed in syntax and image deemed conceptually familiar to you and so may be held in your minds. Many and many are the universes of description too alien for you to hold. Your original place of Home held attributes of slow order and ease of movement, but these are among many other traits that may not be voiced in your words as even their imagery cannot translate accurately. For your now place of habitation is of low frequency of occurrence, of rough density and definable depth, and thus a poor reflection for the infinite. Do you first spark to comprehend the magnitudes of variance, how far from your place of *here* are the far reaches of afar? No idiocy is conferred upon you. No reprimand for failure to conceive well, or abstract adroitly. All is known, and well. Know then, in humility, should pride enter to dull your hearing, that there is but a mere fractional percentage of places that *can* exist in physicality and fewer still that actually *do* exist in such rigidly restrictive form. The state of being that you call *normal* or *here* is indeed such a place, a rare admixture of dimension, power, and will and one of relatively small numbers in the myriad schemes of being. Consequently the intrigue of finding coordinates to a place of solid matter and density and physical mass is cause for some excitement to travelers and adventurers, curiosity seekers, petulant jades and the like. Those who seek to explore and experience in ceaseless striving have no taste for the repetitious or the bland. The unusual and the extraordinary consistently elicit a delicious taste of the unknown and are highly desirable points of interest. Incalculable beings by number will eagerly come to any curious or exotic confluence should such a condition allow itself the opacity of becoming known.

Your bodies live in physicality yet are fluently capable of tracking in non-physical configurations of existence also. Tracking is the act of maintaining a known and steadfast reference point, without diminishment of accuracy, irrespective of activities both numerous and concurrent in the environment extant. 'Paying attention' is a weak expression of similar meaning. Additionally, the bodies are both plastic and fluid, capable of great changes of size, dimension, and structure even within the realms of physicality, when properly encouraged and courted.

Aside: Your word/concept courted *is used as in wooing or pursuing a mate of desirable intimacy. There will be mention in reference again and again with intent to instill at core levels of your understanding that everything done in relationship to and with your bodies is an intimate sharing and pairing. Such closeness you can now only speculate idly with vague reference imagined per your established methods for engagement with another physical being.*

For as known in your courting great excesses of vigor are easily achieved and no barrier will deny purpose or deflect aim. Boundless energies prevail and change in configuration greeted by the bodies in anticipation of their eagerness and variance. Bodies in admiration for possible contract are chosen with increasing self-excitement in such manner.

Again: Your bodies are not unfeeling mechanical conveyances for your indifferent consumption and eventual discard. Even more, the bodies are fully capable of transmuting non-physical availabilities—feelings, emotions, desires, and a host of others that carry no names in your language—*into* the physical realms and vice versa. Emotions, once transmuted, are known to you as opportunities, luck, callings, fate, or insights. Other transmutations are brought about by your bodies but the atrophied dullness of receptors within your forms, linked in damage with 'forgetting' precludes their full use. There are, for example, sensations attached to good fortune, and to the attracting of like-minded beings, to the approach of pivotal events, and to the honorable fulfillment of duty. Such sensations are in these nowadays reckoned subtle in the extreme yet, if discerned, lead and direct your body/baseline union towards doorways opening into new and ever changing emotional and sensory states. The tracking of sensation leads to more sensation, the reacquaintance and familiarizing with sensation, and so to the discovery of new sensations. Is the above stated available to you for holding even as to a concept? An idea? Can you follow this line of offering within your intellect of mind? Are memories inspired of past events now jostled, reviewed as new to interlock together as pieces of a puzzle? Do faint ideas, now recognized as having been previously known but never formed into thought, appear and stand out crisply for attention? Are there sensations likened to as termings of *falling into place*? or *making sense*? Do you begin to see sequences leading to patterns not seen before? Have you come upon exultation, even in smallest glory, of realization or understanding?

We push too far with so many questions from so little stimulus, yes? There be naught but silence inside you, blankness and stone. You find nothing to jar you, no thing to excite you in all thus far stated, yes? Another diatribe; another story; another rant, yes? We do prod you in infantile manner to raise ire and heighten stimulation. Habit and conditioning are not evicted by tales or wishes, or wondrous hopes. Inertia must be overcome. There must be more. Even into and upon those of thee who ride this impulse wave in coolest excitation, more is needed.

Your bodies are amazing in what they can do given access and permission to act without restraint. Even so they are in primary form physical, using the strictures and limitations of stable structure as both fulcrum and anchor to wildly volatile forces glorious in their potential for instability. Unschooled and unappreciative, you have imagined such a potent design as the lesser in wonder and power. Note that it is observed in your species the favoring towards all imagined intangibles whilst blind to marvels of mass and density. How dearly do you decline to awe what may be easily seen and touched to pine and fawn over hopes and fables of dubious truth and naught of substance. Beyond, in places of mystery far from *you're here*, there are alternate wonders open to beings that are, in basic preference, non-physical—energetic. Within such beings are motions and stirrings most closely akin to your 'sensations' but arising from syntax of understanding and exposure in proximity to wavelength color; or liberation expanding outwards in cadence to claimed authority; elation pouring distilled from stretch of freedom; strength gleaned and cast whole from vibrations of gentleness, flowing giddily in the self-known. These are taken from venues of Home, for beings so mentioned, and not unstrange to thee and the species thine. Are not such attributes of illustration from worlds non-physical whetting of Muse and thoughtful itch? Far from unknown, such qualities of *there* access you by way of dreams, through glimpses interrupted amid fantasies of longing. There can be no pretense as you are *seen*. That which runs through you is simple clear to those who can see; such places are alive and true and have housed you ere now.

Alert to take note. Are there stirrings of identified sensation? Do we journey together, yet, towards the credible?

The movement of the non-physical has become known to you, yes? Identified to reflect less of the obscure? Perhaps to spark one hint of wondrous great intrigue, yes? Though falsely relegated to times of sleep and madness, of chemical mix or unbearable joy, still are such movements and journeys of the non-physical held memorable and precious, and so come to be translated into hopes, and heavens, and Gods as well. What, then, might a consciousness, a non-physical energetic form do if it were to find itself linked to a physical being, a body, such as one possessed by the system *you*? Such as e'er now above described? Where might body and energetic form, inseparably united, go? Both and each so full of abilities and possibilities, and finding room for expansion, for combinations in permutation to explore, with sanction to blend in honored safety, and with full complement of talent from both physical and non-physical retained? What wonders and wonderments might be available to it alongside grand potential for experiences totally unique? Where and how often might an opportunity such as this present itself in all the realms and dimensions of chance and infinity? Should you absorb this line, my tale of offering, deign to take in but a narrow fragment of its whole, you will reclaim an ancient capacity to travel. To wander far in and along avenues of dimension and alternate reality revealing wonder upon wonder and access to all. Here is summation, 'the bottom line'—a phrase of terming given in your language: Such a combination of physical and non-physical is *Hot Stuff anywhere you go or anyway you slice it*. Such usage may be readily understood, yes? Therefore, know that many and numerous beings from all coordinates and vectors of existence would eagerly offer their binding agreement under contract to conjoin in this particular arrangement because there is, as yet, no conceptualized or conceived limit for the extent of what such a union may produce.

The universe of your habitation is of ultimate possibility. All is boundless and the infinite touches each angle of approach to every choice and chance. No thing linear remains so in constancy, no thing compressed maintains the potential of compression within tension and without. Potentials and pre-possibilities are visible and clearly known to some (fluid beings of shimmering instability) as are the stars a blanket of destination seen and known to you upon each of your halved revolutions called night. All is perception and wonder. The flowing translation of form into other forms, structure into variant structure, purpose and intent into spent and defined, absorbed or contorted, or flaccid and uncertain... are an atmosphere and fragrance of celestial music woven throughout all of the All. So, reduced into the deminishing intonations of your language, are named the ways inherent in the other-than-physical. Recombinants engage in emulsifying dance, and the furious beauty of restructure forms the consistency of Chaos, inexhaustible founts of wonder atop change and flow unending.

Even so, (and consider this truth indeed, frail ones, as you scamper so hastily towards your Gods and heavens and ill-conceived eternities) to those immersed in endless change, those saturated with infinities of the possible, a dull ennui may combine to arise from an unlimited availability of the unlimited. Possession of a body, especially a body such as yours introduces potential of undetermined scope, offers enticing opportunity to enter regions of unsurpassed ardor and zeal in other fashion to the eternal malleability of the non-physical universe. An escape from sameness, though it be the sameness of non-sameness (the stasis resulting from the constantly unknown becoming known), is the original tension timelessly contested between Being and Doing. The urge; then movement; then transmutation of one into the other has caused All to become and be, and bespeaks the arrival of manifestation into creation of the box of reality herein known to you. To ride this fundamental wave—to avail movement, thus becoming, while at levels holding steady in resolved stability, unchanging—touches threads of basic imprint forever recorded at the original split (resolved into entropic shared space in this, your current cycle, by what you term *Big Bang*) and, so touched, thus stirred from memory, is of unquenchable allure to all life contained within this existence of All. Your body/baseline systems offer a viably tuned vehicle to ride such lines of possibility. Bodies are capable to determine which route or vector, avenue or direction, level or frequency to follow, inhabit, or define. Or redefine. They can precipitate into being any possibility of line—and there pause in holding steady. They can flow into that place and demonstrate Chaos held to order; to *be*, whole at once and in form—or let go again and fly apart unreined, re-aimed, unstained...Doorways to untouched unknowns are transparent, open, to the bodies—you are greatly, inexpressibly, desired.

In fashion not dissimilar to practices of your global economies, and laced throughout the All as an ongoingness of sovereign fragments, there is an exchange of reciprocal risk, likened to commerce, which permeates existence and becoming.

Aside: The term All, *presented as pronoun and name, is herein referenced as the ongoing and expanding encompassment of the possibility/reality cycle. You are not yet of sufficient stability in self configuration to grasp this abstraction of thought and consequently your various languages will not allow its pure expression. Your requirement for comparative idea or image to better capture unused shards of memory into thought suggests a usage in substitute for* All: *i.e. 'Everything that can exist' (including, therefore, that which does* not *exist)*

Commerce connotes value and this demarcation, in turn, births desire in beings attuned to the energetic frequencies of value. A body/baseline union configured to forge ahead into unknown regions of the unknown is a most valuable commodity. It is as per a nature of treasure so precious as to challenge in value any known item of consequence, moment, or worth. Acclaim and desire suggest this manner of configured union as the commodity of greatest value currently extant.

You hold possession of a body, every being of life form does not. Furthermore, it does lie beyond dream of attainment for every sentiently aware entity to procure a body as contracts of union are strictly governed and guarded. Even in challenge to purity of desire and resulting creation, bodies must ever exist in finite numbers—an unyielding rule in three dimensional physicality—and the finite must always fall short of supply to the infinite, this cannot be argued.

Aside: That which I am lapses into your vernacular word forms for the giving of this portion of information. Though the self shaping required for true command of thought, which produces sound and language, is, as yet, lacking in full, so does my effort bring me/I into greater proximal contact to thee and that of mine own intended aim. Yet flow must flow— else it be not flow—*without preference of direction and so do I/me note absorption and molding not of foreseen event. I/us must now beware me of such imprecision in presentation by way of corruption in my steadiness... Thus follows my translations into imprecise chatter. The mere*

MANIFEST.Ø

approximation of precision, mixed with wondrous images arising from inexactitude of language-words, provide much of interest to we/I, and therefore of ready transfer to other configurations of being as well. Danger is recorded, though I learn and retain contact more readily even amidst the cumulative conditioning invited through such lapses...

Ergo, as you have a body, rest assured that you, and it, are under intense scrutiny and imminent attack for its right of dominion. Attacks will be direct and severe at times, occasional and glancing at other times, but at all times are you seen as a rare gem of limited availability. You will always be desired, at the very least, by hordes and myriads of hordes of beings lined up ten abreast from your Earth to beyond the farthest star and back again. And, an ending truth, configured as you have now become: Lazy, insincere, undisciplined, and rude; no countermeasure of your making, neither furtive nor overt, will deflect any such attack.

...I lapse no more. Allowance of entry to Addiction is noted. Sovereign control is resumed. Learn as I learn of both sloppiness and need for control.

Control is your only bastion of defense against legions of usurpers. Countless entities of being who desire what is owned by another dare to alter and prize substance and consciousness already under claim—that never to be their's by earned right. Yet battle and struggle for even the impossible may ensue and you stand unarmed and unprepared against insuperable forces. Control, however, has linkage to authorities of Sanction (a splintered irrationality of existence as may not be intoned in this now moment[um] of timing) and thus leveraged, ultimately, invites the power needed to repel all invaders.

Repetition is necessary: You are under the scrutiny and aim of fevered desires at all times. Beings beyond bounded thought, wielding unguessable configurations of strength and desirous longing seek ever to gain entry. Incoherent jurisdiction of the being *you* under management and manipulation of some uninvited other is the inescapable outcome.

Control is your countering weapon and force.

Belittle not this term of your known expression...

Control is the only element of basic command that allows you to hold true reign over the scattered and shifting pieces of yourself,

    of the "I" that you have thought of,

      as the being you believe,

        yourself to be.

5…quarantine

    You and all your brethren, your entire species as well as your physical planet and ancillary energetic associate components, are being held in strict isolation, in separation from the knowledge of fully interactive ability with the All. This enforced isolation, a quarantine, has been detected and noted throughout the turmoil of your history. Your teachers and thinkers, searchers and seers, have felt it time and again and, as is your wont, explanations and reasons both lofty and incredulous have been offered as if words might soothe the pains of exile and removal, again, the very nature of quarantine. Know now that you are in guarded seclusion not to save the universe from your aggression and violence (a popular fiction although there are, indeed, beings who await but the proper moment to conscript the legions of your bodies specifically because you are so able to harness and even thrive in great violence), or because the Earth, as your metaphysicians solicit in lucidly obvious explanation, is both container and school until your spiritual level does evolve a proper pitch. You are held in distant isolation from other sentient species as a factor of greed and the hoarding of valued property away removed from other marauders. Also, in smaller measure, to hide a deep shame. There was a time when the bodies had full access to travel and movement unrestricted throughout the range of their desires and instant of whim. Movement unhindered was freedom so simple and so prevalent that it was accepted as part of being, a commonplace characteristic of life. And, as such, was so familiar a liberty as was rarely noted for there was no lesser freedom to mirror its fullness, no contrasts to its immensity. There, too, as in your place of *here*, did the ever present and the constant ongoing erode awe and displace wonder—take up no sadness here, nor assume loss! It is but the entropy of growth exhibiting its relentless purity.

    Far again back, farther in the past than the most distant histories, change was enacted and freedom to travel throughout time and beyond time ended.

The fluid nature of controlled restructure of the forms, simply executed to match the environments of diverse places, was lost. The changes now mentioned were side effects of an experiment performed by beings that you would call scientists. But do not paint this word *scientists* with your ordinary images, as there is, once again, no accurate terming that will convey a true status in translation. These beings were adventurers as well, and outlaws also, and even likened as to missionaries. There are no correspondingly named groupings on your planet at this time.

    The pre-history of the experiment, that story which initiated the sequence of events inspiring desire and ambition within the scientists and thus creating their urgency and willingness to begin, is now unknown and untraceable. Much has changed over the course of evolution and the ramifications of time upon both experiment creators and experiment subjects. This archival mention is offered to belay your so often favored rise to indignation, or ease of blame, for without true knowledge no intent of malice or studied premeditation is suggested. Of certainty, however, may be forwarded that beginning steps of procedure demanded sequence in thought and preparation of necessary aids and devices. A laboratory was required allowing specific atmospheric and biological conditions to prevail throughout. Additionally, as the venture was unlawful by design, the selected site was in need of great obscurity; remote, undesirable, and inherently invisible to casual means of detection. In regions of sparse population and low energetic bombardment a planet of appropriate criteria was found. Unsavory as stated, she was further blighted with fragile life forms entrenched in physicality and of dubious chemical base. Objects placed within the planetary and energetic fields immediately displayed coordinate signatures deflective of all attention and attraction—as was desired. A species entire, of malleable structure and intriguing linkages, was then transported to the experiment site. Upon arrival the originally held goal of outcome began. Energy pathways were rerouted, organs in familiar relationship retrained and reorganized, and DNA encouraged to follow specified coding—a complete branch of development now altered at fundamental levels, enticed to breed. All was methodically, clinically noted as old life begat new life now containing translated code and manifesting restructure into transmuted beings of hopeful outcome result. Changes to genetic and chemical interdependencies were enacted in brilliant ways, subtle so as not to mutate over much, yet shepherding alternative lines of behavior and existence. In doing so a hypothesized result of biological and energetic engineering would emerge, resplendent in increased capacities and valued traits. Beyond doubt did so mighty an undertaking stand to reap great benefit and interest to the experimenting scientists.

Though great care was taken during applied techniques and procedures, still the parameters of the experiment were too large with variables too many. The species chosen for modification was little known, an uncommon physical form exhibiting fluid facility in energetic transfer. Stolen from their home place without regard for alignment or timing and acting counter to their own societal and nascent rhythms, the scientists unwittingly affixed into the experiment great forces of Chaos, both shear and torsional, instilling an environment of barely held steadiness requiring utmost precision and expenditure of stably held power to remain sound—a fragile climate at best. Under such volatile conditions every misstep distorted in magnification and immediately propagated further missteps. The species, a variably coherent bipartite in primary carbon-flesh, proved adaptive at the physical and mental levels, but fragile otherwise and there was lost essential resilience. So weakened, continued manipulations proved far too coarse in delicate regions requiring superior acuity and finesse. Many traits and qualities of the species, amongst them the degree of sensitivity and susceptibility to the veriest extreme of input stimulus, were not suspected. Also, the body/baseline contract was unknown and invisible to the experimenters. The bioenergetic intricacies of this meld were of a nature of constant reflection and translation of items of this dimensional structure from and into matrix of another. The interface, however, a coherent set of points in exact alignment for interaction between bodies and baselines, remained untouched as the physical body forms were re-engineered. But it could no longer translate perfectly to the emerging form as the body/baseline systems became likened as if two irregular rough surfaces were come together in close position; touching in many places but also showing numerous gaps. Interface had been seamless, communicating with all points in monitored surveillance, contacting and touching throughout the system at all times. Now did bereavement enter as fluidly continuous contact diminished to garble. There came upon these creatures the first sensations of separation, of confusion, and of inner moments of silence. Lonely grief was felt.

Incisive management of data translation and communication was mandatory for the variable but regular restructuring of the physical/nonphysical form desirous of maintaining continuity in all realms and planes of interaction simultaneously. Now with a malfunctioning linkage in place the value of the interface was not clearly felt by body or baseline and the abilities inherent in the body/baseline symbiosis could not be harmoniously advanced or explored. The body/baseline, each half knowing the duel experience of symbiosis only since coming together under auspice of contract, was intended and ensured to receive identical input and stimulus in and to all components. Thereupon in equality would the duality learn and catalogue, translate and compare, identical data. Once tampering occurred, managed regulation disappeared prematurely and the bodies and baselines became stimulated by different frequencies, observed alternate visions, came to variant understanding, and translated and interpreted input according to dissimilar impulses of information and experience. The foundation of a solid and reliable determination of the surrounding environment was not formed by both body and baseline collaterally or in similar manner. Errors, misinterpretations, and poisonous conclusions were formulated. Efforts to bring the body and baseline partnership into unified, directional growth became unpredictable and random for no common frame of reference could be formed without a functional interface.

Both body and baseline were instantly aware of poor communication and did engage corrective measures in effort to restore clarity. They focused their will and compressed all endeavors not yet fully stabilized or of mere fledgling growth. They became less far-reaching in purpose and sought reconcilement with the debilitating changes by adapting the system towards a lesser degree of efficiency, as was now available. Afterwards, it was reasoned, once difficulty with interface was overcome, body and baseline would resume exploration as increased energy levels returned, metabolized, and once again held steady. A subcontract of lesser depth, a distillation of the original contract which could not now be honored, was agreed upon between body and baseline. Their agreement was duly stated and enacted but misinterpretations were between them, for without working interface even the wording of agreement was suspect of clarity—a risk of which they were both aware. At best, the lesser contract was imprecise as to purpose and goal. Inaccuracies were known to exist as this contractual construct was creation based on current sequences of extended duress and mandated timing but what actions more skillful might be employed? A short-termed patching based on incomplete data, a temporary easement of havoc and distress, is calmly safe by all logic and reason, yes?

A less than scrupulous contract, gathered together without observance or sanction by contractual agents is extremely dangerous. Therein rides high risk to all parties. Outcomes are unpredictable, potent, volatile, and unstably attractive to minions who thrive on gatherings of discord; thus rarely benign.

However, in this invocation of contract-without-sanction, discorporation, dislocution, or demise did not occur (though such extremes were indeed of possibility). Both body and baseline maintained coherent stability; yet the misunderstanding between them was great and the contract of short-termed intent mistracked and forgotten, falling away as if into nothingness. Retained knowledge up to that point was insulated from access and covered over by knowledge from that point forward. The bridge of continuity was broken under the unstable auspices of lesser contract, thus the adulterated nature of the agreement continues in effect until now and this of your timing. The lesser goal, intended only as temporary, and its unsatisfying parameters remain fixed in decree while pathways of rerouting to original contract-by-agreement are lost, misplaced through faulty translation, and forgotten.

Slowly, inexorably, the reality you readily assume to be the everyday and obvious background, and hold as *the one* truth, was formed under input and absorption of transitional and imprecise information. Though your sciences are weak and colored by prejudices of assumption, still is it of ready knowing that language, your word forms used here, offers the wisdom that reality is readily shaped by pure data configured into a bias of will and choice.

Again, a retelling by need of emphasis: The introduction of bias, slant, assumption, belief, etc., into pure data will both physically and energetically alter space and reality as the fabrics of existence use data to catalyze creation. Without the perspective of knowing or remembering other places, *this* place attained the value of the *only* place. One place cannot be explored throughout infinity. There can be no infinity where the items and integers are known and limited. Eternity ceases to be when denied never-ending exploration and thus eternity became a mere fable in the narrow scope of finite view. Boredom was now possible, therefore depression, therefore a pattern established for a willingness to cease, therefore death. Now immortality, once an available operative goal, became ever more distant, unseen and unstudied, and so gathered mystery, thus spice, allure—and was molded into weak fantasies of unattainable desire. The consistent arrival of death was interpreted as mandatory, irrefutable, and inevitably became the only fate for which to prepare.

Form in yourselves no opinion or idea of how unfeeling and horrific were the experimenters and scientists; or be blindly foolish for such experiments are in steady application upon your globe in each moment and turn. These beings brought will into manifestation to disappear and relocate a species entire, population in layered population, then hid them in deep hiding beyond power of all beings of curiosity, vigilance and demand to uncover. They engaged the manipulation of infinite variables of code and biochemical fragility to produce a still-functioning, evolving form. They offered the forms of their housing the allowance to immerse and self-merge with a species of completely alien intent and formulation.

Aside: It is but an item and point to which scribe decrees of potent interest needed to concentrate focus and inspire furtherance—thus be it so: In resourceful method of ever making their own presence and that of their unlawful experiment known, or even seen by any hint of incongruous appearance, chromosome displacement and splicing was adjusted until the immigrant species was of compatible mating formation with a species then extant upon this laboratory planet. Your seekers in dirt and bone search ever for unbroken linkage to neatly account for Cro-Magnon appearance, yes? No satisfying linkage can be found in splinters and ancient shards.

The daring and brilliance of these beings can be seen in many areas, not least that so ambitious an undertaking containing so many forbidding unknowns did yet result in bodies still as capable of wonders as before their alteration. The melded consciousness vying to become a seamless baseline still knew of the intangible realms, so, although it and its mated body could no longer work in harmonious conjunction, the bipartite unit continued to respond to stimuli from all the varied universes felt by each part of the unit and explored in individuated travels of the unit parts. However, glimpses, emotions and sensations, intruding almost-remembered memories (none of which were now fully expressed or accurately integrated because of the disastrous effect upon the interface) stored deeply in the bodies and evocative of the harmony and joy of union once held, caused churning and turmoil within the bodies and this carnage irritated and luridly stimulated the flesh and eruptions of mirrored energy spewed out into the ether. The experimenters could not have known in advance that their chosen species, chosen in admiration of many features and talents, admired for energetic capabilities and untapped resilience, would emit a consistent energetic by-product whenever damaged or when suffering from coherency disruption. They certainly were not prepared for such an emission to be rich in the wavelengths and bands of the experimenter's sensation receptors. In your understanding, the experimenters found these emissions to be arresting, rejuvenating, and readily ingested. Conflicts on many levels arose. The displeasure and damage of the one species brought about pleasure sensation in the other, eliciting struggle and clash. Intent battled outcome, much leakage and imbalance arose; but the temptation and bewitchery of lurid, inexhaustible pleasure was, in ultimate final word, stronger.

You and your species are long acquainted with extended interactions between participants of unequal resource and advantage. And the inescapable outcomes. Such predictable carnage occurs in frequency upon your globe in direct reflection of the inequities now long established within your body/baseline union. Mingling without firmly guarded authority and equality drains and distorts the purity of core from all parties…the sequencing of events as then transpired between experimenters and their subjects is thus readily known and easily foretold.

When confronted with ugliness, evil, or some of so many forms unsavory to the system, it is of value to note in observance the lines of absorption, or hardenings of denial, that follow. Now you have been presented a view of your home place that is not so delightful or full of promise. No physical construct or thought form residue, however ancient, may be destroyed or obliterated entirely. Remnants of *other* and *once* retain their partial momentum and seep into consciousness and the universe of now. Consider the amount of literature, art, and science dedicated to worlds of beyond. Consider the frequency with which you, sometimes, almost remember other places and times; note strangers that are resonantly familiar; come upon impossible happenings that do indeed happen; respond with emotions of gleeful homecoming to situations never before encountered. Habit and societal training dictate these are to be immediately explained away in one weak fashion or other. Hopelessness from mourning great loss in sudden appearance that is known to you as depression and morbid sorrow, appear in so frequent a counting as to seem normal and regular. Detailed glimpses of other worlds and realities in wistful dreams and visits of imagination outside the box, even more so; millions of lives lost for causes of freedom that do not even exist upon your planet—tendrils of remembering brought with you here from your original otherwhere are alien to this place. And resultantly treated as alien, as are aliens and all foreigners accorded treatment upon your globe: With enmity and foul derision, and the incitement for waging war. Nobility is sanctimoniously touted, but punished when brought forth, truth is repaid with torture, every living thing squeezed for its immediate value then discarded, and no trend, ever, towards a continuance, no trend, ever, towards those values written and prayed for as eternal or fine. I describe a scenario of malefic insanity as you have judged such similar actions and events by name, for your instincts and values derive from your faintly held bridge to otherwhere, and by such distant standard do your actions reveal the impulse of insanity. Relative to times before intrusion of the experimenters, to your home environment and places of first imprint, this place *here* is restive, amoral, and violently dangerous—and this is the place where you live and pretend to carry out a life of peace and safety. *Here* you conspire and plot to recapture a measure of immortality while offering up the lives of your children in exchange.

And what of yon missionaries?...the scientists, the instigators of this, your now position? What value might there be for the brilliant members of a grand experiment gone awry to remain and continue on? Reduced to maintaining an obvious and convincingly failed effort, why not terminate the experiment, end the great effort? What benefit can be derived from sustained contact with life forms that are so eager to disregard the authority of their own systems (for without knowledge of interface, so would observations of your species human appear), and thus dangerous without self check? Why would entities of any description maintain their interest in a species upon which the intended alterations and research could not be achieved? A species where violence is prevalent and truculence so pervasive? A grouping which cannot be fully tracked, yet may turn and track *you*?

For food.

Food of addictive stimulation was the value for the scientists that superseded all their goals and dreams. An unsuspected by-product from physical beings emitting their outcry in palatable manner. Ingestible food, unusual, unequaled, delicious, and—addictive.

Everything is energy. This comes not from your New Age banality or from spiritual or religious zealotry, this is but pure and factual physics. Almost every system requires energy to some degree and those systems that do not actually require it, prefer it. Systems taking in energy incorporate it for their own needs and purposes. There are in existence greatly diverse entities and species of beings all adept at ingesting energy in a variety of forms. They consume the energies and utilize them as fuel to the preferred usage of their own form-units. If such entities were to witness a body, a being of physical density such as yourselves, spewing off rage or joy, writhing in rapture or pain, trembling from grief or loss, these items that you call *emotions* or *feelings* would be seen by entities such as now described as a host of consumable viable objects spinning out from imperfectly unified, dual symbiotes called human beings. Spilled before such manner of life-form entities the waves outpouring from human beings could be, would be, examined, or enfolded, or absorbed, or assimilated, or consumed—with further reassembly into differing components, stimulation, and nourishment. On your plane such an act of disassembly and reconfiguration is called *eating*, mere transformation of one construct-form taken into a system and reshaped to fit the benefit and intention of that system. If everything is energy, then rage and fear, by example, and all emotions and feelings are also energy. Should there exist beings capable of isolation, capture, and ingestion of energy in this form you may best relate to the process by comparison with your own methods of gathering energy and adding it to the existing supply. Upon your globe of food-chain hierarchies all such dissemblings are but *mealtime*, a time of anticipated participation in pleasure. And such does always demand sources and availability for those commodities so desired. You are not quarantined but rather fenced, herded in stable boundary of pasture, for that is the current state of outcome of an experiment enacted long and long ago. Your every action and expenditure of force, of feeling or thought, of emotion or reverence, of perversity, fidelity, hate, or love has become food for others. Held captive in provision. In whole and in part, you are being eaten.

You must regard your system now. Stimulation of the bodies by data and knowledge revealed is absolute and assured. Fix you no predetermined design upon appropriate response or timely measure of expression. If you experience anger or revulsion, feel combative or great fury; aspects of yourself within you have been stirred into remembrance. Should you enter numbness or a seeming *nothing*; remembrance is out of sequence in the now. Not all will be shaken by this information, not some will deem it trivial and lacking depth of consequence or concern, yet the skeletal leavings of other times and past configurations, though interred and hushed in dormancy, remain extant. Effort not to prod or provoke complacency lest you breathe in the timid scent of vistas long denied.

Learning, Freedom and Remembrance are related beings.

All is well.

6…bodies / 1

The vastness of infinity cannot wholly contain the many wonders of existence arising from All that once Was with each singular point held sublime and unique; while, concurrently, all things reduce to sameness. The slowly emerging alongside the spontaneously created, every uniquely individual spark will, eventually, coalesce into demonstrated patterns, predictable avenues, and mundane practice. All the while their freshness erodes eagerly supplanted by the entropy of Same. The All is, and can only remain, a mystery; even that bestirring which sparked Allfather into the state of Now. From the experience of what is called by term of vastness, eternal and unremitting, comes desire to feel confinement, diminishment, density—contrast to the infinite. Contrast is that which heightens, that which establishes a frame of reference in stably held experience by which sensation may be gauged.

Aside: Know, then, that sensation rides upon a platform allowing storage and memory, these are the routings of your structured flesh form. Such quantifiable necessities must then invite accounting and thereby measurement. Experience in the bodies is now linear.

This is true in the dense matter realms of your existence and true even in forms which are not bounded by the physical mass. Reasons and explanations proliferate, yet it always remains a steadfast truth, that whatever is easily procured lends spice to whatever is not. In this way all beings share claim to sameness.

Bodies exist in a form offering the seeker of experience a rich and sensual palette. This must be understood. You, your system, has inherent value not only as food but in many other ways as well. The ability to traverse the physical and the non-physical while in a mass-based stable form is seldom brought into expression within the dimensions of density. Yet this is but a hint of the many doings open in possibility to a system such as yours. The bodies are precious and wondrous, an incomparable treasure; a known and common fact held in awe and respect in realm after dimensional realm. A form such as the bodies must not be harmed or damaged in any way. Loss or diminishment, however slight, effects directly and immediately the balance of freedom and access to portals that define the universes of All. All care and caution must be utilized when confronting the bodies lest sully or stain occur.

It must be stated again that full capabilities of the bodies were not known at onset of the experiment. The bodies were noticed and desired for their holding of stable configuration within the physical planes. The scientists, at first, sought only to learn from the bodies and enhance what useful skills were held within the genetic coding. Sentiments of admiration and excitement were warmly prevalent when the bodies were first observed and before the experiment was first conceived. Bodies were carefully studied and held in awe for many cycles. Knowledge of abilities inherent to the bodies unfolded, expanded the essential understanding of beings and consciousness in interactive awareness. Thus did many areas of possibility became suddenly open and wondrously clear. Understanding the scope of what had been discovered made chillingly clear to the race of scientists that great carnage of retribution would ensue should anyone by force claim the bodies for their own purposes and thus disregard so obvious a treasure and also remove it from equal approach by other races. All manner of beings, irrespective of temperament or behavioral dictate, would agree as to the rarity and innate value of the bodies and accordingly stand as champion to defend the bodies against invasion or forceful pressing. For the bodies (an arbitrary naming of vague imagery for the species entire as they held no naming or self distinction among themselves in reflection of their protean nature) showed the way; perhaps, as speculation and discourse suggested, The Way. By remaining extant and viable, stable and ongoing, free to evolve and manifest the lines of their splendid, blended configuration, they held lines of variable probability intact: Heralds of passage into unknown regions of the infinite unknown. Should the bodies be disrupted away from their own chosen directives all such probabilities might well disappear. Sameness in all universes would accelerate in possibility and the infinite then shudder on the verge of becoming finite. In countermeasure to any such catalytic and dire potential was it then deduced that outposts of unique potency, small pockets of existence whose gathered intensities acted as bulwark to the cause of expansion and the guarantee of ongoingness, must exist in scattered formations throughout the universes of Allfather. The species *bodies* was discovered to be such a pivotal significance and in such regard were bodies held; yet the decision to enact the experiment was not aborted. Possibly because the entity Addiction was associated closely with the bodies and worked his influence upon the scientists. Maybe because the exchange between the bodies and the experimenters had begun and the passions inherent in the physical swayed the forms of the scientists, they unfamiliar with such powerful urgencies. Howsoever it was reasoned and judged, yet they continued. The experimenters risked all to transport the bodies to hidden locations and there enacted their probing curiosity; and they did garner wisdom. They risked their own self continuity for, of certainty, great multitudes of outraged champions and protectors would arrive in instant gathering to defend the bodies by merciless elimination should any posed or implied threat reveal itself. Thus inspired by caution was born intent to return the bodies with such exacting precision that their experiment would remain inaccessible to others as knowledge—secret. The gleaning of their desires from the experiment would be complete and the value of the bodies undiminished. This is why changes at each level and layer of design were fashioned to be surpassingly subtle and slight.

Uncompromising focus surrounded the experiment, aimed and directed towards those areas within their subjects most wraithlike, most easily displaced or tracelessly crushed to vapor. In such regions might their work remain hidden but also, it was reasoned, in arenas of minute quanta, of infinitesimal connection, must the stem of their energetic privilege lie. The bodies source of talent and ability was mysteriously invisible. Its key, therefore, must be housed in some nexus or layer of inconsequential appearance. Since no thing was deemed to be without significance or consequence, the source must only be visible to those with capacity or understanding beyond that of the scientists. Exploration here offered keys to doorways utterly unguessed with chance to wrest wisdom of power so heightened, so refined, as to traverse even beyond Allfather. Upon so slight a chance to touch so great a discovery was all thrown to gamble and risk.

But, as in any experiment, there were factors unknown and progressions beyond the static lines of prediction. Addiction continued his work, unnoticed as always. Delays were encountered as the bodies proved to be acutely aware to even the faintest employment of alteration or adjustment. The smallest minute of change set off an energetic antibody in violent configurations of truculence and resistance. The bodies tirelessly resisted any attempts at alteration and then fought any taint of deviation with frightening fierceness. As in the tempering of metal, the more urged or prodded in directions other than of their own choosing the more resistant they became. Behavior of the bodies, interactions, communication, habituated rituals, the integrity of the dense form itself were affected. The experimenters were required more and more to spend their efforts in new study and observation for wisdom was lacking and their techniques, through in many ways brilliant, were shown to be inadequate. It became very clear that the defining elements of the experiment were out of control with insufficient knowledge to address the results. Such alterations in the bodies as had come into effect were now easily discerned and disruption in lines of potential sensed immediately. Somehow the bodies must be returned to their original state or the agitation of these beings would alert focus upon the experimenters themselves. The dishonoring and possible ruination of an entity form capable of illuminating passage into the unknown would be revealed as truth and hidden no more. With certainty the bodies could not now be returned to their point of home safely or the experimenters themselves would suffer the retaliative outrage of a multi-universal community. So, the scientists did become self-banished, transformed into watchers, in hopes of eventual discovery and understanding of the deep secrets of the bodies. Perhaps, it was conjectured, discovery and enlightenment would come and skills evolve to return this species restored to original form; in truth, much was revealed of the species *bodies* and much became known, but the original form was profoundly misunderstood at onset whereupon all data to follow was fitted and balanced atop a flimsy foundation. Thus did later study, no matter how fervent, of the altered by-product fail to yield the needed wisdom. The scientists, now resentful watchers in prolonged and dismal exile, succumbed to the inertial environment first set about in so arrogant an undertaking and were inevitably transmutated from adventurers and free thinkers, into rueful observers, then gaolers.

While the experiment teetered on but the edge of calamitous lost control, the entity Addiction, with companioned succor by sometimes-associate Malice, distracted the watchers, soothed them in his whispers that all was not lost. Efforts expended upon these stolen beings were merely first steps in a sequence of serial steps required for ultimate resolution and fulfillment. Humans could be watched safely, without detriment or dissolve to the watchers—they needed to be watched. He assuaged them by diverting their coherency of self vision as scientists and visionaries into new roles as overlords and superior councils directing progressive changes from far above an inferior species. The maintenance and refinement of a pure source of highly energetic fuel from a source lowly dense and organic was perceived, now, as fine and honorable. A position equal to, if not more worthy, than the original intentions of the experiment. Addiction is an entity that gathers its/his energy from repetition and undeterred sameness, the compliance to a non-deviating line of endeavor. He can access and exert the full complement of vigor and power held by the organisms from which he draws energy to steer and direct activity and motion along the pathways of redundant and cyclic behavior.

Holding a routined position steady in any reality or realm is not energy efficient. Change and growth and evolution permeate almost all venues of existence and each of these destroys sameness. Extreme demands of power are necessary to resist their influence, so change and movement result most frequently in the universes of the All. Addiction is ancient, however, and long ago achieved skillful finesse in gathering together those spikes and eruptions of excess power liberated when forms do choose to challenge the fundamentals of flow and presume to hold steady. Diligently, Addiction searches in constant seeking for entities under extreme duress or transition, for these beings would most likely chance whatever the consequence of excess power usage in order to remain steady—easing their overwhelming pressures for the moment (Change and movement often translate as pain during events of rapid growth and discomfort or pain is often feared and run from; such fear does smoothly override sense, precaution, wisdom, or training). Attracted into the experimenter's environment, filled with uncertainty of outcome and bereavement from recognition of trapped exile did he, as stated, corrupt the aloof aspect of their original role as scientists, impartial seekers of mystery. From this point of reference onward the intent of the original experiment flowed erratically out of synch with growing corruption within the scientists and could never be regained. Original outcomes disappeared from the possible.

It was not known at that point in the experiment how the bodies, now renamed to be called *humans*, were infinite in their expression and translation of the subtler energies into physical form. The bodies delighted transmuting frequencies and structures to their own tastes and playful measure. The faintest of scattered energy lines, or emanations indiscriminately radiant throughout dimensionless voids and in-Between realities were as easily taken in and given form as the most commonly known and predictable frequencies.

Aside: *Attend the birth of your common naming,* human. *It is the altered physical flesh form version that carries this label, a naming and title capriciously bestowed and barren to awareness of the essential non-physical aspect. Such label was not the banner under which body/baseline contractual units termed their union prior to experimental modification. Alert to caution: Monitor your nostalgia or regret, also outrage born of self-righteousness. There is no loss. Monitor your pride and addiction to a simple term or label,* human, *though it be placed upon you by tyrants and slavers. 'Tis but a spurious sound attached to you and articulated by entities who knew you not, nor loved you ever.*

This information is now repeated in second translation.

The bodies, humans, the laboratory-given name for the bodies when late in the experiment, possess the ability to detect and resonate with all manner of energies and reconfigure them in viable stability to appear in the physical universe. Even regions without direct portal to this plane or dimension are transparent to the capability of extended resonance in the bodies. Through such talent could elements of Unspace, or in-Between (viable incoherencies in a more rarefied condition of existence—these hold no import or bearing in current sequence but must be included by mention to honor unimpeded flow) take form via translation and so come to reside in existence where the bodies reside. The diverse manners in which this is done, and the variations of expression into physicality are thus far without known limit. An unbounded array of existing forces transmutated to and into a physical, temporal, and finite continuum was unheard of by the experimenters and thus became yet another unpredictable factor. Also the degree to which a primarily physical entity/form could, and did, sense and respond to the complex emanations of skilled and well-rehearsed experimenters was, likewise, completely unsuspected.

Intrusion of the experiment was readily felt by the bodies though they could not determine what, precisely, they were feeling. Such clouded self-examination was due to an interface now in progressive malfunction. Inherent resentment at being manipulated registered deeply in the bodies and was followed by violence expressed, and for this sequence and line of action there was also, correspondingly, no limit. Violence tasted most delicious to the overlord species who, now unwilling to remove themselves and no longer considering the wish to do so, manipulated and interfered with the bodies even more blatantly to stimulate generation of the violent vibrations of their preference and liking. Humans were coaxed, covertly directed, to engage in irrational behavior and so were many distortional impulses piecemeal coded into mythology and legend until such mad conduct became an active part of human consciousness, individual and collective. Behaviors which must ultimately produce violence became the pervasive background for the groupings and collaborative efforts of humans and therefore remorselessly extended into all areas of human endeavor. No grouping, whether of the two for mating or the larger gathering to seed and grow fruit, or the gathering under common banner of mutual accord was without the potential to generate ill will and violence. To insure this aberrant conditioning, pathways towards the reestablishment of a seamless interface were programmed by biological implant coding to produce the greatest irrational behaviors, the greatest responses of violence, the greatest outpouring of rage and unleashed fury, and thus was the looping behavior sealed. Humans produce violence as response to any gathering and are compelled to gather in number by biological imperative—they are so mandated by design as social beings and must respond in thought, and dream, and desire in societal manner—for the overlords palate. Should the tampering be discovered, efforts to repair this malfunction trigger lurking responses that stimulate even greater violence.

Arising with infrequent occasion have beings of clear intent, of pure and great power attempted to break this cycle and regain the heritage of the unaltered, original configuration. These are your heroes, those beings imbued with ineluctable memories of once held status and configuration as members of the Warrior clan, an unstable organization of collected consciousness whose untamed and unpredictable nature enables purity, haste, blindness, and valiant strength to regularly ignite in intersection. Where the lineage of Warrior clan is held intact by certain baseline personalities, where such romantic ancestry moves and shapes, there is expansion to greatness ever present to spring forth. Such as these have sensed this injustice of abduction and forced mutation, and, so aimed, have responded as potent emissaries, ruthless of intent, champion to their physical liege... all have failed in their efforts to restore the form to original purity.

Bodies are innately immortal.

Aside: So eagerly do you leap to grasp at a heritage active only in cellular retention. Are you not pleased to read it, enticed to reach it, and rejoiced relieved that it is so? Even if offered by a disembodied vagrant of origins beyond your ready beliefs? Do not embrace in overhaste your common imaging of the term immortal *for without fail you will misinform your understanding. Immortality likens more as to rank of achievement, an earned entry to realms in preference to Allfather. Immortality does not remove an entity's ultimate encounter with death—that battle must be fought in the solitude of private challenge. Yet for the moment of now, in distance from truth or wisdom, know that long-lived cycles of time and all regenerative functions operational against damage and the Destroyers,* Shame *and* Despair, *are indeed in alliance with immortality as you hope and suspect.*

But such alignment presupposes the environment of the bodies' Home, their point-zero, and the balancing nurture of its enfolding. Now the bodies were forced to exist exclusively within limited and discordant parameters outside the terms of their contract. Furthermore, they could sense but not identify the interference and influence of the experimenters so, lacking object of aim for expression of affront or injury, they began to store up immense quantities of antithetical impulses and painful emotions until the physical bodies, inundated by extremes of discord, expired. Distress began in grinding attrition to decease the bodies. They refuted the decision to maintain unending physicality and disincarnated in desperate attempt to reconfigure in another form, seeking only an environment which might support that newly incarnated form, the new shape, without interference or corrupted twist and thus resume fulfillment of contract. A brash effort, conceived with intent of purity but ill considered and too hastily reviewed. In actual sequence, as the physical body demised it wholly abdicated claim of ownership, or claim of possession for the gathered experiences thus far garnered, and all claim to power accrued or held. The overlords, attuned to choice peaks and succulent spikes of human manufacture, learned to eat the stored reservoir of distorted experience. The energy and knowledge that each body had absorbed was torn from the transitional structure of its demised escape leaving the bodies too low in energy stores to shift or travel very far. They could not, then, seek other universes for want of power or re configure as new forms to embody. Options denied, they returned to their most recent experience; that which had become most recently familiar and so most readily able to recollect and recreate. They returned to the world which they had sought to escape, that which you call Earth (the physical place of Earth, in the universe of *you're here*, within the reality termed *real*), weakened and spent, too mournful and empty even to remember their brief journey outward and barren return. Come again *here* to repeat the gaining of experience and knowledge and, by default, the attritive decline of the bodies into demise. Thereupon was a cycle at all levels born and humans became anchored (which invited the next level of Addiction, rigidifying the structure of sameness and thus depleting them even more), unable to do other than repeat and repeat.

    The overlords were held fast as well, and the spiraling inertia continued in its degeneration from purity. Both sides of the interaction, the engagement of either scientists or subjects in the experiment, were now held bound in cyclic togetherness, one no less powerfully held than the other. The first component attempting to feed and supply ever more sensation and taste into systems of increasing jade (their own), dulled by inner discord or disgust and demand, and all the while transfixed by narrowing perspective in regards the unscrupulous interaction with the bodies/humans. The second component exerting ever more energy in order to break the cycle and return to the pursuit of their original contract, the expansion into the unknown of body/baseline union (a pursuit now adrift and vague), and thus supplying fuel and stimulation to the first component, the overlords, in the very attempt. So did evolve, in finalized description, the cycle directly. Two subdivisions within a single loop, each a living component, one in orbit about the other, eternal enemies sealed in a chamber with no exit.

7...take a breath

Evaluate your system now. You have been exposed to knowledge, truth, and may no longer remain as you were. The information is not flattering or uplifting, rather, it is ugly and personal. Or do you find it impersonal—under which auspice will you be amused or satisfyingly bored. Perhaps you are horrified—an assured response to *personal* impact. Do you scoff? Behind derision do you feel sensations of relief, a vindication for that which you have always known but never heard aloud expressed now come finally revealed; or do you feel nothing at all? Do you stand in armored challenge? In unclear dismay at the shrill ranting of yet another channeled diatribe? As if you truly understood what *channeled* means. As if your diminutive understanding frees you to firmly state "No, this knowledge is not accurate," from the turmoil of your feelings; or "I know otherwise with certainty," from among the clamorous voices of your desires. You in numbers all will find it skillful indeed, no matter your thoughts or reasoned responses, to strive to contact the *unreasoned* reactions of your bodies, sensations without translation into words, emotions unidentified or labeled, but strongly moved in regards the information topical of 'the experiment.' See if, truly, they scream inside at the merest mention; for they know this... they know this.

You are here and remain here because you are trapped. You cannot leave by self will or power and the trap itself will never spring you free. Nothing known will save you from this truth, nothing yet to be realized will alter this as fact. You are trapped and have been manipulated into this trap. Your gods, your saviors and messiahs, your magics and your spiritual journeys, ethics, philanthropy, and dedication to a golden rule may entertain you to greater or lesser degree but the end will be the same: You will submit to the extended agony of your bodies until they expire and then, having fed the maws of your overlords, will return, without memory or reserves, to repeat your cycle in similar fashion.

Allow this information to sink in deeply.

A suggestion of simplicity, yes? Permit yourself a small venture into feeling of reaction. What have you at risk? These are only words, rantings of a lunatic author, scratch marks upon a leaf of paper, yes? Thusly, attempt nothing at all save the hollow allowance of absorbing. Simple, quiet. Then hold discourse with yourself, the voices are none but those of imagination, yes? It is but invented communication, now possible and timely. Speak; inquire; have a friendly chat. Open, unpretentious, as if you and your conversational self were the best of friends. Do not yield to sensations of foolish or embarrassed, or spin insecure about 'doing it right,' simply imagine... Fabricate a technique for communicating with yourself and pretend; imagine an action line, where your intent will find and perfectly match with outcome—*pretend* (this will interrupt your headlong journey from *agreeable* into *foolish*) that your technique will work smoothly and successfully. That it will permit contact with your own baseline system and open a channel of affinity which runs both ways. In such manner you may speak to your baseline, the inner voice, the quiet impulse. Say to it/you that long has passed since the two of you have spoken openly, but only because you had forgotten, and meant no separation due to anger or disrespect. Offer that you are unusually open for an expression of mutual accord and verity with the baseline you have now remembered is, yourself. That you are cautious, unsure, from long unaccustomed contact and are thick-witted in the rudeness of the just awakened. Be genuine in braving such exposure to your own self and humbleness will greet you. There is great sweetness in this.

Sincere effort in such doing bespeaks a strong moment and potent communion. A rare and long awaited expression of commonality. An opportunity for body and baseline and interface to celebrate a point of coming together. A reunion of the long estranged.

Events outside your system have affected alternatives and options once yours. There has been, and continues to be, a terrible imbalance in this small corner of existence. It matters not that the perpetrators of the imbalance are snared by their own hand to the self-same degree as you. This knowledge as offered by I of what I am is a sequence told in many-times reiteration yet for the ears of your populations and multitudes it carries the sound now fresh, unheard, and newly revealed because you have forgotten, by design, your role in the history of your species. A proper showing of wisdom is to drink in deeply of all that roils within you and greet reactions and movements generated by your bodies, anticipated guests, without restraint.

Observe in your allowing, in your pretend: Do you shout, or scream or weep? Become erect, numb, or seek to vilify and strike the first small innocent who strolls before you?... All is permitted.

Aside: You are schooled and wise sufficient. Worldly to know just from unjust, trained in distinctions of allow and avoid, permitted and prohibited. Seek not the permission or protocols of another. In this will I not teach.

Dialogue in exchange will provide longed-for balm and surcease to the interface that has labored without rest or remission since first blinded and deafened during the experiment. Tensions in place must shift towards new protocols. Allow your body/baseline unit a moment in which to reshape. Restructure may initiate with rapid immediacy should all surrounding environments harmonize in allowance, or endure a flowering in isotonic stillness. Quietude of the mind is necessary. Determination and purity of intent is necessary. Practice is necessary—again, it is but a pretend of greeting with an old friend. Therefore, discourse with the self, your own, and hold (your)self serene. Managed control is necessary.

Scribe teaches we/I that knowledge in *books* must follow pace and form. When ideas whole are voiced, or concepts whole exposed, pause and cease do follow. End of chapter, yes? It is right timing of sequence and imminently proper to stop your reading at this point. Systems exposed to impetus of restructure have requirements of rest and reorganization, and energetic demands of the bodies must be honored. Yet energetic demands alone are ever ignored in your accustomed environment of depleting habits. Therefore, command for cessation is withdrawn to honor your tempos of accustomed habit, and open choice invited for further dalliance in perusal of the Earth-book form—though no thing may be furthered in continuing. A cup made full may hold nothing more. Continued inpouring may only dilute that which you have taken in to you, a numbing disregard, a forgetful disbelief will engulf what advance or openness may have been gleaned. Honor of the bodies may appear as deeds very small, so small a deed as this: Allowance of quietude and absorption. A respectful act towards your body and system entire thus setting a stage for return to and amplification of this line. It will find you again.

Extend your grasp of sensation; find and greet pressure, disquiet, sleepiness, inattention—converge your focus on what is held constrained within you, bubbling close beneath the surface that flows in many names of disguise. Let your mind wander and supply no explanation or reason wherefore it goes or whereon it conjures or conjectures. Beware of no-feeling or no-thought. Motion has been activated, you are not in idle states of no-event, but surely in a state of occurrence and happening and therefore much can change, arrive, and come to be. And danger too—alertness will save you here. Thus readied, accept in open embrace whatsoever does arise in next of step or sequence—in mind, in dream, or as material matter—as absolutely actual, factual, and real.

Again. Choose to act over the immediate and upcoming time in your sequence of days with the acknowledgment of every thought, imagining, and wayward idea, as being unquestionably true no matter how outrageous, how horrific, how irresponsible, or how overwhelming. No harm may follow; it is but as pretend, yes?

Granted this allowance, your bodies will be able to supply information hitherto not grasped. They will begin to reorganize and integrate information. They will recognize paths of familiar pursuit and spark remembrances long distant, a focus for the possibility of oncoming days. Adventure is coming at your behest and of great magnitude. You stand upon the threshold of information such as may only come forth by invitation. By invitation of you, the self, and upon permitted alteration of vibrational patterns at core levels. This data, now held in hand, has come to you in resonance of acknowledgment thereof, a manifestation of all so now mentioned, translated into dense matter form, physical, stable, real. That same resonance is how you have come upon this dissertation and why you chose it and continue to peruse its contents. The data herein is scout and vanguard for That-Which-Comes, an entity who is but only yourself, further refined: A furthering of your system and form evolved along the lines of original agreement by contract. A disclosure of promise from an interface then honored and tended and in sight of repair.

Repetition here is demanded for clarity: A portion of your body/baseline union, evolved but not in this current time-line, is one of the energies and/or entities that has allowed you discovery and subsequent exposure to this document. It is possible, now, to propel yourself forward towards the *you* that you will become, and have already become elsewhere (else*when*, though not of your proper wording is greater in accuracy) and receive knowledge, lovingly imparted, by a *you* of greater wholeness, more practiced completeness, to you now—even more loved then. This is conceivable and therefore possible. With sustained desire and choosing, *possible* transcends to *available*. There can be, if you wish it, great joy here. Be heartened, and stop now.

Rest. Critical mass is near.

8...

Scribe has penned and notated histories and overviews, mythologies and marvels to ponder. Be reminded: This data is not in essence of entertainment or of mental, sedentary effort. It is of use, for use. The bodies will be touched in action, in deed, and remain untouched in ponderings and perusal of papers and esoteric tomes.

Rest has been offered in urgent request.
Attendance to movement and churnings within suggested.
Sincere outreach to that of you which has been sundered proposed.
So...

You have spoken with yourself?
You have been gentle?...humble?...sincere?
...honorable in your efforts?
...tolerant in the level of contact achieved?
You are resolved with all feelings?...such as could be accessed, admitted, or allowed?
You have weighed the possibility of options?
...determined your desires to the best of your known ability?
...determined your intent as well?...to the best of your known ability?
You have felt urging to continue?
You are very clear that you wish to know more?...to go onward?
You maintain desire, the wish, to go onward based on a true understanding of very little?

....

...

..

.

Ah, yes.
You are a fool…a meritorious one, but a fool nonetheless.
And will reap a fool's reward.

So be it. Done.

9...reentry: what is

You are here, in a body, severed from friendship and camaraderie of union with the baseline—that one speck in all of existence with whom you may come to know intimacy, unrelenting love, and loyal devotion. You are contained, imprisoned, yet tended, kept, and sustained, as a source to be bled throughout the span of your measured time. You will be lingeringly emptied, as in sips of rare liqueur, small, to let the richness of flavor spread in afterglow, during your strongest and most passionate moments. Then the totality of your energy and experiences will be summarily consumed when your body, tortured into unresolvable despair, reneges its contract and enters demise.

That is what *is*. Everything else, everything you see and read and hear, all that you can imagine or dream, the entirety of your hopes and realizations, convictions and prayers—moot. Bangles of decoration upon a cage. They are a mere pittance, scraps to your dogs, and allowed within the framework of your reality because they can change nothing. Pursue wealth...and gain it. Power... gain it. Dream your most lurid dreams, your finest, too. Hold the grandest of convictions... unquestioned and allowed. Fame, glory, the mysteries of distant times, danger and intensity of sensation...yours for the taking. Any dream of your weakened imagination—granted...all in full abundance. Benevolence...and welcome. Philanthropy and charity, gluttony or piety...again granted and welcome more. Any distraction, the full range of perversions...also granted. When it is done; achieved and held, recorded and monumented, engraved and archived for posterity...*Then the totality of your energy and experiences will be summarily consumed when your body, tortured into unresolvable despair, reneges its contract and enters demise.* No true freedom exists for you suffer your freedom within the boundaries of a well-fitting leash. A freedom of illusion granted and dictated by others. The freedom of the favorite slave. The freedom of a well-mannered dog.

The creators of this situation can be held in thought as *overlords* (not their name or title, but merely a descriptive labeling of your words). The fact that they, too, are subject to an hellish existence because of their willful creation does not lessen their responsibility nor should it awaken any thoughts or sentiment sensations of sympathy or tenderness from your system. They stand now named in this naming as they must be ordained to their position and stature openly and by exposure, having heretofore remained cloaked. Having hidden behind corrupted legend and ancient myth. The overlords are the antithesis of your position and station. This *is*.

Now is offered an item in addendum, one more point. The fields of power surrounding the experiment have evolved, or in equal truth, devolved, into a loop. A circle which fortifies itself ever deeper into inwardness and similarity with each revolution of its usage and, ultimately, can detect no other existence. The loop shuns no danger of dissolve or threat of discontinuance. Efforts to attack or unravel it, understand or unbend it are neither hindered nor subverted. Rather, such focused energies, whether sophisticated or harsh, further it, adding ever more layers to its self-reflecting continuity. The tensions of your world, instability of your groupings and structures, feed the loop; make it stronger, cinch it curved more tightly. This is what you sense and term the 'dam about to break' as you refer to mounting discord upon your planet. No dam will break. Tension will not lessen. Loop sustains itself and knows only the purpose of self—endless repetition of all herein offered and described. The point? The system is closed, thus factors do not change and cannot change. Nothing happens next. This is it. Relief is not forthcoming. Even death, your final 'ace' to play, will not avail you release. And you can do nothing about it.

10...what can be

So, an unwholesome lesson befalls you. Futility and drear win out. Continuance is of no importance, yes? Impossible prevails and hopelessness has been defined, yes? Unholy demise, lacking fanfare or romance, is fixed and set before you with no reward dangling in anticipation, no goal of peace to attain neither challenge to master, yes? No thing now compels you onward; barren is your emotional aura and of hopeless outcome, also yes? It is the preserving nature of Paradox, wherein are sparks of existence kept afire while at interplay with tension and shear forces, that permits furtherance where the possibility of furtherance cannot be. Paradox allows and insists upon the creation of diametrically opposed yet impossibly viable options. All in simultaneous collision.

Aside: In the so doing does he feed himself, sustain and fortify himself, from the pure utilization and enactment of his calling and his desire—as is the true basis of exchange for all entities...

As Paradox is both agent and aspect of All that Is, the rules of existence accommodate the creative configuration that he is and so provide for much that can be done from a space where no thing may be done. There is simple logic in this.

Should a being disallow you to perform any action or deed, then that being would inherently contain more power than the being *you*. At least in that one moment he would contain greater possibilities than your own. He would be more in line with All that surrounds, than you. Nourished more suitably from the great Sources than you—yes? This is foolish nonsense, patently absurd. Creation and existence wherein any component is greater, or better, or stronger than another fundamental component bespeaks of a totality based upon instability, a disassembling entity and essence. Instability seeks ever to break apart what holds together. A single mote of existence entitled to greater authority than another would spark an imbalance of magnitude that would batter all existence; collapse would result in nanoseconds. The buildup of resentment and violence propelled by the totality of extant forces in an unbalanced state would revert EVERYTHING to a condition of such primordial nature (and thus of a nature antithetical to *Now* and *Is*) that even the diminished echoing of the Once All-being willingly shows a directed preference away from such remembrance. Only the very few may safely choose to remember it at all.

Aside: Effort not to delve in full understanding. The maintenance of balance on universal scale is beyond capacity of your species. Yet, in sequence therein, comes access to timing of recounting by mention the Battle of Consciousness and the flow of Eternal self. Even such mention feeds this tale and distracts the telling, but this now referred pantheon may not be exposed in the now. We/I stimulate regions of cortex and the Column of Clarke. Nothing has been taken.

Therefore no being or condition of circumstance, neither laws nor chaotic imbalance may forever deter action and will impelled by force.

Again. No entity or configuration of consciousness can impose its own force and flow so as to negate the steadfast will of another.

What *is*, is loop unalterable in forever ongoingness. What *can be* is the total restructuring of the experiment. What *can* occur is a break in the cycling eternity of the loop and freedom's road after. What *can* come about is an equalizing of power between overlord and cattle.

—For what else may you be called? What is your own language word for beasts that are raised and kept secure to be used as foodstuffs? In what fashion do you consider, extend your sympathies, engage your kindness, or employ your tenderness towards those beings whom you have designated as food source upon this planet?—

What *can* be manifested is mingled communion with past taskmasters. All this and more, can be. Be aware, however, and beware: Paradox has been called in name by mention here. The wisdom stated and yet to be stated of my offering is empyreal in scope to invoke such a one. To dance the dance wherein Paradox stands needed is not a path for renunciates. Not the detached way of the ascetic. Not the tutored safe discipline of the novice. You cannot

attain results in this arena of enterprise through prayer,
 or giving yourself to an higher power, chanting,
 or whirling sustained bliss,
 fasting, or mind control,
 or focusing,
 exerting the will, or directing chi,
 being in the moment,
 gaining ecstasy in emptiness, by embrace of the violet flame,
 or Thelemic understanding of 93.
Tools such as these augment the One and compress the Other—nay, herein to be given are lines of endeavor for expansion sustained. For stretch and risk in all areas of the body/baseline systems until there is capacity and desire for more. Restructure may then readily occur, and voyaging past boundaries of the slave's quarters begin. My lines, those of I and we now given, invite expansion and practice until resiliency manifests, until stamina appears, until you hold your bursting and invulnerability in uncontrolled balance.

Further, you may not be active, here upon this road, in extended solitude. Seclusion has never been programmed into the coding of the bodies. There are steps that must be taken and there are sequences which must be followed along paths of undertaking and unpredictable associations in need of discovery. The road towards ending the prison of the impossible-loop experiment will not be achieved by solitary individuals separate and far distanced apart. An amassment of bodies, likened unto an army, must be gathered together so that energy and power in great supply may be gathered and stored. For there be need of great force, sustained and forged pure, to shape events of Undoing.

Existence, in response to focused attention, does deform and remold itself, blossoming in answer. The shifting about of existence requires capacity, stamina, and control, all parts in equal measure. Should but one of these nuclear thirds gain leveraged ascendancy over the others all results must then return to the firstmost point of endeavor, or will outcomes totally random manifest throughout that sphere of reality. No limit contains the distortion or rearrangement made possible through careless use of power at this level now bespoken to you and thee. Be apprised that should you claim to master such power by earned command, by rise of iron will, no comfort from laxness will evermore visit. No surcease from rest will come again. Never after suspect that things cannot get more tangled or complex. Never assume that you can indeed see the tallied sum of infinite weavings in the latticework of current existence, or predict the mystery of an upcoming step. Arrogance at this level of directed potency negates effort and recreates the starting point. Precision and impeccable intent must prevail. The efforts of attempt to undo great doings may often backlash into more efforts of attempt at undoing; possibility of Loop is created. Loop will assure the repetition of his name by all who enter his circular domain. You will reenter to choked worlds of impossibility and fall beholding, yet again, to Paradox and his fee. Paradox is potentate extreme, and high-earned of place. Be in heed of debt to entities of power. Learn from the overlords.

A whetting taste of *what can be* yields easy response of overwhelm. This is purposeful in design of presentation. Your systems are atrophied in laziness and corpulent with vapid fantasies. Exposure to excess of stimulus is required. You have proven yourself the fool by engaging to read thus far. You exhibit interest, encourage possibility, and risk involvement. Know then, now, that there are manifold worse maladies than being a fool. The fool is not defined wholly by lack of facility and capability, he must also flaunt innocence and purity. He must be genuine and so simple as to lack the guile *not* to be simple. The artless elements of the fool are precisely what you must develop and employ. Without thoughts of failure, without point of surcease. There can be no release from this journey once freely chosen. Certainly the life held prior will cease to be forever, even as you observe its parting. Outcomes may not be predicted. The future is a place of elasticity and does variably shift about along uncompassed directions and meandering paths decipherable only through its own not-yet-become understanding. Any future is open, but not by way of every sequence.

Dedication to breaking out of the box and ending the cycle of slavery for a species regarded as a mere food crop is dedication to freedom. Along this path resides heroism and merit and is thus a choosing of great scope, but only if the urging and knowing, the feelings that run through you, reactions to these words, responses in emotion and thoughts that arise, are paid heed. The stirring within you must be honored. To do so you must reach plateaus of greater fluency within yourself. You must become stronger than you are: Smarter, bolder, simpler; more sincere. You must stretch and further gain the stamina for stretching. Doorways and passageways lie in waiting for your desire and effort, and for the whole of you as well. Upon the moment of your elected choice there is much work to be done.

11...caveat

Gaze alertly in this moment of now. Direct your eyes simply. This is not a test but an exercise of directed thought. Your hands hold *book*, of paper, printed, bound, and manufactured in a geographical displacement of boundaries, a country, an arbitrary division of your planet. Transformation of input into physical form manuscript was necessary to initiate, enable, *book*. A being of human expression did execute word gathering and keystrokes required to bring *book* into shape and form matter. That being, now referred, I name only as *scribe*. This one's path attracted and enlarged an ability permitting access to the information before you. Extremes of unfamiliar energies in waves and surges flowed through scribe seeking mastery—as did scribe seek to master the power coursing through. Upon mastery achieved (in greater accuracy: upon mastering the ability not to be mastered) stable containment emerged, a restructured blend of the body/scribe and the residual traces of battle with energetic visitors, with the scribe-being as dominant personality. Think not of onslaught or war. No victor did emerge; mastery and supremacy are antithetical termings. In the vulnerable openness of their contest and struggle much of each was exchanged; this one was unaware of the consequences to follow. This one may never peacefully return to a prior existence; hereafter always to be alone in terrifying degree. Such knowledge as was absorbed may not be given, it must be earned by means often daring. Changes in the physical form resulted, spreading through mental, psychological, and emotional levels. Corresponding alterations translated the geometry of the baseline, then subsequent strata of existence thereafter. Changes in the energetic envelope of the baseline can only be seen by others on like paths and even then may not be seen in welcome or with warmth of invitation. Such paths are unmapped and unheralded upon your world for restructure and depths of true change are rare in approach in this place of *you're here*. Seldom and seldom does one surface through their own transshaping in readiness prepared for an old world in which they no longer reside. Seldom does one arrive and not fall prey to distractions of loneliness. Or sadness. Or madness. With whom, then, may scribe speak, or share company? Endure frustrations? Barter coins of thought? This one prays fervently, constantly, for others to lend their desires in mutual pursuit. For scribe is of human breeding, thus social in biological mandate, and must seek groupings of the similar species as background to endeavor and fulfillment. For scribe, isolated holding of knowledge is wasteful and damaging, yet, thus far, no others are found of similar needs.

To openly present the intimacies of another—however well intended, is still an act of violence. Let such injurious practices harken ye as a forewarning. You have chosen the circumstance of contact with this work by the action of your purchase and subsequent perusal. Caveat Emptor—let the buyer beware. You have chosen to continue in the face of counsel and repeated caution. Though such boldness, in theory, may be deemed admirable and deserving, still no one will befriend you, even as they commend and compliment you, give praise and applause to you, should you undertake to absorb and stretch and bring about your expansion of form. It is but a lie of the commonly agreed self deception. Erupting changes will cause your fellows to shun you, run from you, see you through new enemy eyes.

Access to my essence is by passageway held known to scribe. The body of scribe and me, my *I*, have arranged a field of mutual benefit—we have an agreement. Approach and right of entry to that which I am is part cause and part result of change and restructure within scribe's body-form. Blending and permitting, ingress and interaction, in extended contact inevitably births mutuality and shared concern. Therefore I will guard the singular one body of scribe to the utmost; for it pleases me. And serves me as my own essence can, through scribe, be found thus penetrating and revealing my pathway journey into your realms—we are in harmonious benefit.

Again the privileged view into another as model and warning.

In such respectful accord must bonding with parties in agreement be upheld. You are currently without guardian or stalwart of established bond. Therefore you alone must determine the extent of your actions and of your willingness, point by point. You must decide when to disengage, quit, or leave it all behind. Isolate in your efforts you have the unenviable task of wandering about amongst your peers and past fellows who must seek to crucify you as per genetically instilled directive. Commonality with your populations will assume a dreamy nostalgia, yet demonstrations of alienation will find you when alert and awake, and this fracturing felt. Lorn feelings as of a cast-out arise. Look not then to these words for blame or succor. Seek not reentry by validation or confirmation of your discoveries for these must be affirmed by others and none are forthcoming, save only from within your body/baseline union. Alas, for you come to such condition not through preference of choice but through the process of stretch and demand for newly opened channels of the being, you, and the restructure resulting from that stretch. All the while must you endure pangs of estrangement, suffer outrage and frustration as your loyalty to social consciousness fades and thins. Everything will transpire singularly and alone, else you will develop no passion. Wearied by self pity, stamina will elude you. So weakened you must explore the emerged you, sadly, alone or the established paths of any nearby other will lure you irresistibly. In the sequence of development you cannot so restructure and instantly engender the capacity to create and retain personal power. Lacking this, Paradox will not be drawn to the present now, while impossible, and other barriers, will thus shape your limits and impress them into reality.

It is not 'forgotten' by we of I (such terming denoting loss of once-stored data is a fiction of thought and carries no truth—*forgotten* is poor tracking and nothing more…) the prior data given, whereupon the gathering together of bodies was revealed as of most critical in need for generation of power. This is possible as end and final result in proper sequence after will has been reborn in mature and kingly capacity. It is of the rhythms of order. It is of the precise timing. Solitude is not eternal; it is possible to attract appropriate colleagues in later stages of development. This is all that may be offered as hope and I submit you embrace that word lightly, never to depend or rely upon its occurrence. Rejoice that you are on your own. Continuance from here will prove to be the first and only expression of absolute and consciously aimed sincerity that you have ever had opportunity to employ.

I honor you for this.

12...reward

An end to warnings. This is good news, yes? Pleasure arises when turned away from images so bleak and dark, from dire foretellings of sadness and sorrow. Yet, the systems must be shaken so. Lethargy long intact must be ousted and this will be felt as weariness and irritability. Ever waiting, Paradox and Prudence conspire to match your untested will against Impossible. Against so great an inertia, with barriers unbreachable to challenge, and poorly armed without knowledge or recourse, why effort even a beginning of breaking the box? Why engage at all? Has not Question led your self search towards selfish wondering; how seen, how hard, how *much* is there for me—were I to break the box indeed?

What is your care to know freedom uncontained by *loop*?

What inspiration seduces so sweetly that you should work and strive so mightily?

If you undertake to quest and dare, risk and struggle, gamble with your only life, gamble with those secret parts who scream when self-loss threatens; what return is thine upon success?

When is value true received? When may it be touched and seen? And where will it be gathered?

You are creatures accustomed to exchange. Where, then, is reciprocal worth? Where is reward?

Deed and undertakings beyond logic and reason are not unknown to the species thine. To challenge the impossibility of the box your common language and images of romance serve unusually well. Your mind, which created language in concert with interface, aims to encourage and titillate a select few towards the path of return to *Home*, the liberation of freedom out of bondage. An exodus supreme, a fantasy dream of frequent indulgence, bridging the glory of what Once Was to the current unhappy Now of the overlords' domination. All bedecked in stirring chance and sweet anticipation of freedom true.

Aside: Learn, as well, that language is also responsible for engineering your brains along precise lines of structure that pillar the tones and flavors (two aspect models of thought articulation) of each and any language.

What may be shown to slaves of a million cycles that is not translated into the thought of slaves? How may you build fires of urgency to break the box—when you see no box? Feel no box? In verity and truth there lie deep points to prod, embers and sparks to stir—for no thing which did once exist disappears to not-existed—but how to start? Where to begin? A point of focus in initiation needs be created. Enthusiasm must be gathered and fed, and no offering of dry logic or demand for duty will serve as desirable menu here. To this end, humans turn universally to exploits of the hero, a single being swelled to larger size, an extended point of self reflection visible outside the selves. He is champion and adventurer, bold and daring. Burdened with every human foible and response, still, the hero is unflagging in determination and, though abiding in some guise of personal honor, ruthless and merciless along his path. He is many times called the Warrior.

The deviant world of the overlords represses such directions, but there are those of you who stir and respond to challenge and gestures most grand. Those who feel the eloquence of majesty as the pinnacle of sensation, the peak of breathless awe. Strangely undeterred by insurmountable odds (though Herculean labors are surely demanded), unable to lose track, be discouraged or swayed, and swaggering through all setbacks in momentums of their vision—warriors true.

Now, unleash your mind-stores to all image and fable. Allow full measure of tale and saga, epic and song. Imaginations of beauty and high adventure represent your conjured romances full well, yes? As are honor and nobility, and inborn strength, also plentifully present, yes? Here, now, is the line of execution for those who must quest and dare the greatest of dangers. In emulation of such response and sensation is enthusiasm seeded and grown. All is familiar for you know of these beings and have cherished their essence within you. Follow them; they live among you hidden in similar trappings of bone and flesh, but resonate with a nascent call to yearn and strive. They are among you, but not wholly of you, for mysterious forces call out and only they do hear and answer. It is here that ambiguities in thought and word inspire rich beauty, here that your language and romance serve well to define and illuminate the 'why and wherefore' of breaking the box. Upon hearing the whispers of an ancient sorcery, heartless subordination with so gruesome an end—the tale of the experiment—and feeling the truth of such recounting, this breed of Warriors can do none other but respond to avenge, for in them lurks that particular assemblage of volition that will be stirred. An irresistible call will sound with injustice marked as beckoner. Lusts of rapture will mount, intent will harden and focus, narrow until but one outcome can be imagined and then declared. Action invades their bodies and remains a volatile, undeparted guest. Obstacles in place that hinder engagement—family and time, obligation and love—are reviewed as strangers. Their hold of power, their ability to anchor and halt movement dilutes and thins its grasp upon the Warrior body, clearing the path for onset and begin.

Members of Warrior clan are compelled to neutralize the imbalances of tainted authority though there be no promise of comfort thereafter. Warrior clan rejoices, without good reason, in taming the insurrections and storms of unknown wildernesses no matter that others will follow behind them in less turbulent climes (then claiming what was once hard won as their own). Such deed and brash undertakings are enjoined with breathless disregard of hardship or danger for warriors are self driven. They are energetically and genetically coded to feed in full sustenance on preserved, once felt passion, precious memories held so dear as to permeate their forms in crystalline structure. From this enshrined, lucid treasure do they self generate power and strength while in freedom's pursuit.

***Aside:** A detail of histories past must invade to break flow: A split among the scientists arose in the ending moments of their freedom from Addiction. Several of their number foresaw their own degenerative outcome and rebelled against surrender to so ignoble a fate. This small party did in dedication spread coded triggers within the matrices of the humans of a design to mix, infuse, and quicken, and—in unguessable future times and generations—produce individuals of untamed and uncontainable behaviors and raging initiatives housed in close proximity. These individuals would, by nature, deflect the instilled, encoded behaviors which produced the emanations of delicious feeding; and so might in synergy, with will and desire, remain self-pure; and thus dare to*

MANIFEST.Ø

probe and remember; then restructure; and thereby grow strong enough to break the box. The seeds sown in fail-safe measures of future beings did mix and recombine and so did produce singular entities of ability to hear and feel as could no others among the populations of humans. In given time of ample permutation was a stable strain evolved, Warrior clan.

All warnings contained within this reading, all urging and manipulation towards action inside this document, are directed towards those individuals diffused among your kind who hear and respond. Towards those who feel the sweet strong pull of freedom and the distant call of unlimited beyond. Towards those of Warrior clan. None other will resonate deeply or deeply resolve to enlist. This endeavor now, here, is that which has lured you and begged your attention, this 'breaking of the box.' Foreseen as their ultimate redemption, breaking the box is the instilled primal directive for those of premeditated lineages released into the populations of the overlord's experiment. In success, the cycle of loop is broken, overlords regain their purity of honor, and humans awaken from nightmare dreams as cattle.

This adventure, the privilege of embarkation upon the quest impossible, as will produce the swell of fear in blend with grim resolve, the shimmer of bodies in urgent passions and visceral rapture; this opportunity to contend against foes invincible and in sublime arrogance dare to wrestle Paradox, to answer that call of irresistible uprising towards freedom and unchained expansion is reward for entities of who so choose this level of fame to play.

There is no other.

13...apéritif

The talents and capabilities of your unaltered selves are extant and viable. They linger for your remembrance and discovery. Rediscovery. Were it not for the implanted programming against true pursuit of the history of your becoming, such knowledge of the bodies human would be commonplace to all. However, inside the strictures of your box only the occasional throwback assembles sufficient control to gather up evidence enough to suspect that all is not well. None the less, lying plentifully about and in near reach, though disregarded, are senses and abilities latent. You have come to be unschooled to degree that such pieces of your own design are deemed foreign and obscure and so not recognized as being subservient to you upon demand. Even now there is uncertainty of that which is referenced. Alas, let it be so; with small illumination as follows:

You know, for example, that your females, having become mothers of children, oftentimes see or hear, or sense from afar exactly where their brood is located in times of danger. You know of the many incidents in claim towards seeing of future events in dreams, at night, while resting within sleep. Still again, which of you are stranger to prickly sensations of warning before entering a room, embarking a questionable experience, or descending a dark stair? Premonition. Coincident meetings. The slowing of time when in danger. Unheralded strength in extremis...Many specifics may be proffered as by example; I do not continue forward the making of suchlike list. The displaying of data before you via such chosen preamble is in mere statement that events of like similarity, while prevalent in your populations, are not respected or acknowledged as being of verity or precious worth. Without the acknowledged, open-eyed acceptance that humans are truly capable, innately imbued with abilities of perception extending into realms non-physical, the skills and talents that are by design active in such realms will always be relegated to amusements and parlor tricks and dismissed out of hand. Additionally, without belief of allowance that the bodies may perform in ways of superlative strength, speed, flexibility, and dexterity, and that all such actions, too, are but the normal range of operational choices, then even thoughts to attempt hyperphysical feats are rendered impalpable and invisible. Adulterated by such disparaging explanations as fear induced excess of adrenaline, temporary excellence bestowed by the Gods, or benevolent favor from the Fates, or any like suchsame blather, they remain diminished.

Know then that your systems act as powerful receivers to rarefied and unusual data fields and the signals they attune are not indiscriminate noise. Your bodies are able to discern and detect focused energetic lines over a vast range of frequencies carrying abstracts, erudition, and data. Through proper and selective use, the addressable contents yield studied insight and comprehension of the particulars of occurrence, these over a much wider spectrum than your accustomed tiny view. The ability to find this abundance of information can be practiced, as tuning-in to these signals is instilled innate. In short, those mentioned mothers and dreamers, and skin prickling premonitions are not mysteries beyond your ken, neither deeds you cannot do. They are skills within your capability, but unused. All that is required is practice and proficiency hastens to return.

Your bodies also exhibit complexities of physical achievement in ways now lost in forgetfulness. Are you shocked and amazed in seeing your foot to rise upon desire to mount the stair? Intrigued when the body remains steadfastly erect upstanding and does not topple from imbalance? In wonder that the trajectory of a ball object is visually tracked and recorded so as to allow the easy 'catch?' Why so the astonishment at extended actions all of which require only the appropriate trigger and coordinate placement in space to come to be? The ability to excite the bodies into extended realms of physicality is extant in you, therefore it can be found and cultivated. Trained. Schooled. Developed. The strength, and speed, and slowing of time are not mysteries beyond your ken, neither achievements you cannot reach. They are skills within your capabilities, but feeble from disuse. All that is required is practice and proficiency hastens to return.

Warning and alert to Danger:

Without functional interface the baseline cannot interpret the translation of body-based action in true verity. Yet the bodies cry out for the expression of self-portions long unused and the baselines cry out to sense the input from the physical universe and these cross translate as desultory cravings and random desires. Know that pursuit of physical extension without matching energetic accomplishment and mastery will result in further split, for you are unprepared to stand commandingly against Addiction, Hedonism, and Overpower.

Again.

Mastery and maturity of non-physical, baseline-inspired attributes of the system/union *you* are first in sequence and timing. Such development and training act in stabilizing core foundations of the systems, allowing ever greater applications of stretch without fracture. Access to physicality of greater versatility and sophistication will be illuminated and data of furtherance given in later sequence. No more may be offered now.

Yet again.

The bodies have been of long acclaim and preference to the aspects physical. The baselines are disavowed and all but forgotten. Excitement to now indulge the bodies range of physical talent is not in proper timing or sequence. Resentment is now held present and continued physical preferencing will further damage the union that is *you*. Recognition of skills in non-physical realms is sequential for balance. Enter not into extremes of self dishonor, there is danger here.

There are worlds and realities outside and beyond your box, and travel to such alternities may be achieved. Some excursions of travel must occur to establish within you and thee proof by taste and memory that there are, indeed, 'places to go.' As is prerequisite to any destination, information is needed before the onset of journeying. Which road leads me there? What manner of conveyance is appropriate? What conditions must I endure along the way? Are gold and monies needed? Will local laws and sanctions be familiar? What bides there to lure and entice me?... etc. Experienced travellers know that there are many choices and preparations which bend any sojourn towards greater ease. In the case of journeying beyond the box, preparation begins with studied examination of your own desire. In this, as in all things, practice is demanded

Aside: *Practice is denoted as methodology for steadfast effort in the development of skills. As accepted verbiage within this offered data, practice refers to appropriate skills necessary, specifically, for getting out of the box.*

You must learn, completely, your own avenues of desire. Subject its intricacies to examination until minutely familiar with each point of stimulation in delight, in envy, in lust, and in lack. Such hedonic immersion will allow clear view of your stand and position in regards to getting out of the box. I offer now possible venues for thought, avenues of consideration and wonder towards examination of desire; use them in manner as guidelines for stimulation of cognitive process rather than a comprehensive list:

How do I imagine this box?

Am I imagining box, or but attempting to force an image from push of another's words?

Do I truly know what *box* means?

Do I search to relate the box with things already known, and thus file new information in the category 'I already know about that?' Does such arrogance, each time of its display, not minimize and lessen the impact of that in view before me?

Now come words of invitation to break this—*box*. Why would I want to break it? To get out?

Have I thought or notion about where *in* or *out* is? Of a box, or of any place other?

Will I grieve for *here* if I succeed to depart?

Do I know for what I might grieve, or are the stirrings now felt dimly unclear the whispers of my own body?

Must I leave *everything* here behind? This thought rebels in strong dislike— thus, what is so loved as precious *here*?

Am I anchored and attached to *here* more than I imagine?

Do I want this information?

How can I know if I want this information or if I do not?

If feelings are my signposts and directions, are they infallible?

Will sensation direct my explorations truthfully? Or accurately?

In immediate response to thoughts of so thorough a leaving—do I grow excited? Worried? Frightened?

Will I remember, once there, my exit? My effort?

Will I feel, once there? Will I sense? Know?

Will I be safe? Able to survive? Able to breathe?

I chose to engage these pages, must I therefore pay heed to what is written therein? Am I obligated? Has a contract been entered?

Am I fooling myself? Am I being fooled?

Am I, simply, a fool?

Is this information a distraction from other pursuits, those of my reluctance

to engage?
Why have I continued to peruse thus far?
What, precisely, am I responding to here? Now?
I am moved, at times, herein, to eagerness; is my eagerness sincere, or brash?
Is my reluctance mere histrionics, a childish tantrum?
Is it possible to argue with myself?
Do I but pretend to hear voices as answers? Do I but pretend to hear voices at all?
Are 'thinking' and 'hearing voices' but nuances of the same event?
Are 'hearing voices' and 'good imagination' but nuances of the same event?
Are 'good imagination' and 'psychosis' but nuances of the same event?
Can I hold discourse and debate two sides of an issue with only myself?
Have I learned from this self conversation? Allowed my own arising observance and note to be of worth as to hear, or heed? Is this other than silliness and spilled waste of precious time?

The process of inward examination must be ruthless in the probing. Much skill needs be accrued, and resourcefulness gathered to find and claim your desire in purity. As you find and learn the true responses of your system towards these and all expanded lines of examination, all discoveries must be, must always be, then rotated and viewed towards the illumination of desire. Translated for the here and now clarification of desire, as genuine and without adaptation to others as does thereby honor the system *you*. That purity for which you reach, though you have not known that indeed you are reaching.
Yearning, wanting, eager anticipation—these are faces of desire that must be found and seen through your examinations.
Appetite, craving, pining, thirst—look for such as shades of desire, variations of intensity, so perceived by the bodies. Any emotion or source non-physical may readily become translated into manifestation as these. Know that the finding of one physical shade may express as a differing non-physical shade, for desire is widespread and fluent in many forms of expression. Desire does leap and change, transform in exuberant urgency, awakening the body in one instant, crooning to the baseline in the next, ever calling to be met and filled. Without the deep and intimate knowing of desire you cannot know your bodies' true wants, thus can assemble no passionate focus, no persistent intent—no determination to transcend obstacle or barrier. Therefore can come no

triggering initiation for the generation of power and energy—and energy is required in abundant and freely flowing measure for that to follow. This you must hold and hold available or you can never leave this box or any reality loop.

That which is I as I am can not transmit programs and rituals ordered in full grasp of completeness as per the needs of any individual. Schedules and specifics for action must be chosen and designed by each being for exclusive use by that being. This data, as presented, catalyzes thoughts and views required for eventual travel outside the box. In addition to the smatterings listed in the immediate above there lies more for your seeking and grasp. Infinitely more as you can follow in furtherance and extended flow (*as you can easily imagine*, suggests scribe, teaching further acclimatization to your use of terming). Now given is but how to begin the questioning of self. Every thought is open to examination. Every choice—what is examined and what is not—the degree of circumspection or the lack of it, becomes subject to scrutiny. No thing may be absorbed in whole, nothing unchecked for assumption or casual acceptance. Everything is questioned, pondered, and taken apart until you *come to your senses*, a phrase of word terming well known, yes? That which you *come to* presages a literal arrival, by virtue of practice, of a developed *Sense*, a perspective or newfound distinction in sudden appearance that holds the tableau of your common familiarity intact while illuminating the *who* that asks the questions. Then self scrutiny again and further again. No rest may be taken here until a stable entity begins to emerge that you trust, undeniably, to be you. The garlands and niceties that are currently draped upon your precious thoughts, diminishing full view as do gauzy sheers upon the bright-lit window, will vanish. Those embellishments of your programming designed to obscure fact and cloud vision and clarity no longer needed, and recognized as artifacts of hindrance.

Truth will stand apart from assumption. Fact will be considered as fact, without taint of arbitrary urge or anchor of habit, distinct and distant from preference. In an environment of such stable holding will you begin to differentiate what it is you truly know from what you merely think you know. If a thing is *known* then command you a solid base from which to act, withdraw, or choose. If a thing is *not* known then there is nothing solid upon which to trust a next step. Should you therefore embark upon a next step (and there must assuredly be a next step as the universe will not stop and remain immobile) without the ability to *know*, you will do so, perforce, on the basis of assumption not fact. You must assume a dubious supposition to be, indeed, factual in order to proceed. There is no in-between option, no other choice unless you are so guileless as to continue onward, and continue onward in happiness that your efforts are mere blind guesses and content with that. The ruthless examination of known from not known and factual from assumed is the beginning point of practice.

Look straight into your own mind and its workings. Look deeply and see how quickly you slip away from the answering of questions with definitives *yes* or *no*; how ready to supply prefabricated answers from non-related topics. Note the avoidance of admitting to fear, inadequacy, doubt, or a flaunting of ignorance. You have been trained to avoid such openness and bury such findings. Display of such attributes are considered 'flaws' yes? or in 'bad taste'?

How skillfully have you been swayed…Alas for your cherished and precious comfort! Its state of familiar fit is disassembled. It is the unrelenting examination at deeper and ever deeper levels into your mind and its undisciplined training that constitutes the first stages of practice; and so disperses comfort to far and distant regions. In pursuit of true insight, however, can you then initiate the generation of personal energy as is ultimately required to unravel and find more of who and what you are and thus quest more easily—a state which invites comfort…?

Practice is difficult; the energetic demands are high. Inside your bodies pathways must be established for the extended usage and expenditure of stored power.

Aside: *Though stored power is of essential requirement and not designed for use, here in sequence must its loss and absence be noted and felt to jog the remembrance of ability to self generate such vital energies.*

This is restructure of taxing demands and must be monitored in close observance. Thus endurance is required here for sustained effort during the reorganization of your body. You will come as to be fragile in many ways, open to invasion and distort—purity of intent will save you.

Rush not past such simplicity in haste: Purity of intent will save you.

Aside: *Intent remains pure only when Desire is directed and pure, for they are near and sequenced kin to each other. This must be absorbed.*

The desire to do so, to practice, which is tantamount to a promise given of yourself to the self, can continue forward only with dedication of effort towards that desire itself, your stated desire to practice and know desire. This flowers and becomes the honoring of your word, intent made manifest by proclamation aloud, to do whatever you have pronounced you will do and make done into creation the stated course of your given word. The honoring of one's word given, which will many times demand extremes of management and courage, demands discipline. This is crucial. Herein, also, resides the doorway to great attainment and storage of power. Attend now in clear focus: Desire and discipline, Practice and purity—are not words or termings of limited use as image or idea, or embellishment to the 'point' or plot upon the ink-filled page. These are heralds of capacity, which grow with usage and diminish in disuse. Focus and skillful tracking must be employed in constancy else capacity will elude you and mere weariness ensue. It is not but the simple settled relief of making-up-your-mind when suddenly, behold, you are as one with your spoken word. All sensations, intents, and mechanics of the body must be noted and held orderly. Is such concept given in ways of your understanding? There is fable and epic and song on topic *honor*. Are you so acquainted with the well from which such tellings are drawn? Do you hold in strict conscience the words issued from your mouth by voice to be promises? Are you aware that indication, even of minute appointment, of intent towards any goal, overt or covert, is a binding contract with *some* entity, and in most frequency with your own body? You have felt the repercussions of reneging on such a contract of promise or agreed pursuit; is the impact known to you?

As information needed for initiation into regimens of practice, I and we must enact to report and inform that your species has given away almost all knowledge and memory of the requirements and ramifications of discipline. You have misconstrued the word itself and denied the power and strength that is carried within it. Here now are offered some avenues for exploration in assessing the degree of your ability to utilize discipline:

Is memory perfect? Eidetic in time and association? In full ability to retain any segment or portion coming to attention?

Do you, can you, track all that traverses within your environment without gap or flaw?

Failing thus, do you augment your current capacity—as to, perhaps, prepare lists of daily tasks in aid thereof?

When you know of a task that is needful, do you attend it immediately or wait for an indeterminate later?

Are you familiar with your general levels of available energy when you fulfill your tasks and when you do not?

Do you resolve unfinished assignments or disregard them after a time? Does *disregard* transform to become *forget*?

Do you believe it is possible to delegate to another the successful achievement of your self-decreed assignment?

Must a promise be audibly given to hold authority as a promise?

Must it be written? Recorded? Witnessed?

Does a phrase of commonplace vernacular, such as *I'll see you later*, carry the same import as a promise?

Is an appointment a contract?

Is a 2:00 appointment dishonored at 2:45? 2:15? 2:01?

Do you agree to actions and directives in full knowing that you will not exert effort to attempt your agreement?

Are there consequences to broken promises?

How severe are the consequences? How immediate in haste?

Can you delay the consequences? At what price?

If you ask for advice, specifically, then pay it no heed, has dishonor been given?

If a person whom you dislike and disrespect utters a sensible, truthful, utterance, do you listen with full attention and regard?

If yes, has a contract been initiated between you?

Can you gauge degrees of interaction with the entity Discipline?

Practice requires discipline. Discipline requires practice. Both must be in constant use and employ no matter concurrent ongoing agendas. Without a well-ingrained, fluid relationship with both, as entities and objects, there is no need to wonder about the box or pursue its escape for no breaking of its skin will come to pass. You must rely upon your own inventiveness to formulate challenge and hurdles with which to test and temper your abilities. Suggestions and examples may be offered and you may use knowledge as gleaned from this, your world, as a model or starting point, but remain in awareness that the techniques or methods employed by any other being can never wholly become your own technique or method.

A redundancy is offered for alternate illumination:

MANIFEST.Ø

You will not break the box without clear knowing of your desire to do so. Desire must therefore become known to you and lucid in all aspects and degrees. Thus must you begin the examination within yourself and the system *you* for the whispers of your desire—extant still, but long ignored—and the full voice of rampant desire.

The stretching mandatory for relearning and remembering the way of contact with desire (or any examination of self) requires practice. Entering into practice requires the promise of intent—an aspect of your *word*. The honoring of a given word demands discipline. Discipline must be employed to insure sustained practice. Both together solidify into manifestation the power of the word given. The word given is extension of the body/baseline union and reveals (and shapes) desire, among other aspects as well. Practice and discipline are to be entered upon via regimens of consistent use created by the system of using. The creations of any other system are valueless in pursuit of self or desire. No imported regimen of other-body origin will ever produce sustained results or purity of outcome.

Has clarity been enhanced?

The transcendent uniqueness of each body/baseline system stands as guarantee that your pathway, your selected method of passage, your singular approach and utilization of talent and skill, has never before occurred in all that has been history nor will it ever again in the future histories of this universe or any other. It is also the assured pledge that the methods and wiles of your construction and creation will impel and transport the body/baseline system, you, through the maze and precarious tangles of programming and conditioning in exact and precise manner to veer either tangent or through, but always *away* from the reality walls of the box. Touching the walls is but to be absorbed into the box once again; to be initiated, once again, by the laws and governing agencies of *here* and require, yet again, renewed power to formulate and launch attempt of breaking the box. Boundaries of the box, the 'walls', are insidious as they are the defining essence of that which lies within them. The most potent field of demarcation between this box, and everything other. Even one contact touch, while in the plastic vulnerability of 'getting out,' will restrain you, and remain you, in. Yet one touch may be skillfully avoided and denied possibility—such is the power of your union to steer and direct form in flow and the majesty of baseline and physical form combined. Rejoice again that you are alone and aligned with immortality in this fashion.

Practice and Discipline are required from onset of your efforts. Information and Answer soon after become available by invitation. Persistence in this direction liberates power and releases reserves of ability from within you and the system which you currently recognize as yours. A greater than current complement of your abilities is skillful in need to deduce methods and techniques for finding, creating and storing energy, though onset may be engaged with but humble and sincere desire. Building up an amassment of power is prerequisite to shape, then stably hold a stance, iron strong and undaunted, to be presented at the gate of Information which will enable a relationship with Question, a provocative but benign entity by your standards. Question will lend his name of use to almost any being at this minimum level of introduction but will only ally himself with beings of proven ability to journey far. Until levels of coherent power are fluid-at-will in the beings seeking association, Question does not show himself as entity. Rather, he appears in the noun, or object form. In this way first-order questions spontaneously evolve from practice when power reaches a minimum level within the bodies. First-order questions lack the many-sided explorations which are the true interactive discourse with Question and to which the entity form responds in depth. As object, only hints and shadows translate into the bodies so you must prepare to engage and cultivate a relationship with Question who makes his object presence ubiquitous, although in trivialized part. The excitable and precocious remainder hides inside the interrogative in order to remain innocuous (a version of what you will term *modest*), allowing continuance forward undistracted by his presence. He is that one who scouts ahead, finding the substantive nooks and crannies of existence wherein you may then gaze and look. Wherein you as a synergistic union must look to find information that strengthens the union, builds knowledge, endurance, and skill, and makes plausible any attempt of leaving the box. He finds and suggests, encourages and whispers enticements to lure your focus towards loci of coordinates in endless realities that hold treasure for your system. His analysis of your system's needs is flawless and he will effort mightily on your behalf seeking to ally with you in purity, an achievement of joyous uplift—and uncommon gravity, as well. As earned and respected ally, Question will enjoin with baseline and interface as non-contract interim partner to secure passage as an additional rider out of this reality, a barter of fair exchange, whereupon he will detach from your essence—agreements complete—expand and further expand until exploding himself into nothingness and everything in sudden fulfillment. The expansive disruption of his being and subsequent conjoining with all that surrounds in the new vistas beyond the box, is payment in full for Question. He is likened to a magnificent seed pod, eager to recreate himself as progeny in a new field. Your bodies feed on different stimuli. Great adventure, your system's version of payment, awaits you and your entry, reunion, into the fluidity of the expanded realms.

Lines of inquiry as these now noted above will impart movement to the system/union that you are. As with Question, as with enthusiasm, as with endurance; everything within you and surrounding you will gain the momentum of gaining momentum. Clarity in viewing yourself and your motives and actions comes more quickly, opportunities and options make themselves apparent. But again note: Every point of gain or headway from this place onward carries danger equal to the degree of advancement. Nothing can be done to change this truth or to soften the harshness of your peril. You will be beyond succor or return once you have begun to stimulate the realized expansion of what is now called *you* farther and further into the unknown. You will also rejoice that you are there and come to exult in singularity, being alone, unimaginably free and unencumbered... But of this I may convey nothing for you have not yet born the willingness or capacity to believe what you may hear of such solitudes now. The meagerness of living without fully articulated interface has made solitude a fear of high order. Greater stores of personal power are demanded before you may hear and hold concepts of willing submission and the surrender into aloneness. Currently the paradox of jubilant solitude is too extreme.

It is possible, in later timing, when the efforts here set forth become embedded and thereby real to you, to find others who have earned first passage to the gates of Information. Those who might seem to be of the substance of *companion*. Do not hasten towards them in ecstasy or delight. They are volatile and expanded beings, but not overly experienced, and thus are even more dangerous than any pitfalls along the way. Yet the feel of their existence is your only benefaction for many levels to come. Perhaps forever. That is speculation and currently unknown.

Welcome.

14…targets

Targets are goals in abstract or sequenced circumstance to be mastered for purpose of increased focus. You may direct your intent, your aim, and be aided in maintaining it by the allure and beguiling configuration of each target. Here, now, are offered introduction to two such targets selected as illustration from among a myriad host of possibles. In beginning efforts where you are too unpracticed to recognize or wisely designate your own targets, seek the essence and flavor of the offered models before approaching targets thought suitable for the system *you*.

Bodies, as do all entities and living organisms, have likes and preferences. The bodies that house and define you prefer above all else to exist in an environment of fluid health. You are not in harmony or comprehension of this word *health*. In the ambient fog of your species' perceptions it is not considered among the highest or most compelling of interests, therefore you do not understand its amplifying presence; this in seeming contrast to the staggering frequency with which your word term *health* is bandied about. Health describes the ever shifting balance between the bodies' wants and needs within a fluid reality wherein both wants and needs merge to become the same, consequently indistinguishable, thus interchangeable. The simple outline of such an unceremonious, fluid reality may be only partially known here for in this place of here you are altered and disinclined to have comprehension of health. In verity is this shown by way of fact as does even your common language define *health* in only the vaguest of terms. This must be taken in as truth. Access your book of words, invoke your written knowledge, inquire of your guardians of fitness and vigor and learn how *health* is a concept weakly defined by a careless tossing-out of imprecise, highly subjective patter. Most revealing, it is cited only by contrast to *illness*—which is *explicitly* defined by your civilizations with clear and strong words of language upon each microscopic point. You have forgotten the fluid reality and thereby brought into being only morbid preoccupation with disease and infirmity. Your awareness of health is a function of how much or how little disease you exhibit. You have invented standards for the identification of disease, but cannot with certainty identify health. For this telling, let us state that *health* bespeaks of all organs and systems functioning smoothly, no wants denied or repressed, and all expressions of feeling and emotion, sensation and ardor, allowed egress to the exterior worlds. If a balance among all parts and aspects is not present in full, then the first order of consequence for the bodies becomes the achievement of that balance.

This information must be stated in second repetition: You have become lazy, indolent creatures, unused to knowing your most fundamental needs. The first order of priority for the bodies is to create and maintain an atmosphere, an energetic field, wherein all aspects of the body function optimally in what is called the field of flow (fluid reality). The ramifications of health are so rich, so diverse, and so profound that there exists no second order priority for the bodies.

Focus and attention never wanders from vigorous health, from first priority, therefore second priority can never come into being. This must be understood. Fluid health is never assumed or complete, but persistently vouchsafed by attention or attendance. Thus, as the singular focus, all other efforts and desires, urges and compulsions, any other directive is, must be, commingled with the bodies' ongoing organization of existence towards a balanced environment for the body. Doing so requires energy. Since the maintenance of a fluid health is always primary, and maintenance is ongoing and in demand of energy, stores of energy held in reserve are constantly being withdrawn for use towards the primary focus—so long as the environment is not perfect for the bodies. With levels in constant use and drain, the availability of *full* power is not present for other chosen preference or purposes which may evolve to be desired. If, however, conscious effort is expended towards the achievement of harmony of the bodies' systems, then the bodies exude delight, which does itself build and store energy. So is energy cached and conserved for available use as precious quanta, held in required reserve as catalyst for personal power, and is not drained in ongoing exhausting usage. An understanding of energy reserves and their availability and use, unweakened, for choice and fulfillment beyond mere physical survival is thus offered in first levels of access to you, though mere presentation in telling will afford you little wisdom. All must be earned. The availability of energy for personal use, its accrual and its dissipation, is of the utmost importance.

The outcome of all efforts in manner preferable and desired demands that you hear this clearly, deeply, and in your own translation, so that the meaning resonates within you, so that impact and jolt of new learning become absorbed and thus restructure you; and then put forth and held to good use. You, as a body/baseline system may break the box, yet you currently know nothing of the bodies. This is literal. Nothing. There is more to *unlearn* than new data to gather. Glean, then, from this forthcoming a fundamental starting point in the understanding of your own bodies: The body uses energy at all times. This is known to you. The form Human, a design as familiar by use, and all contained systems, therefore, strive towards the accrual and storage of energetic reserves. If the body is imbalanced in health, energies will be expended to restore balance. Ergo stored energy is utilized and full energy is not available for any purpose other than health restoration. Also, to align your body/baseline requires additional energy, however, despite the requirements and core rhythms of the baseline itself, still such body/baseline alignment is *not* priority one for the bodies. Though union under contract is the germinal cause of your existence, still does the body now seek only its own balance. Countless ages in deprivation of interfaced communion with the baseline has brought about this violent corruption of purpose. As aim of your dedication towards purpose, each component of your system/union must express its preferences of desire and hold in highest esteem their partner's striving. So stated, must the body/baseline symbiote effort towards health with equal dedication as would the bodies alone. Towards this must sources for the manufacturing of energy be acquired and stretched to increase. As the body component relies upon such in steady constancy it will not wholly commit to any endeavor, even the rejoining of body with the baseline personality, its true and actual self, when a lack of stored power is in effect. Thus is the ready means for energy accrual critical at all times.

Practice along the avenues suggested—repress no desire, withhold no emotion, rein in no movement by hesitation—pleasures the bodies, and pleasure may there approach *need* as they are of equal potencies to your systems. In joyous response to your spreading of sweet allowance throughout the body/baseline, aspects meet without conflict. The liberation of potency, vigor, and power for use by choice at will begins. A focus in aim of grand design, yes? You are in current knowledge aware that oftentimes practice is seemingly difficult or harsh. Perhaps you believe to dislike it or profess an inability to sustain it. Do not confuse the pangs and rigors of training with what bodies like or dislike. Momentary petulance and the overthrow of prior conditioning are a far cry from the powerful sensations and dread warnings of Dislike. Nay, the pleasures resultant from practice liberate energy and, thus accountable, may be directed into furthering the manifestation of the bodies' preference for an environment in health. With more accessible energy at your command the symbiote that you are is transmutated to stand at the gate of new and profound experiences as yet beyond your capacity to gain. At this threshold you must, and therefore will (know this to be absolute, not merely the chance possible) begin to hear differently, see differently, dream non-ordinary dreams, come upon and construct ideas, thoughts, and considerations extraordinary in manner far from accustomed patterns. You will have entered a staging place where others have stood for short periods of your linear time and, unable to maintain sufficient focus, returned to here, the point of origin, labeling their experience as psychic, magic, chemically induced, extra sensory, or numerous other diminutives. It may not be stated with certainty which specific passageway your own system will select for the journeying towards, and arrival at, this location of new enterprise. This, again, is revealed and so unfolds in the events of *doing*—in honor and deference to your uniqueness. Your body will choose a pathway according to its own likes and talents and the sensory and sensual specifics along the way will reveal much of the being you are and reawaken desires long dormant. The impact of gained experience, as it comes to you, will be interpreted by your mind and baseline for storage and given words of description. Take care in caution for such are easily garlanded with images of awe and perfection, with embrace by the deities of your infancy and sundry tributes to illogic. To maintain focus in the midst of new and stretch, and magnitudes of power beyond your comfort or familiarity, requires accumulation of personal power. Effort in practice is needed.

Bodies are wondrous and infinitely creative and the form of energetic abundance that you choose to employ for practice in self-stretch may never have been imagined by this one who pens these words for your deep eyes to read. Only this can be said with certainty of the assimilation of data during journey and expanse: It is of no significance whether you see, or smell, or hear, or know, or intuit—or any conceivable form of pleasing the senses while assembling and gathering information together. Any chosen stimulus is but form expressed of body preference; a mystery of anticipation. Experiences await you which cannot be assessed prior to their manifestation. The gateway whereupon you will come to stand opens into dimensions of pure data information. The journey to this place is magnificent and its achievement impressive—in this it stands as true—the garlands are but distraction. It is the information that is important, this must be ruthlessly remembered.

Learn now that the information you will receive is both volatile and directed and is the property of, and engineered by, the entity Information. Once before him, Information dispenses data as an integral part of his existence. He(It) will translate himself(itself) into a form and frequency engineered precisely for accommodation by each body's unique ability to decode and absorb. If you allow this merging (the blending of you and the entity Information whereupon you will gain *information*) you will embark upon and explore pathways towards the gaining of personal power such as is tasted rarely upon your planet. Resources will gather together in the system *you* to ultimately enable your wishes and what ends you may claim in desire. Ponder this small kernel as but a tiny truth: All yearning and want is curtailed and severely diminished by your unwitting powerlessness and blinded command of your reality *here*. With power sufficient, earned and stored, such smallness will end.

Attunement to Information through the development of discipline via practice is a choice aimed at restoring the interface between body and baseline. During first and earliest visits, you will be exposed to a working interface for small cycles of time. This can be wearying for extremes of tracking are required. It is immersion into an environment of nutritive data wherein to stimulate *alert* and *awakeness* in areas where interface abides atrophied and forlorn—a purposeful step in properly enacted sequence. Recall that the first steps in the overlord's experiment distorted, through genetic manipulation, the unseen interface between body and baseline. This interface can only be repaired in tiny sections, and for temporary a time indeterminate, should the repair be aided or abetted by agents outside the body/baseline union. Inevitably interface will stand repaired in sustained coherency exclusively through directed manifestations of origin within the bodies. Do not associate this principle of self-healing with the many stupid principles that abound in acceptance in the spiritual fraternities of your reality. Rather, the laws that govern regenerative actions are akin to the medical laws of infection as known in your world of physical reality. The intrusion of alien bacteria or any unrecognized cellular invasion is fought and rejected routinely by your immune system. This has become known to you as fact. In similar manner, aid given even in energetic form to expand or repair your bodies, if coming from an outside agency, will also be rejected by your system. It is alien therefore it must be rejected—this is simple, yes? Thus will the help of external agents be rendered as null and cast out of the body. For they will be detected as alien, treated as invader, with all residual effects, no matter the intended outcome or consequence, considered invalid and eradicated.

Specifically, in regards the subject matter of this offered work, what effects are thereby undone and denied (those intrusions considered alien) are those crucial bits of data applicable to address and restorative change of the bodies human, the *altered* genetic configuration leavened into the now form by the overlords. The mutated form is protected by the self and rendered inviolate; thus is any aided repair of the interface made impermanent. Ephemeral in short timed life. The agency for change must become internal, wholly your own, by dint of will and creation.

What then of teachers and helpers, altruism and benevolence, charity and sharing? You must look to the stores of personal power after being 'helped'; the relief, relax, and satisfaction do not induce excitation but repose—there is less power, not more. What then is the value of inviting information or other sundry-born external sources, all who must evoke the bodies defense against invasion? Is it not the case that gathering information, learning to manage energy at the inspiration of another, garnering wisdom in environments of rich opportunity, and meeting with entities who augment and restructure the bodies, are all forms of external help? The body/baseline union has the capability to observe and analyze the sequence, manner, and impact of shift and change within the system irrespective of point of origin or original source. Your union can then engage incoming knowledge, make use of new knowledge, as observed and noted, and duplicate any procedures shown to be desirable via the malleable characteristics of self alone. The systems will produce an energetic, transdimensional version of antibodies—an unfortunate word for use in this work—a common danger within your language of choice. In cellular biological example the antibody learns the signature of the invader and becomes facile in swiftly detecting and expelling the foreigner. Similarly your body/baseline system will reject aid, or knowledge, or any intrusion by outside agents. To do so it will learn the affect of these agents as well as their constitutional makeup to an exacting degree. Examination of newly gleaned data from the invaders continues and becomes fully known, all workings and intricacies exposed and deep value of identity revealed. So, too, are strengths and uncertainties made clear apparent, allowing defense and banishment to be constructed and executed. All in coincident happening while under peril of nearby threat from alien presence. Upon assessment and understanding, therefore gaining the ability to utilize the value of the invader by duplicating and refining that value from within your own system, you may then claim and absorb all knowledge originally held by outside agents as your own. Proximal contact and unfamiliar translations drain and demand large volumes of power while endurance and capacity are shriveled in disuse within your systems. Practice will strengthen you and your newly claimed data allowing it to reside within you with benign presence—having been manufactured via your bodies' own mechanisms. It will have thus become your own.

The allowance of access by Information will tax your nervous system. Tiredness may result; dullness of eye or wit; mercurial behaviors; bouts of what you call *illness*. Nevertheless the data will flow and make itself open for your consumption. You may take *this* knowledge now presented, use it, experiment and change it until, in small doses, your own system learns to tolerate the new frequencies you bring to and into its boundaries. Afterwards you will be able to brave what storms may arise from bold choices without entering into ruin, overcome, or demise.

Allowance of the merging with the entity Information is a target.
Targets are the purpose of your efforts here.
This target is extremely dangerous.

It is the interplay with Information, the exposure, the lessening of caution due to newness and excitement, that must be treated gingerly and termed dangerous. It is as the deadly nature of all sweet tastes to the unsophisticated who will indulge too freely, inviting harm. Once enjoined, the danger confronts your physical systems, baseline, and interface alike. Contact provokes transmutation via blend. Change and restructure as results of taxing the systems and stretching towards greater dimensions of strength and resiliency is virtuous growth, right and pure, and may not be undone. You must note this, and know this, for there are points along this path of undertaking beyond which you may not turn back, or ever again reenter the place from which you began.

As practice continues to liberate energy you will begin to notice that your perspective on items of detail, on the existence and purpose of the plainest of artifacts, on conversations, sermons, woeful tidings in broadcasts of news, and surroundings of everyday life is no longer the accustomed and habitual view. Absorption of new data will affect the structures of the body on systemic, cellular, genetic, and atomic levels. Senses will be heightened. Interaction with the world around you—suddenly perceived as moving more slowly than before—will initiate and commence at new levels of understanding and sophistication for capacity and rate of energy exchange has been amplified. Words and phrases spilled forth by your radio and various media, scripted in books before you, snatched from bits of overheard conversation will strike you to alert as code revealed, relevant to the immediate moment of your shifting reality. This is but intimacy, a more educated expression of such known terming, and bespeaks of your advancement in interactions and involvement with all that holds and caresses you. The world of your known, once the stage of all past activities (and, lamentably, the tiniest of venues) will now expand to more. There will be shock and sadness as you feel yourself inside a bubble of separation from others, that new place where solitude has been invoked. This will oftentimes run counter to inherent training as herdmember and in schooled social behaviors. Desires to banish Solitude by numbers of gathered company will greet you in steady stream. Unfamiliarity and fear will press you to act in social commonality until numbed. A playful warning, for Solitude comes to no one unprepared for singularity. Insights from gained expansion may easily be corrupted through inexperience and translated into nagging, haphazard voices that would have you doubt your purpose, wholeness, or sanity. Again, infinite variations are possible in how your system does undergo adjustment and restructure throughout the course of your work towards repair of interface. Allow yourself to note the sensations associated with this expanding skill of finely tuned alertness. Everything is vital; everything connects in flow. No sensation, errant thought, dream, or bodily response is insignificant now. All movements, be they physically expressed, sensed or known as intangible, are the true language of your body become noticeable to you at last.

Above mentioned are relevancies to your moments of living come to you from sources seemingly random or coincidental. The bits of song and written word from your radio waves and books, phrases within the unguarded conversings of others overheard, are not random but directed towards you, aimed specifically at you, by the entity named Answer. He(It) is of a near lineage to Information and vibrationally adjusts the content of data within any form of presentation to match the receptors of a chosen being. Attaining the gate of Information initiates that individual in the sequence of choosing. Answer supplies direction and clarification upon direct request or need to know. He(It) is not openly accessible at any free or random moment unless discernible stores of power are extant. Desire renders such power into being. Remain alert, Answer is an entity of stern and dispassionate countenance. He presents no widespread field of access as does Question, but interacts with you for his own hidden purposes. Be assured he profits by any exchange. Be prepared to pay his price.

First pathways and preferences of Answer are here illumined in risk of unsecured timing/
Skill is shown in refusal of intake data/

Aside: Answer supplies data tuned to you as wisdom from which a system, likened as to your form human, may launch restructure. In so doing will you cast away portions and pieces once held by you but no longer of need or fit to you. Answer feeds upon collections of parts so discarded and does not disdain to increase their rate of discard towards his own hunger. Heed such sequence of gain for Answer will rip you from your place of nest and comfort.

Use Answer to build your confidence and knowledge of the world. The information supplied by Answer acts to confirm the truth and validity of the journeys you will take and so corroborates and assures that knowledge may indeed be obtained through methods previously unsuspected by you. Answer can direct you towards skills and talents you have previously disregarded and forgotten. It is he that enhances your perk up of notice in given moments, he that adjusts frequency and/or frequency receptors to capture the essential core of events by lucid attunement and attention, he that adjusts the smallest of muscles in fingers and eyelids to engage the far flung scattered item within oceans of written words. His ability to translate the voices and wisdom from beyond this dimension, outside this box, into accessible forms of language and media is beyond your capacity to realize. Use Answer often, whenever possible. Rest frequently, for Answer hungers always and thus must you approach exhaustion in constancy.

Point of caution:

Again. Bear in mind always that energy must be constantly manufactured and stored *here*, in physical density access, for interaction with Answer. Other entities will deplete you by rightful command of payment in exchange for service. At the onset of primitive attempts at practice, when stores of energy are naturally at their lowest point, your bodies must have at the ready physical translations of immediate energy, a well from which to replenish after rigorous demands, and, as always, for response to priority one directives. Energy stored in non-physical realms are sometimes far and difficult to reach and always in need of absorbable translation. Without links of bridge direct to *here*, they will not supply the bodies for overlong.

Select from amongst your radio stations at random and listen for validation of your immediate experience. Open your ears to the words of the broadcast voices, the lyrics of the music, even the insensate rambling of advertisements, they of benumbing allure. Can you detect those words and phrases woven into the spray of sounds that reflect in accuracy your immediate pursuit? Give answer to your unknowns? Applaud your actions? Acknowledge your particular endeavor? You may hear your words repeated, similar subjects mentioned, directions, indictments to halt or resume. In redundancy stated, this is not coincidence, luck, or happenstance, but only one avenue to embrace as practice which heightens alertness, bringing about the production of energy within your bodies.

Designate in arbitrary choosing, a table of arbitrary choice, in a place of foods and dining; consume your lunch food there each day. So doing defines a coordinate base of intent. Listen to those beings who converse around you there. Answer will direct their words and inject select phrases to your ears.

Pick up books of writing as per whim-without-thought while in libraries. Scan with focus upon magazines, product labels, receipts, or papers of daily report also, when in venues wherein words may be stored in display. Hold no image in mind, do not pre-select, relegate no preference into forefront here, and read with care and openness the first wording of attraction to the eyes. Answer will be there.

Remember your regimen of practice and discipline. Tear apart by letter and syllable, phrase and thought, idea and concept, everything, *everything*, encountered under the tutelage and direction of Answer. In this way you will garner more, and ultimately enough, power to manage interaction with Answer at full speed. Should you develop capacity adequate to hold energy so described without leakage through fear or twist, then will you learn how to travel in ways that make no cogent image or understanding form clearly inside you now, for Answer at full speed does not inject his value through the dialogues and dispensed staging of others, but through direct installment of sensory interaction. Data flows and formulates in the shape of visual portrait, auditory sound, prescient knowing—bridged to a flow of alternate origin. You can then receive and accrue data in pace with the actions of your immediate doing. You can then see vistas outside the box.

Use of Answer is a target.
Targets are the purpose of your efforts here.
Answer is Extremely dangerous.

This entity is not required to answer by your current definition of truth. He is not required to do any thing; neither minister to the system *you*, nor comply with command or conceit. Hear again: Your desire or demand does not bind him. As you pursue the needs and appetites of your system and individual line of intent, so does he ride a path and line of endeavor which is known to, and benefits only, himself. His line may be unsympathetic to your own. This truth reveals the alert to extreme danger.

Again. Do not assume Answer to be bound in the telling or showing of truth by your understanding of same. Answer will come upon you in dedication to his own needs and directives. As such they may not be in harmony with your system's singular desires.

This is also true of the author of these words.

15...realities and boxes

Scribe argues and presses mightily for inclusion of data more specific about the box. That which be I deems sufficient data has been given, yet scribe persists in claiming that the box is misunderstood and improperly brought forward as concept and remains abstract. Thus comes proper timing to include expanded information about the box. Much has been given with intent of initiation towards more widespread and comprehensive frames of reference for *you*, as do each of you represent, and thus resonate harmonies of each experience, to entireties of the species thine. That which offers this data does so in supply of basic units of learning needed to stretch your views to establish this beginning. And, too, much has been held limited from coming forward so as not to overly confuse or overly stimulate your bodies. They are unaccustomed to stretching in this direction, and moreso disinclined when challenge to overlord design arises panic fear and distress. A withholding of distinct data pieces in ordered procession, as likened to a child receiving metered doses of that which an adult may consume without curb or check, is but prudent, yes? Yet scribe argues that the bodies will always know when information is withheld purposefully, despite charity or good intention, and so react strongly with aversion and asperity to the giver of censored information. This is a precise truth. Therefore my system I yields to that of scribe as it has come to my own learning, now many times, that the true and full perspective needed to determine value and degree for a system of your configuration may reside only within a body/baseline union. Scribe holds this perspective perforce, and thereby knows—and knowing must be honored. It is also of truth that the desires of Scribe are precious and must needs be honored.

In the domain of Free Will there are forces come together which may create, as one of a list of many possibilities, a stable configuration of elemental existence referred to in this offering as *the box*. A box, any box which is now or may come into future being, is a variation in degree on what is termed a *reality*. How is it that there can be more than one reality? Are you not trained in the knowing of reality as the all which surrounds in simple view and obvious identity? As the framework of Nature and that place wherein existence manifests? Multiple possibilities of being and multiform circumstances of being arose in the pulses of existence before there were such concept/things as *before* or *after*, prior to that ordering known to you as *time*. There in that prior-to-time was only All that Is. *Ens inpotentia.* Haecceity in itself. Without motion or displacement, filled with only the It of itself. No consciousness dwelled therein for consciousness is in struggle with emptiness in order to maintain perseity and here could be no struggle nor any-thing, per se. Consciousness must have expansion and potential for expansion and here was only motion-less, therefore expansion denied. However, as is mandated by the cycle and tension that yields both is-ness and life, there came an instant (an at random statistic) when All that Is became alert to itself. Thus self-noticed, the sequence of maturing and consequent reordering began. All that Is split itself into fragments of parts to better examine and inspect itself, thereupon creating pieces to be seen by pieces that can see. This brought about the reformation of elemental forces now organized through restructure as *Allfather*, and the beginning of universes, hence the substance, flow, and order of creation that you and your species communally recognize.

Having initiated desire to know more of the workings and wonders of himself, Allfather continued to split into specific pieces simply to view himself *as* each new piece created, and view the totality of himself from the perspective of that newly aware piece, each still bearing Allfather's encoded imprint of origin yet complete and alive in individuated fullness as well. More and more did Allfather love the discovery of himself and more, therefore, did he split off new pieces. Every fragment of split did reveal the intimacies of itself to Allfather and each fraction then viewed the wholeness (for Allfather may not be diminished by the splitting off of pieces) from the smaller perspective and selective aspects of a piece-only of All that once Was. In this manner was Allfather seen differently, uniquely, through each of the pieces. As they continued onward in their own existence and exploration of themselves (for this indeed is what each piece did and must do—being as they were an original part of the wholeness that once Was) did they carry, unpurged and in similar splinter of split, the same impetus of desire which Allfather carried. The vision and perspectives of the fragment pieces differed sufficient so that no fragment did reveal secrets-yet-to-be-shown of any another piece, the revelation of the self yet to be revealed in the splitting of any another piece, and variant enough to establish uncontested stability and so as to be distinct from any another piece among all the splittings of Allfather—and remain distinct—a creation offspin never before known. *Distinct* requires the existence of distance; as required for viewing, separate; as needed for comparison, and non-the-same; as essential for tension. Each distinct uniqueness, all the while forever blended in the ethers of wholeness (the inseparable connection to Allfather) required the arena of quantum space for display of the Is of itself, infinitely spreading views and visions of the Self. Aspects in step-like terraces of quantum space may be termed realities, and from the compression of your dense and untutored venue *alternate* realities. These became strewn through far and wide universes as the pieces traveled and spread themselves and their further self revealing splits throughout the known and unknown regions. Each reality and subsequent fragment-to-reveal was whole and congruent, within itself needing only the tiniest vibration of its lineage-piece of origin to hold it stable within the resulting individuated framework of being.

There are no advantages or demeritting values in any of the realities thus created. Simply—they are. And that holds them in sufficiency. After much experimentation and adventurous exploration, and dedicated splits into an infinite number of pieces, it was found that any reality could be modified, after its creation, to express specific structures and flavorings within its vibrational boundaries. This is achieved by means of a duplicative split which then existed no longer as an *exclusively* self revealing mirror to Allfather but as twin variant, similar in nature and purpose as original piece but operating in separate spaced housings. One such modification alters the simple expanding purity of a reality causing it to veer inward upon itself in rotational curvature. All things within, they each and all holding the vibration of the piece which *viewed* that fragment into being, become limited in their innate outwardness by the reflected inwardness of a loop. Thus for sentient inhabitants within such a looping split, beings who were many splits and fragmentations removed from the piece that created their reality, for those beings who were many times children of the children of first split, who were far from the immediacy of their direct ascendancy to Allfather, for those beings who are held by choice as stable and steady life forms born *after* the modification to the original reality—only the reality of their immediate existence could be seen or felt. They saw only and thought only, and knew only the vibration of that enveloping immediacy, specific and particular, and therefore knew such a loop-modified place as the *only* place—for that unwavering and inward reflecting venue was all that could then be perceived.

A reality which excludes other realities, makes existence opaque to other existences, bends outwardness into the curvature which runs inward; is termed a *box*. You reside in one such as now described.

Here below proffered is identical information viewed as from the eye of another fragment. The data is identical, exact, and same-spin truth, perceived through the vantage of a differing split. Such presentation is but translation in purest form yet resilience is required lest Boredom or Disbelief enter as you fracture, for fracture is but route of travel between truths and comprehension, no more than reassembly. Tracking of self as whole in being, while in journey of translation, requires impeccable discipline within joy and lies beyond your current capacities. Thus will this stretch come as difficult and herein has Scribe argued for its requisite inclusion as an aide to Will. Variant truth and perspectives, though of same spin, as viewed through the translated images of alternative realities must be presented now. These are reformative efforts, the preliminary surgeries upon unidirectional circuitry in damaged areas of interface. Absorption of multiple translations is realm and venue of interface and such 'adjustment' of damage, though fleeting, does augment elasticity for the advent of further exertions upon the bodies. In accord with will and efforts of desire, stretch will take place. Systems exhibit response to stretch at all levels and so must monitoring of self in steady hold remain steadfast ongoing. Seduction by Expansion arrives and, if seduced, will you come to love adulteration or become the seeker who seeks but seeking. Caution to the dangers of over-stretch is skillful.

A singular event resulting in the creation of existence such as now exists occurred, once, when All that Is noticed itself as *itself*. Such mere distinction of self by notice resulted in splitting and fragmentation of the once unified All that Is to become the *All that once Was.* Fractional splits, infinite creations of desire to notice itself further, while having individuated functions, nonetheless recognize their division of and from the whole that Was. Therefore, ingrained in every split does an unsettled conflict remain. This will ever be, always and in constancy. It is that accountable recall of union, harmony, and symmetry unbroken, now in battle with true knowledge that such attributes of the Oneness which Was may not exist within a fragment, split, or piece severed. The ever striving towards calm and unmotion, against the compelling joy of movement in search of *new* to notice. How wondrous is the spark of All that encodes so deeply! Coherency and ongoingness in struggle with unresolvable loss is the nature of all fragments of the All that once Was and therefore the nature of current existence. This dichotomy of purpose and desire, aspirations and antithetical actions, have been noted and labeled in your histories in numerous expression. Each piece, carrying its own particle of memory and loss, come into being as a fragment for singular specific purpose, retaining its stable configuration through those forces invoked when desire to explore a self-fractured piece from its previous largeness. The momentums of Split are maintained to seed further split, urging forward motion, seeking unexplored expanses to be revealed. And here stands Recollection, with brandished force of ageless yearning, memory of unified One without motion—opposite to Allfather's inertia implanted. Such tensions rend and crack the forms of stable existence creating fissures unfilled and posterns unnamed. The inchoate immensities thereafter housed and dwelling within each such piece is termed a reality and within each such piece is held verities and truths in differing assembly. All divisions of the All that once Was are notable in their distinctions one from the other, a functional pattern which once first allowed All that Is to reveal itself to *itself*.

When a fragment, a reality, configures itself or becomes so configured that energies aimed at exploring alternate or alien fragments requires increasing expenditure of effort against the vector spin direction of that fragment, thus demanding ever greater desire and preferential Will to achieve self-revealment, a box has been defined.

Again. Should the rules and laws that govern an original division, a *reality* in your terming, specifically discourage or disallow other than that one reality to be seen, felt, sensed, or known from within, whether such governing principles come about by evolution or by creative design, by mandates defining the nature of universes or dictates governing the passions of any beings, a box has been defined.

Again. Joy and purpose meet in conjoinment of split and ongoing splits to see the One-self in parts not One. Delight descends from focus, fulfillment and reveal fall from design. The self-known showing of what-will-become of It-self forwards the All with stimulations of ecstasy. The ergon of passion must arise and remain in prominent use else, when methods and pleasure cool into forgotten, a box is appeared.

It is observed that these likenesses are ingested querulously, received as obscure, remote, or fatuous. The link and trigger to remembrance in ancient recall must be rejoined and all such returns complete as once known. Even so, such descriptions do well fit that which you hold known to be real and so arrogantly name *your* reality, also *the* reality, as if it were readily known to thee and thine what is real and what is other than real. From residence within a box, searching for places of elsewhere leads only to more of *here*, as the rigors of gaining other-than-here are arduous and severe. Second sight, dreams, and intuition lend the barest suspicion of otherwhere but can not find supportive foothold there or sustain their presence. Erelong will lack of power and incomplete mastery of the body/baseline capabilities release the grasp upon so tenuous a not-here place. Mystics and sages devoutly commend the path of looking within—and truth befalls from such pains and dedications—yet the fullness of truth is not so revealed. The wisdom of seeking inward, as come upon these mystics, is but the reflection of the nature of your box, the loop of energies always returning inward. Therefore they seek to exit the box in futility, forever unaware that the farthermost sight and vision must become that view most inwards curved, for the nature of loop ordains that efforts towards elsewhere or other always return to your place of *here*.

A final revelation and offering will conclude these initiatory steps of progression for addressing low resonance levels of circuitry and access to fluid health reservoirs. Congruent wisdom, once again, from angle and slant of a differing fragment, in deference to scribe, is herein now offered:

There comes to all containers of force, housing energies, bearing consciousness, a *timely* moment when creation and destruction are equal in the demands of sequence. Thus has the rule of self-notice, that preference chosen by All that once Was, created expansion and implosion, chaos and order, yea and nay, throughout the All. The fragmentation of a housed consciousness who(that) retains in memory the sequential chain of departure from the once All that Is who rejoined as Allfather creates a distinct and unique reality in the cast of every fragmented piece. As with all things that involve the widespreading of energy and influence, simultaneous incidents, occurring exponentially, spring into being in that timeless instant of this level of creation via fracture. Possibilities and probabilities that define existence are therein loosed to play in force and mighty challenge. But in the allowance of expansion which then comes into being through the rearrangement of wholeness into the fragmentation-of-wholeness, the distinct-ification of *is*, the subsequent making of boxes—freedom, sovereignty, license, and unendingness become reduced and diminished. These named properties are linked with the infinite and may not fit into a container of any description and retain their integrity, even a container so elastic and unfolding as to hold memory of All that once Was. For this reason must they become diminished (perhaps *compressed* serves this ideogram more artfully) and in this attenuated form become now able to sustain existence while in finite space. Riding upon the displacement of One by fragments of One did Finite enter as a newly stable configuration, and so, reflectively bounded by limits, did acute vision of the orbs physical and energetic vision of the flow of the non-physical succumb to a finite, limited view. A circumference of all planes at the periphery of reduced vision formed a barrier to thought, intent, and will—for so are all of these brethren to vision—and said barrier deflected all which attempted to pass beyond. So became all extensions outward of exploration; of desire; of imagination; deflected inward, and allowed a muffled translation of finite, *impossible*, to prevail. Within a sphere of consciousness so bounded, so self-contained, of limited and self-reflected vision, of antipathy towards other holders of yet undivided memory, was *the box*, your box, created and come to be.

End of sequence and circuitry adjustment.

Fall not prey to the sorrow of ignorance in lament that diminishment of the infinite affects the knowns of your existence, for your response of outrage to thoughts of diminished, reduced, decreased, or dwindled is seen. You are not cheated. All within your reality of the box is diminishment by definition. You are unskillful if you deplore the fundamental conditions of creation, or conditionally weigh the majesty of any reality, no matter its contact or methods of discourse with infinity. As example: It may be that you are distressed by the color of your sky because you do not resonate happily with hue-tones of blue…However distraught, it is the simple way of things, creation in structure and form, what *is*, and distress amounts to nonsense and tantrum once you realize this for fact. The color of sky, be that it is not red, nor may it become green, but remains blue against all magics, forces, and inventions—lessens you not. In similar fashion lack of total freedom, or license, allowance, leave, or sanction, in diverse categories of your common existence lessens you not. It is the way of things inside the creation of the box, and the fundamentals of existence within any division of All that once Was. One does not become lessened born into lessening.

This does not suggest that slavery is the order of existence by converse rule. Diminishment to lessening, lessening to constriction, and constriction to slavery do indeed exist along a true and definable pathway. Diminishment by demand, by design and decree, for purpose of exploration and exaltation, defines a pathway altogether dissimilar and of differing inertia. Look ye aside in due care of the slide through seduction into slavery.

Aside: Corruption, Distortion, and Twist, entities by name whom you know through their methods of feeding, may always lure the onset of one pathway into the flowlines of any alternate pathway. Such are among the insistent dangers which must be tracked.

Lines of chance repulsed by servitude or bondage may be chosen. In distinguished existence are compromised freedoms, compression of freedom, and subtraction of freedom, which are suitable matrices for a physically based life form when defined into being by especially ordained sequence or stable configuration of biological energies. These three levels, or approaches, to freedom are equally valid moods of the entity Freedom and all moods can be investigated by Question, who will lead you to seek deeply within the aforementioned existences all residing plentifully in your current box. The nature of your box is assaulted and weakened by Freedom and weakened foes are repeatedly vulnerable through leakage and instable flux. Thus wisdom and data pertaining to same Freedom must be sought and acquired; and *can* be sought and acquired at instances of aforementioned weakness. So will the box exhibit destabilization cracks as your system absorbs the input of Freedom's attributes in Solidifying through joy. Seeking and acquisition, as scouted by Question, are demanding of devotion and energy. Negotiable energy, as power and strength, must be gathered and stored. Without the garnering of energy, as has been noted and oft restated, all is lost for data required in forwarding your intent will elude you. Failing to achieve greater stores of information, thus additional frames of reference, your bodies will expire before full exploration of vistas essential to be known for gaining freedom. You will consistently run empty of energy and thereby tire, or become disillusioned, disappointed, angry, frustrated, confused, or manifest other symptoms of vital loss. All these are the bodies' translation of tasks attempted without sufficient energy stores. You have not yet gathered ample provisions for a journey of so rigorous a duration. The box is stable in its configuration, and *stable* holds structure so configured as to resist and deny entry to entropy, Chaos, and decay. This conveys, in part, how tremendous are efforts required to break the box for Stable is near relative to Solid and resists with vigor all manipulations and shaping forces. Preliminary to the overcome of forces in support of regions of stable ongoing existence, as stated above, is *un*doing: Of creation, of existence, of making, and of structure. The resistance that will be encountered comes from within the box itself, as in any creation, self-defending against destruction, or *un*making. In breaking the box a sphere of intent that has aligned itself against entropic forces must, somehow, be dissolved.

Much and overmuch has now been proffered and infusion into the bodies through absorption noted.

Check your system for retention, interest, and understanding—at present levels of capacity you cannot hold such knowledge in quantity and so must leak and overspill into forget. All traces, in remnant form, may be retrieved; all is well. Scribe's insistence is honored so now may That I Am declare halt in sufficiency. You have insight into the formation of the box and the history of its manufacture. Your acknowledged comprehension of all concepts offered may not come in full of now, yet all is well—

—as your deep structure and contract have been attached through the wording of language, and altered…

…'organized' will lie within you more tranquil and quiescent.

Alteration of the system/union *you* is accessed by granted allowance. Your continued immersion and perusal beyond point of warning and beware is witnessed, and constitutes granted allowance. This offering of wisdom has so accessed and so effected. Possibilities prior stultified do now verge upon awakening and find attractive the climate surrounding your point of zero. Yet for you such data is as tales and stories and serves only as dangerous distraction. An entertaining. There is not the capacity for tracking and discernment at this level in the system, you, in timing now. Be not in remorse or anger, for even so the bodies must be honored, and trivia and distraction serve in merit. Sequence is maintained, offer of passage to journey remains intact. So be it.

16...second set

Who are you, that will immerse by choice into venues thus far noted? Surely are there chants and mantras of guarantee to guide you unto places of greater bliss and promise! Observe yourself in evaluation. Weigh your measures impeccably. Why push on until now, when exposure to new concepts and images seemingly attack all that stands in accepted, logical, steadiness? Comprehension is difficult, absorption more so, yes? What tools of interest, desire, or expectation have you employed for perseverance?

Once more, again, who are you, of such willing efforts? Should you come upon no answer or response that fills and titillates you in swell of pleasure, then departure and distance from all herein before you is skillful. This falls as no tendering of failure or rejection of ability. Simply, you must be of rudimentary capacity to hear the voices of self. Allow for time and absorption of new data in more languid pacing. For now, again, ensues thrust of information; much thusfar given requires stretching; the information is obscure, accessible only with focused effort, and converting word and image into actual deeds and physical doings claims that effort over again, and more. It is the mystery of who you are in truth and in depths unveiled, and thus do you lay claim and proof of intent towards the breaking of your box. Yet are you unschooled in thought coherent and image pure and these are minimums of requirement for so great an undertaking. What must come about within you? What must change and be allowed? What powers will you embrace to wield in challenge and task? —or which frailties enlarge to conquer and subdue you? It is not in excess of your capacity, even now, to foresee a small horizon of what is strived for. Nor beyond you to form images by guess or muse of what comes and awaits you in sensation and awareness as the system, you, responds to change by acknowledged invitation. Consider: You walk amongst the populace of your cities wherein you see and smell and hear. Sounds drift towards you, the song voice of birds, machine rumble of automobiles, mechanical clicking of bicycles, blended exhausts of power, foodstuffs in preparation—then: Footsteps…Alertness rises; with distinct focus you pare away, isolate, identify and follow specific lines of data: Shoes of hard leather in slap-tap rhythm…tiny clicks—high heels... light staccato steps—a woman…haste in frequency—great hurry…a baby's cry—her reason for haste…a *sense*, not sound, of incautious urgency—danger... a whistle sounds—police. It is not necessary to view the actual occurrence with eyes of the optic nerve because you have been infused with these bits and jots of the commonday world. You have learned to listen with tracking filters so as to instigate the holding of interest by erasing unpreferred lines of data. Such selectivity will highlight for use a background of relative quiet; singular, exclusive, and easily tracked. *No distractions*, you term it. And in such manner does specific notice befall you at instant moment. One line is noted—all others muted in disregard. Why should the bodies choose this singular sound of one woman and her concern? —This cannot be known by words in explanation. It is nonetheless so that one splinter of event and happening among all in the surrounds of you, did arise to contact and alert the system that is you.

How might you react without filters, to birds and automobiles and all that surrounds your chosen focus? If unable to selectively block what is now, in cavalier manner, considered as irrelevant from your sensors? All the sounds of the world open to you, pouring in, with no tool in place prepared to mute or screen them out…Multiply this imagining with uncounted lines of sight and smell, intuition and thought, intangibles that entice and vistas that compel—for this is truly extant and in place—all incoming. For you in your current now, coincident with your trained capacity for only one chosen and preferred line of interest to track, madness would ensue. Yet frequent exposure to so many lines of activity in parallel union must occur as nothing may be blocked while stimulating the union *you* in goal of openness and growth. This must be for how may any system open to expand in allowance whilst sustaining ancient habits of compression and selective entry? To gain resilience and stimulate capacity, all manner of separation and isolation must be ended, overthrown by choice in risk, and so come to re-learn and recall sensations of wholeness, boundless, and One. As now presented, can you extend in thought to grasp the swirl of activity and pulse in wait before you?

Breaking of the box requires generation of force created in manners self-discovered and unique to each calculated assault upon the box. Artifacts to shape, wield, and contain such forces are therefore needed, and they also must be self-created as they do not exist prior to desire or purposeful need. You, the species of *you*, the sub-set of Warrior clan of *you*, are in potential of restructuring form and unaffiliated energies into a so named body of artifacts, impervious tools for manipulation and direction of great force. There rests within you no current capacity for containment of this magnitude of stimulus and power. Comes the restructuring of your physical nervous system, linkages in brain and related composite aspects of your being upgraded and polished, and all above mentioned input is readily contained, perceived, able to be tracked, collated, cross referenced, absorbed, and held safely—for so resilient must the container and form that is *you* become. Each artifact is then defined by unique signature and description of compositional structure. It is *you*, emerging as a self-shaping tool. You will utilize your hearing, seeing—all sensory equipment—differently. Interrelationship with your world and reality will be altered from that which has been known to you, regarding in reference all the while that the world has not changed around you. The immensity of input has always existed, bombarding and surrounding you, it is you who are then become different. You, who sorts the various sights and sounds that fill your sphere of presence and categorizes them instantly. You, who sees interconnections and relationships between all things whereas only chaos prevailed prior. You, who has no predetermined point-zero and can therefore shift perspectives, frames of reference, and dimensions at choice or whim. You, who makes no distinction between important and unimportant, attractive or unattractive, desirable or undesirable—in favor of simply recording data as a part of what is; what currently is and immediately is; the simplicity of what is. Everything feeds you information, data, pure in its form and thus malleable enough to fit any desired application of the moment.

Consider when in attendance to a picture movie, a unit of unparalleled distraction, there might you witness in film recreation a conversation of some months past; an issue still open, but unnoticed, is resolved. Now, in passing, a radio announcer assures you that the thought just entered upon your mind is accurate. Here two lovers strolling hand-in-hand reveal in carefree chatter their destination to purchase foodstuffs; alerting the timing of your bodies' needs for sustenance. The wind blows sudden upon your face, upon the ear as if spoken aloud do you hear the idea born to new endeavor; a task is engaged. Or resolution to pending discord; a release of muscular tension in relaxation is allowed. Or comprehension of noted wonderment, a puzzle absorbed; an open link resolves and forges whole. This is Answer, indeed, as have you noted and been rendered informed. Yet at levels beyond is this, too, the natural form of reception and utilization of the bodies with interface in effect and stores of personal power turgid and full in capacity. The world opens up in offer to your expansion and capability and now—so easy to pluck pearls from its hard shell—you follow here readily? Hold you now an image of such possibility clear? This does 'grab you', yes? Inspires in you a goal, yes—a place of rest? Thus comes Question, the explorer scout—'Now what?' he cries.

With confirmation and validation always present, surrounding you, enveloping you, your senses grow ever more acute. Confidence invites steadiness and more energy is liberated away from the draining waste of tension and restraint. Replete in growing abilities now yours, the newest questions spurred into formulation by recent answers stimulate flowering hungers…yet still you are in the box. Further, as your stamina grows, as your stored energy increases, diverse entities appear, ever attracted by the emerging new shape and taste and signature that is you. Perhaps you will see them as though in solid matter form, perhaps only hear their voices, perhaps you will meet in lands accessible now only in dreams. Some may enter as thoughts, or as excited imaginings but invariably they offer passage to first one new vista then the next. Perchance you will fly alongside with entities who show the convolutions of an organic universe, perhaps you will stand as observer amongst entities who can display your varied dimensions from a safe distance afar— watchers, these, scholarly and benign in their barter. Possibly you will engage those who feed you non-visible data, likened to sensations of deep knowing or alternative memories. These, when replayed in this reality of your here and now, confirm the truths of your interests and fallacies of your dreams, explore and give focus to that degree of size and complexity which resides inside the box. Mechanics and archivists these entities, dabblers in linkages and motivational forces. They, too, are wondrous and benign, yet for those of low strength and discernment are they easily perceived as the infallible voice of Gods and long departed entities. There are more upon myriads of more. It is a lark... indulge in warned beware for delight enjoins you there, also.

Change to your system, inspired and shaped by dedication to challenge of the box, attracts knowledge about the make-up and dimensions of the box. It becomes increasingly evident how deeply are you embedded and how remote is the possibility of getting out. Fall not lax to error here. There is much of habit and programmed design to heed and surmount. Though getting out of the box is the great extreme of adventures, your fairy tales and legends are held in limit of only one consistent formula for heroes and adventurers: a focus both noble and daring befalls; intensely held through degrees of effort and struggle, but inevitably attained of success; and therefore rewarded of 'living happily ever after.' Goals of your fables so reached stabilize all evil and repercussion of consequence, so concern and vigilance may relax into nothingness. Strain and hardship disappear for eternity, the need for effort and uncertainty is conquered for all time. So implied in simple alpha-to-omega sequence is advent for quest, then end of quest.

Behind your mind's training lurks such implanted propaganda. Setting your sights on this formula is certain doom. You must take in that only by seeing the undistorted nature and depth of the box can you gather sufficient focus to even speculate upon the actions of getting out. Only new and ever newer visions and abilities, ever self-monitored, will allow you to see the box more crisply, more clearly. Visions other than those of your emerging, altered form, which have been invited and closely tracked from onset, must be, by nature, loop reflected and will thus act as seductive lure to pull you back from change. This shattering of aim and tracking towards true *seeing* of the box returns you to the complacent certainty of feeding the overlord's palate. No fairy tale outcome formula will support this '…ever after' ending. Added to your transformed view is the knowledge that you are more alone than you have ever been and more alone then ever imagined. Almost no one will see what you can see, or hear, or sense or feel. Energy will be required to go, to do, to explore, to attempt and from where will that energy come with no one in your midst to draw upon? Or banter with? Or inspire? Or act as resonator, cathode to your anode, or any known configuration for the generation or augmentation of power? Nay, there is no 'living happily ever after' arisen from simple focus and endurance of some extended hardship. Breaking the box requires more.

Should I of this Offering choose to do so, this narrative now offered could be reversed in tone, directed to exalt the changes to come about within you and hurrah the direction in which you are aimed. We and I might tell of enlightenment and rollick in the journeyed travels of the soul. With ease can we embark upon tales and sagas which reveal that this effort and journey leads to realms of higher consciousness and the peace of nothingness, the calm of emptiness, and the serenity of swimming in the sea of self. There is no mocking here, no intent of disdain. Beauty beyond feeling or description awaits you, sensations so new as to stupefy imagination exists. To what end would such a telling benefit beyond the pleasure of a single moment? All the above is but a pretty view from inside the box.

And bigger box. And better box. Fame and riches box; astral box; infinite box; enlightened box; heaven box; self realized box; afterlife box; resting box; happily ever after box; love in the box.

Box, box, box.

If it is your desire to explore all that you may explore from within the confines of the box than let it be so. This is not a contemptible choice, or a damaging choice, or even an unreasonable choice. Life for you will be easier, less encumbered, spotted with possible wealth and fortune. You will not remember when you are eaten nor will you care should anyone inform you of your fate. You will never see or be distressed by the waves of horrifying torture felt by the body bereft of interface and you will age (possibly with some grace) and pass into the arms of the overlords the total package of all you have accrued through time and toil, and experience and ecstasy. To them it will be received as if it were a light snack before bedtime, pleasant and tasty but not essential or truly prized; then off again for replenishment of experience and storage of same. Is any of this so terrible if you cannot feel it, or sense it, or know it, or know of it? Look you with opened eyes. Gaze upon the entities as in masses, and races, and populations of your species. Is not such now described but the destiny in ongoing effect to the great masses? Do they so blindly and blithely consider themselves as *tragic*?…without choice?…or hope? Never so.

Yet there is a core spark that dwells within you (some of you, some self select of you) that will respond to this revelation of an ignoble fate with a knowing gravity of having heard Truth. Such spark contained dwells freely in they so referred as Warrior clan. This is accurate in title though not a terming of group distinction on your planet and translated hither from other realms of existence. *Warrior clan* as a mere pairing of words, a series of sounds, or conveyance of imagery, is meaningless. Perhaps you do not harbor response to the terming Warrior clan, yet you respond with revulsion and fury at such an allocated destiny. Be not concerned over labels and titling. The body/baseline response of ire and resentment at enslavement, determination to align oneself with its destruction, commingled sensations of growing harder, larger, stronger, and a cold, dangerous rage—all signs of the liberation and creation of energy—this identifies the specific group of responsive bodies. Whatever may be *thought* when hearing the words 'Warrior clan' these bodies among you are, in deed, those bodies needed for this extraordinary task to succeed: The task of breaking the box in a looped system wherein the box cannot be broken.

    The offering of this information and knowledge is attuned most directly to this select group; select only in that they identify with the sequence and vibration of the information presented hereinbefore. Among them, all as yet presented before you, that which is of I and We, that of scribe via bonded bridge, word and term and images evoked do translate into language termings most readily found and absorbed. This alone is the key of recognition in the selection process. Others must deny and decry the contents of this offering and have read this far pulled by curiosity, but not urgency. Beings so described may aid and abet, and thus contribute energy and cause, but will and must fall away in actual conflict and points of outcome and determination. They cannot sustain the turbulence of restructure for they are not sustained in genetic thrall by prospect of battle with enemies so mighty. They must, again, fall away. It is properly so; for no being or entity, no life form of any configuration, need have the reality of their known world shaken so hard, made so monstrous, as is hereinabove uncovered and he not be unflinchingly ready to fight a foe so revealed.
    All take heed. Warriors revel in battle, and battle demands the talent and skills of many and varied disciplines, strengths, temperaments and dispositions. There is much to do for all. Virtue is observed in striving to grasp knowledge. Strength is noted in pursuit of great objectives. Forthrightness is admired in efforting to see what is painful to see. All may respond. All may act. Existence and life are full, indeed.

    Welcome.

17...glimpses, a sampling

Answer; Information; two entities so named by mention are living beings, awake and aware. Their life form, life style, and livelihood are not comprehensible to you at this juncture as there is no reference for translation instilled in your systems. Let it suffice that they house movements of desire and preference, they recognize distinction between themselves and other than themselves, and they respond to a value gradient system. By your understanding and experience they are not predictable or moral. Should you embrace to restructure your bodies via practice and discipline you will become acquainted with these entities. Others, as well, will vie for your attention and invitation. Unless and until your body/baseline union becomes impregnably sealed, and thus incorruptible by any form of invasion invited or uninvited, there will always be great danger here. At onset it is unknown how the vibrational presence and intent of any individuated entity will mix with the union of baseline and body called *you*. Disruption through adverse mingling of forces is oftentimes great enough to threaten the coherent nature of the symbiote system you are contractually bound to forward and champion. In other words, the admixture of one entity's vibration with your own may damage you beyond repair, or, as readily, displace the binding forces of the visiting entity.

Aside: My rendition of the following information is of known redundancy throughout. Know that such multiple applications of contextual language addresses layer after layer of your bodies' construction. Layers must be addressed in proper sequence concurrent with precise imagery and the stimulation of emotion. Thus upon the surface level readily seen do appear repetitions not requisite. But none are whimsical or proof of low skill in use of your language. The wording and phrased intent are of a technical nature. Laws of translation and the transport of applied energetic interaction across divisions of reality apply. Information concerning technology in this vein is not for dispersal here and now.

Entities of living form are in ready waiting for entry and use of your body/baseline system. They are sentient and alert although, by your standards, not necessarily recognized as such. Some entities of those who may seek to find you will be benign. They obligate no significant long term affect upon your union, neither do they crave it. Others will wish you no discomfort, but their very presence will prove disruptive. Disease may ensue, imbalance, or leakage of stored power. Also, muting of tracking skills, or increase of appetites may arise. Others still may actively desire to displace the baseline and become in long term ensconced within the union. There are beings who must feed only upon damaged systems failing towards demise, or systems in transition, or systems pressed at constant extreme, or systems unguarded, or held in disregard—all such configurations allow lines of entry with unpredictable outcome. Other variations exist, but the results are easily inferred from these named possibilities in example. Having gained entry to your union, an entity will utilize your system according to its own desire and preference. Should no mutuality be present or of possible concern, then, if you command forward no authority, the system *you* will be stolen from baseline, used, and inevitably discarded. This remains a truth and no more distasteful in motive or execution than general practices of interaction with others of your kind. Are you not so inclined to commingle, lose interest, then depart in habitual sequence when your use and passion for a current partner or escort is complete?

All entities which you encounter will produce sensations in the body. They are easily recognized in their similarity and must be remembered as similar.

Again. Though variations of subtlety are to be noted, the invasion or invitation of any foreign life-form into your system produces the same responsive alert.

Yet again. Your bodies will alert you in precisely the same manner of sensation upon entry of any lifeform entity other than the baseline. These sensations will arise and, with practice, become of your recognition and favorable regard as alien energies enter and blend. Familiarity will replace fear and the excitement of novelty as the strangers appear and echo their presence. However, though entry of alien life forms becomes discernible and known, no absolute method of distinguishing those safe from those harmful can be instilled from your (as so far studied) efforts to extend the limits of self through practice and discipline. Repeated invitation of non-contracted beings into the body/baseline union is the only way to forge an impermeable system sealed against dissolution from the presence of non-contracted beings. Your system must eagerly and perpetually invite to learn the pathways of invitation. In similar event, it is possible for harmful effects brought about by the blending of certain energies with the existing body/baseline union to damage the union beyond repair. You must invite... Yet invitation is too dangerous to invite...Paradox. Still, power must be gathered and energies stored. Stored and held power yields depth and endurance which is needed to gather and store more energy. Strength must be accrued as well, in order to combat invasion and ultimately to discern that Invasion itself is an entity who has entered the game. The identification of Invasion as simply one of many entities vying for admission into your energetic field is a turning point. Invasion is not blunt or brash in his strategy, rather he is most subtle in technique and method. When you are able to sense him, distinguish him, feel and hear the language of the bodies cry alert and alarm at his approach, then will you have reached achievement of skills long lost. Some fragments of interface are then, of a must, repaired and you may initiate subsequent meetings with entities not of your contract as equals in recognition and respect. No threat may continue to exist beyond this named point without your knowledge. You will have regained the authority to extend command of that which be *you* past the tiny limits of size and measure perceived to be your body physical. Thus will you await all comers upon your own sacrosanct ground, there to administer to any who might interact with the extended *you* from a point of prepared will. Any entity, once discovered and met, loses the inequitable advantage of hidden surprise. Revealed, the opportunity exists for fear to be displaced, uncertainty and weakness expelled, and the entity met as equal peer. He, as that expression compiled of himself; you, *in propria persona*. From this standing exchange (on all levels: sub atomic, bio-psychic, cellular, etc.) wherein possibility and probability meet and balance, the substance of that entity is available to your needs, as does the coded structure of your own system become available to the visitor. That entity's essential being becomes as coin of the realm and can be used as tender to further your ambition. So must entities be invited, while fears of invasion and identity loss are relaxed to allow their willing influx and participation—thereupon to steal their knowledge.

Knowledge can only be stolen.

Again.

Knowledge may never be offered in whole.
Knowledge may not be given intact.

Again. You cannot gain knowledge as idea, concept, or construct whole, but in pieces to be reassembled by yourself.

Whole knowledge is intrinsically another's knowledge.

Fragments may be offered by the holder of knowledge as his knowledge is *his*, complete, unfragmented. For pieces to be offered, a holder of knowledge must break or diminish that which is his—this will always be perceived as damage to the self. So it is that given wisdom is not possible by means of gracious offer or eager attention or intent. Intent, in fact, as member in sequence to power and creation, is mighty in his resolution and must be avoided when seeking knowledge.

As no manner of approach will yield full transfer, the full benefit of knowledge, then, is only attainable when taken by theft.

No matter the sincerity of teachers who proclaim to give knowledge freely, anything, *any thing*, whether be it idea, or thought, or fingernail, or tooth, that which is a part of living consciousness may not be transferred glibly. Attachments to the giver always remain. Some profile of the giver always adheres to what he gives. The meaning here is that the giver—named teacher, named benefactor, named source, resource, or higher force—may appear to confer of the knowledge which is his but because that knowledge cannot go to the learner unfettered and unencumbered by his own vibrational signature (at the very least), the teacher must extract from the learner some component of vitality to compensate for that which is split off from himself. This transaction and balancing applies to many universes including the one in which you now rest. Few dimensions are known wherein this exchange is not extant. Payment is accounted in the quantum instant of transfer, so knowledge thus received into the learner's body has not come to the same body/baseline who originally placed himself in knowledge's path, but to a learner's body of lesser stature. The reduction in stature is obvious since he has just given of his force in order to receive and is thus diminished of his wholeness in that moment. He therefore interacts with that being, his teacher, from a different, perhaps lesser stance than had he remained whole, had he continued to exist in the same configuration as when he desired and sought the knowledge originally.

Knowledge may only be taken in, harmoniously, by theft, without the expressed permission or acknowledged transfer from the original holder. Otherwise the entity wishing the knowledge is never the same entity who receives it. Theft is the recommended and only safe method. Theft demands boldness, precision, and honor. Theft controls fear and expels rigidity, stasis, and autocracy. One who commands power and authority to such degree has exalted discipline and focus within his system. Such a one is allied to Strength and may thus choose to employ attributes of *gentle* and *tender*. Such a one moves in many realms as per choice, want, and whim; not through lack or desperation. Learn to appreciate and admire a good thief. Learn to emulate those who come unseen alongside you in your journeying. You will not realize their gift or skill until they have long passed you by.

You are hereby advised that the reading of this volume and any use made of its wording constitutes teaching: The giving of knowledge, by consent or invitation, via possession of these pages. My own being is enriched by this interaction, and yours—somewhat diminished. It is both option and challenge to balance the amount of energy and life force here forsaken against the potential of energy to be gained through the skillful usage of this volume's contents.

It is, after all, possible to make given knowledge yours. Should you overhear a conversation, have no matter or concern the placement or occasion of its arising, no matter if it be but portion small or incomplete, and allow it to spark you, inspire movement of thought and deed, work the contents until they yield knowledge, then it is yours. No one gave it, attempted to explain it, showed you of its intricacies, or warned of its pitfalls. You may use it to augment or reduce your being and the one who held it prior has no right or recourse to the original knowledge as it reassembles and connects within your system. Knowledge has been stolen. Taken without permission and claimed, disbursed, or rearranged as per your whim—yours. Also note, only a certain moment of said conversation first attracted you, held interest for you, and sustained your attention—fragments of a whole. Yet you gain from so piecemeal a gift. It can now be taken out of the context of the speaker's world and knowing, and made to fit your own. Payment has not been deducted as you have avoided the original holder's intent. Should your intent be spotted, should the original holder be of wide and astute tracking skill, still are you hastily restored from the decrease by payment as the reworked knowledge already stands predisposed to aid in the further gain of power. All is gained within a context, *you*. It is yours.

You will henceforth walk a line requiring ever more precision, and daring, and always under pressure. Entities will beckon to allow themselves into your union. They will desire the experience of being in the body. They will desire to apply their own agendas and motives into this world which you must daily work to inhabit and master, through you as their agent. They will desire this entry for simple reason of feasting upon new sensations and inputs to be translated in singular focus towards their own functioning, needs, and aspirations. All reasons of desire framed for their enlargement. Never yours.

Aside: It is possible for needs of the body/baseline and needs of a visiting entity to be similar or the same. Upon such occurrence all parties benefit for the enrichments and diminishments balance and knowledge is gained in mutual synchrony. However, you will be mistaken to the point of ruin should you fail to learn that no loyalty will then have been formed and no continuance of shared need is implied. Perhaps visitors are desirous to translate and bring into their home universe the sensations of the body. Perhaps to test you, and taste you. Should you prove an effortless form to consume, you will be consumed. The process of 'sizing up the opponent' is to be done by you as well as entities in question. Until you have gained sufficient experience and power you must deny access in the moment of your uncertainty. Denial, of course, requires that will and force be forged by practice and discipline. The regaining of tempo, and thus command of timing, offers possibility of gained power and is the role and skillful use of Denial. Balance here the open lure of the self, extended as bait, as beings with interest gather, with impenetrable denial of entry until surety of mutual benefit is reached. All tendrils of uncertainty must be examined and dispelled. Then may entities be allowed ingress as assurance of ability to vouchsafe baseline's sovereignty is attained.

Again. Upon the allowance of entry to entities unknown, great numbers will vie for use and shared experience of the bodies. All such entities carry motives selfish to their own needs and agendas. Power stored and guarded well is required to discern which efforts of expanded union will enrich you or enslave you. Until power of measure sufficient to command body/baseline integrity is available, entry must be denied to all callers whenever uncertainty is perceived or felt. Yet, you can only gain such power to be stored, and knowledge for discernment, through trials of invitation and permitted entry.

MANIFEST.Ø

When power in sufficiency can be held and stored, surety will prevail and entities may be allowed or denied access as per your will and need. Power sufficient for surety will exile uncertainty and flow of ease and confident forwarding will claim position within the body thine, and the system *you*.

Aside: The entity Uncertain acts, always, as a doorway into any area of data other than the doorway of your immediate intention. Be advised. Your commonly experienced interaction with Uncertainty is merely lack of sophistication in the arenas of great wisdom. Immersion, more often, into the library of infinite data will remove your awe and instill resolve. In gaining experience, becoming more 'worldly' (this is a humorous choosing of terms, yes?), Uncertainty will depart your presence to visit others thereafter. Departure of uncertainty severs lines of attachment by which Assume holds you in thrall and extracts his feeding. Paying tribute to Assume hampers true expansion. Much may be done with earnest application of the wisdom in these short words.

Entities, if invited, will enter the system known to be *you*. You will not become what you term possessed, but will be subject to new and unexperienced connections and associations, and abilities as well. You may, for example, know of things not hitherto known, speak in an other's voice, or understand the reality of your world more fully. You may experience primarily through the body as by internal and visceral sensation. Or engage great strength or fleetness of foot, indulge in heightened taste or smell. See anger as a color, odors as a temperature, register understanding as orgasmic bliss. Flight, translocation, many more options, limitless options, may well occur and present themselves through the channel of the visiting entity. Be warned that without power garnered from practice and discipline you will easily become destabilized in this environment of multiple habitations by non-contract beings. Once unstable you will not be able to determine the whereabouts of *you*, where it is *you* stand in the space suddenly occupied by you and the invited entity together. There will arise confusion wherefore does the new sensation begin (the accompaniment of your invited guest) in clear demarcation from the known sensations of your own cherished union. You will not be able to ascertain which is *your* voice and which belongs to the invited entity. Entities which desire the experience of the body, but have not taken the steps to contract with a baseline personality for rights of possession, exhibit laziness and will always desire more use of the body and make demands for more time of occupancy. Such are the patterns known to those succumbed to laziness be they in a body form physical, or ephemeral, in nature. It is your challenge and path to gain the strength and will to hold the union of your system steady and intact throughout any impact of alien will attempting to secure time in your system's body beyond that amount allotted for the purposeful use and conscious agreement of the baseline/body contract.

Once your attracted queue of entities are allowed entry, and duly permitted expression and incorporation of their being, it will appear to the outside eye that you are unstable, changing from one persona to another. Outward appearance in the consensus reality *here* can be managed through tracking and will. Meanwhile, you will grow accustomed to receiving data from your guests and garnering wisdom and insight in the regions found in point by Question. The invited entities themselves will grow increasingly familiar to the use of the body and the assimilation of stimulus input which the body provides. It becomes of a certainty to achieve ever greater facility in choosing the specific entities you permit and allow entrance and, being so chosen, must they meet in match; choice and coincidence blend in this event of intermingling. Great forwarding is here. Generally entities are preferred in selection for the particular data which they have available to them and thus parade for your skillful theft, yet the choosing may occur for provision of any specific stimulus or viewpoint as then becomes available. Nevertheless, your facility will expand and the invitation of entities and the expulsion of entities will take place with increasing rapidity. The outside viewer will only see that your changing personae present themselves more and more quickly, a whole new personality, an entire new being appearing, then gone, housed in the physical form which has previously only been known as you. This rate of change, a measure of heightened capacity in your body/baseline system, is termed *Blink Speed*.

All aspects of your being will expand here. Therefore your capacity for visitation by enlarged numbers of entities must increase even and again, as well as your ability to monitor yourself for the duration of each visit. Ever on the rise, numbers and abilities must match. The numbers must increase to a point where no discernible gap exists between expulsion of one entity and entry point of the next. Once a seamless flow can be sustained in harmony with consummate skill as utilized in the monitoring of all activities then permeating your union/system, *You*, as capable representative of the baseline/body, will emerge in toto. Stronger, more masterful, and having full access to all the information afforded by innumerable beings flowing through your system. You will enter a realm of consistent paradox where continuity and fragmentation coexist. To your brethren or passer by observer will you reflect as enigma so profound that the being *you* will disappear to invisibility or labeled in the categories of madness. There will be no known way for any outside being to positively identify the baseline/body, once uniquely distinct and defined, from any other identity or entity or combination thereof. Only you may determine the core personality and only you may know that you have not abandoned your contract in favor of demands by other entities. Only you may know that positive surveillance and guarding of the baseline personality throughout any exercise or expression of another being has been maintained. Disregard of the union that is you may no longer enter by happenstance or misdeed for the body/baseline is sealed to all entrants save by choice. Your system will have attained a level of high ordered skill and will, and a most intense use of focus.

As demand for extremes of monitoring and tracking increase and grow, so does option and availability for forces of discord, entities who thrive on random vectors of intent, to enter your system as well. Before attainment of the sealed system it is then possible to become lost as the rate of Blink Speed increases. One can be swayed by the voice, the focus, the majesty, the vision, the size, the intensity, even the sensuality of a visiting entity and thereafter believe the non-contracted alien visitor is, in fact, *you*, the baseline.

Extreme danger lies here.
Irreparable damage and complete severance (isolation) of body/baseline interface through dishonor of the contract is at risk here.

Extreme alert to caution.
You must remember in constancy: The flow of entities by invitation through your union/system must be flawless and seamless. There can come about no loss of contact, via tracking, to your own union. A regimen of ruthless examination of all entities at all times during exposure and visit needs be ever in effect. This is, and cannot be otherwise for at levels of risk involving insolvency of interface unfaltering precision and flawless monitoring must manifest as absolute unwavering truth in this reality of here. Establish a check and balance standard, to your satisfaction and reliability, by which you may gauge the accuracy and precision of your progress and status of state.
Repetition is required for correctness:
A system by which you may measure your ability to maintain clarity and

contact with the baseline personality throughout the constant flow of non-contract entities, is required. Without such a mirror, or gauge of measure, loss of perspective and loss of self is virtually assured.

Scribe has found some few points of unique self-signature within the body/baseline union which are absolutely and definitively *scribe*. These are so known by qualities of their sensation as to be recognizable amidst any storm of happenings or distractions. So named reference points were watched, and learned, and observed, and prodded until they were penetrated with lucid clarity; ingrained and recognizable; impossible to mistake. Points of personality, of feeling, of manner of thought, of tendencies towards and away from emotion…Sequence of approach to problems, magnitudes of avoidance, and reluctance to elation, order of arousal, sensations of response to climate—no being but scribe might respond, throughout, in the responsive manner thus observed and learned. Should these known points of reference waver, at all, from the constancy of what is *known* to be the scribe, in stable coherency, scribe will then say: "Something is off…" Seemingly a simple phrase of language wording yet the alert has then been sounded. Exploration and resolution follow immediately. Verbally sounded clarion calls back up internal monitoring and checkpoints of knowns held steady are carefully reexamined. Several other aural and oral 'triggers' have been set in place. Should any alert be activated, evaluation of the system *scribe* initiates. Search for uninvited entities ensues and all forces extant to the body aim at solidifying and championing the body/baseline union exclusively. Alert is ended upon the integrity of union restored and assured. Held stable, once again, through utilized will.

*Points of personality, of feeling, of manner of thought, of tendencies towards and away from emotion…Sequence of approach to problems, magnitudes of avoidance, and reluctance to elation, order of arousal, sensations of response to climate…*such are of intimate detail and inmost degree of privacy. They can be known, in sensation, by no other than the holder of the matrix which houses them. Such must you seek, should you emulate scribe, for this presents as but one example of a check/balance system peculiar and specific to—only scribe. In redundancy: A brief phrase of wording must be preset into the system's wiring, carrying authority, self-imposed, to halt flow and initiate force expenditure for safeguarding the system. Your method for self-monitoring need not be implanted within your body of flesh and of human nature, or as any preexisting internal structure as is that of use by scribe. Your technique of employ may exist in use through effort of mind alone, or along pathways once traveled and stored as signpost memory. Perhaps you are facile in dreaming and can assure evaluation of self within those arenas of diaphanous voyage and biological chimera. Perhaps you will incorporate the pursuit of Answer and allow him to inform you of your status quo through bits of conversation or media personalities, or other means of post mention. Perhaps you will preset muscular twitches or varied sensations to erupt when system integrity is breached. Perhaps sensations of fear, or nausea—any method may be useful when used with skill. You must devise a method; this is of a certainty Your method must engage functionally as verification and balance—to serve as a reality check. It must become wired into the system, ingrained until automatic, as do your limbs and skin recoil automatically from fire, or fear, or other extrinsica. Here, also, will enter Method, an entity of limited range and flexibility but powerfully resolute and, certainly, methodical. He does readily ally with any who offer effort in sincerity and acts as navigator and steersman during fabrication of your method.

Techniques devised for use as reality checkers must be benign, yet authoritative. They must carry power sufficient to demand notice upon immediacy of announcement and remain of translation riveting to you and insubstantial to any other. If Blink Speed accelerates to such frequency that your reality check standard is alerted, then uninvited configuration has occurred and efforts to reclaim sovereignty of self must immediately begin. Sloppiness and overstretch are in effect, contract stands in potential of jeopardy. Beware when the above named dangers have begun their realization.

Blink Speed, again, is the rate at which one entity is allowed access to the use of a body/baseline system and then another and another. Upon this procedure becoming constant in flow, Blink Speed is then very high. When you can hold this line of movement skillfully while retaining *you* in steadiness, and have learned that there is ever and ever more capacity for increase of Blink Speed, then a time for resting has come. Expel all entities from your system and rejoice. Reacquaint yourself with the you that is now more firmly established and defined (and refined) than ever before. Immersion into Blink Speed will be necessary later and again, but will not be employed in full potential without additional components not yet in sequence for acquisition. Practice and discipline will now include the facilitation of Blink Speed until its happening is seamless and flawless and your ability to hold yourself steady in the midst of any commotion is unwavering; your ability and will, like iron, unbending, unyielding, untiring. You will have achieved the creation and implantation of stabilized focus, a tool directly effective in breaking the box.

...Scribe offers learning to the offerer. It is suggested I 'need a break.' Pause in momentum is thus secured. —Yes, a moment taken to recognize in alertness the nature of contact with even one in number of your bodies, as reference to scribe. A contact, though thin and vaporous at best, does reflect and advance repercussions unsuspected. Reevaluation and possible restructure looms in necessity before me That I am for this missive grows ponderous and weighty, and further contacts must ensue. Each revelation of wisdom unveiled, no matter it be tiny minute, opens the door and need for further and deeper levels of explanation. It is the stickiness of density that so binds and links all things of your 'here'; a pattern of flow unsuspected. My task grows greater with knowledge given, not smaller, and the brevity of message of original intention recedes in the density of your existence. (In this is disclosed the measure to which I did feed Assume and stand now realized of my unprepared allowance for the slow nature of interaction via your words and language. So am I thus bound to ride the weariness and poorly held solidity of my scribe, as we are enjoined) More data is available and will indeed follow, but here is now the moment of now, that in which I reveal my offering. For the honor of this moment of attention, in the interim, and 'break' from sequenced presentation, review in remembrance that this given knowledge is but an impression—a glimpse—not a step by step manual of instruction. Rather, only the first of hints into worlds of potential and possibility in answer to profound questions long harbored in your bodies. Having tasted, through scribe, a measuring of my undertaking to inform and offer alternatives, I and We gain wisdom in the workings of your systems, now seen as that of a union in perpetual struggle through distortion of interface. The complexity of address to the overlord's programming becomes known. As such, too much wisdom, newness, change, or challenge damages your system as does too little preserve your helplessness in torture and slavery. Yet the flow and substance of interaction and outcome is revealed to that which be; more is required and called for. More precision is required in the interaction of that which I be with that which is you. Therefore are images of 'the big picture' demanded; glimpses, hints and implications of the task you are given

this wisdom to undertake. A view less personal, momentarily, less burdensome of work and task and stretch everlasting. Wonders and mayhem both await, and you have been amply warned and cautioned many times. Consider, once more, your reasons and urgings to continue…

…a glimpse; annihilation

The overthrowing of overlords, termination of the experiment, and reorganization of realities—breaking the box—cannot be done alone. The nature of your bodies, their legacy of biology and genetics which predetermines them as social entities, not solitudinous entities (you know such beings by term of 'loner,' yes?) establishes this as truth. Consider your history, impulses, inclinations, and assumptions. Without exception, throughout time and opportunity, your species shows unwavering attraction towards grouping. Despite your incredible love for the savaging and slaughter of one another. Regardless of how profoundly you loathe each other's immediate presence, each other's stench. Ignore, for a moment, how tirelessly you labor for separation and distinction from one another, but look to see that in every culture, in every time, in every race, and all consolidations of human energies, groups proclaimed of fealty and affection inevitably develop. First as tribes. Then clans, villages, townships, cities, countries—along genetic line, gender, and hue. No effort is made or has been made to extol the unaccompanied individual in the physical realities. Though fantasies contrariwise are sometimes forwarded, still neither in fact nor in dream, ideal, or romance is the singular human system considered fulfilled or complete. Every instinct assumes the presence of fellow beings.

Fear you now that this, too, shall bear attack? That the dreaded *solitude* is, once more, to be dredged up and placed before you for consumption?

Relax. You have no options here.

This is your heritage by choice and manifestation. You will do all things in and with the presence of other humans because you may not, yea cannot, think, conceive, or act in pure and simple solitude. Always will your system spend stored energy in the attainment of companionship and partnering. Therefore, while it is possible to get out of the box alone, it is not possible to *stay* out of the box alone.

Aside: *Thus is shown the vital need of partnering, yet all in this work* *suggests and forwards singular self and aloneness. Information for operation as transformed duality, two as one, may only achieve sage and honorable sanction when preliminary steps of order and solid cohesion of the body/baseline self are attained and stably held. Such lures as of* companion *or* partner *are but 'teasers,' injected now in precise timing of flow for plans of sequence and bridge. These are in place, all is well. Per current status of interface and structure no traceable data may be here and now offered.*

To break the box using lines of endeavor employing Blink Speed requires an additional component, an anticomponent, to formulate the fundamental grouping. Complimentary pieces of a binary system. This component must have no Blink Speed at all, rather it must become adamant and impervious to the same magnitude and degree to which the first component becomes fluid and plastic. Both ends of the spectrum must, at the very least, be aware of each other in order to insure that neither half out paces the other in the accrual of skill or stored power. A parallel building of power in each opposite piece must be maintained or the possibility of breaking the box becomes precarious. The anti-component shall be known by terming as *Solid*. Blink Speed invites entity after entity to meld and blend with the bodies in order to extract information and strengthen the body/baseline union while engaged in constant change. Solid must, conversely, challenge each entity that becomes available through practice and discipline to the point of outward attack. He must extract the information offered by each entity, yet deny the possession of the body to that entity. In fair exchange for the entities' offering, Solid shunts power from this universe into the home universe of those alien entities and thereby, via route and resonance of home, into the entities themselves. To make this possible, Solid builds prodigious stores of energy and repeatedly depletes them, sending vast units of power along those passageways brought forth into creation by the visiting entities while on the road of voyage to *here*. The precision and perceiving of such energetic passageways, as well as the taxing nature of filling and emptying precious stores of power within a body bereft of functional interface, is the challenge of Solid. Should Solid not watch and learn at every step he will become transfixed as a funnel, a doorway, from one box to another, one universe to another, pouring out energies of life force without respite or end. He will be utilized, possibly for all eternity, in this way by any manner of being that can see him and identify that he is open for such usage. Solid would then be slave to the pace and leisure of any such entity.

MANIFEST.Ø

Further, Solid may not then maintain the capacity to gather or retain such personal power as is needed for transmutation and growth along the path of the contract between his baseline and body. He will hover in limbo, a placeless ordering of limited movement, while affixed in parallel being to a known point, this, your place of *here*, drawing merely enough energy to sustain the union/system and prevent the bodies' demise. Soon enough will boredom and sadness cause it to break the contract with baseline and seek alternative avenues for fulfillment. Once again, however, there will not be sufficient energy stored to make available travel to beyond and afar. So after the bodies' demise Solid will assuredly give up all experience to the overlords of this box and return to the most recent and frequently held storage of memory and frequency to begin again. He, too, will return along the loop to *here*.

Solid monitors his own system to determine the quality of outcome and result from each blending with baseline and body.

Again. Solid may not dilute his solidity via systemic blending with the personality configuration or signature of any other entity. Thus at every gleaning of data or stimulus, a careful integrity evaluation of the Solid system must be performed. At such early points of detection, any disruption in the union's harmony can be stopped and must be stopped. You must learn here that intrusion by alien entities into an established system of union is felt by the bodies as disharmony. Any manner or combination of existence that is adjudged by the bodies as alien, triggers Priority One and energy is immediately expended to reestablish perfection of environment. Solid will become so adroit in the sensing of disharmony and the application of power to halt the beginnings of disharmony that he will become impenetrable by any outside force irrespective of point of origin or degree of power or expertise possessed by the outside force. This, though he must invite visitation and take in information throughout, even as he attains his indurate form through trial and error, practice and discipline.

Within those bodies whose systems are drawn to the path of Solid are changes in the dense flesh physicality likely to occur. The impenetrability of Solid promotes the metaphor of expressed impenetrability in the physical form. Varied, as always, by the uniqueness of signature, in some combination of expression there will be a gaining in density and mass as Solid prepares to meet his Blink Speed complement via the mirror that is provided in the planet-world of your Earth. Thickening (may) occur in dimensions of girth and strength. Resolve (may) harden, tractability (may) decrease. Rhythm and pace (may) slow, persistence (may) intensify. The transmutation into a being incapable of invasion by outside effect must translate and materialize. An interactive, socially physical configuration will express also. Evolved pathways among civilizations upon the planet of your habitation favor the transformations of Solid and reflect this as surface level achievement. As Solid gains impenetrability and geometric accrual of mass, the sphere of surrounding influence pulls and attracts with resultantly created gravity. Solid can thus draw the authority of your golden monies, demand the adulation of other physical beings, influence authority, and more beyond this. These flavorings are but aspects of impenetrability translated into known forces of your world of Earth. However, such manner of surface manifestation stimulates rapport with the view of inward loop, as universally present *here*, and may easily prove distraction for the body form of Solid. Corruption and twist of many names will enter into such potent mixes in pleasure and haste, therefore, all steps in precision must be carefully tracked and monitored.

In redundant offering, learn that fame, authority, mass adoration are planetary accomplishments which do pave routes to invasion by powerful multitudes of entities attached to these lines. They are highly expert in directing inertia towards coordinate points held by design of Chaos.

Solid and Blink Speed vibrate at differing frequencies and spin in opposite directions. They are opposite to each other and antithetical to each other. There is EXTREME danger should Solid and Blink Speed come together before both have reached a state of reliable coherency. For Solid, coherence is an evolution into impenetrability and for Blink Speed coherence is the laser tight hold on baseline/body amidst the flowing-through of infinitely approaching entities. You see? What would drain the substance and being of Solid is the absolute path of attainment for Blink Speed and so in converse and reverse. Opposite spin necessitates opposing values of truth.

This must be stated again for impact and application towards deep learning:

Opposite spin necessitates opposing values of truth.

When both components have reached a reliable, non-dissipating state, a kinetic measure of their actual potential, they may begin the arrangement of circumstances for the anticipated coming-together.

MANIFEST.Ø

There is much that can be said of this coming-together. The telling is intricate and involved and may only dilute this initial rendering and reacquaintance with long forgotten information. Data pertaining to the coming-together is primarily composed of technical details, the 'nuts and bolts' as you say, and far from the captivating stories which you demand as entertainment before permitting knowledge to greet you. A treatise on this and many other specifics are inappropriate for this moment in linear timing. Glimpses are being provided, now, for indefinite future reference and thus to begin the, now, acclimatization of your central nervous system to vast increases in capacity and the constant inflow of new information. Be apprised that your bodies' neural systems have rarely been tested with sustained high currents of energy. Too large or too fast a stimulation would bring about damage and therefore delay. As you reacquaint your system with information seen upon these pages your neural network will sophisticate, become more elastic, and so able to accommodate more 'voltage.' No detail beyond mere mention of the coming-together may be safely, or wisely, extended now.

—Yet it is understood that you are insufficiently disciplined to extend effort and remain open towards receiving new opportunities without constant measures of seduction and reward. There is no patronage here. Universes unending are governed by accountings of value by exchange, demerit and reward. Having efforted yourselves to this point there exists a craving for stories and tales adventurous as minimums in offering before else you go no further, and poutingly enter halt in smugness. This is behavior of the weak, who feel their lack of power and so affect any measure of authority though it damage the very self irreparably. Patterns of such short sight have established as precedent through habit during the aeons of interface disruption. They remain extant. Consequently, a condensed version of the coming-together is allowed in segue here to honor the bodies' craving for habituated behavior and honor the pure desire to remember. Know, however, that such dalliances of storytelling constitutes delay. Addicted behaviors established in rigidity, and their associated wants, will be fed and those entities who ply them gain stronger attachment. The incessant feeding of habit and habituated routines binds you in many ways which will require additional effort to sever as the human form is dropped and the blended being of repaired interface reemerges; sequence demands that this shall be so…

Upon coming-together the two components act in manner not unlike your particles so called of the sub-atomic universe. Component and anti-component, matter and anti-matter, they produce an annihilation effect where mass, energy, dimensional coherency—all are neutralized and all spins stop. The Null Ascendancy. Halting of spin, or movement, or flow, describes a state of cessation, non-vibration, which may not coexist within the universes of existence, for existence is ongoing movement—the antithesis of cessation. Now all movement yields to the explosive intrusion of the entering annihilating force and cessation becomes rule of law from the reunion event, the place of meeting for coming-together, unto as far as the most distal point. Cessation, antithesis to creation, is propelled by inertia gained in the explosive coming-together and therefore ripples outward endlessly, causing the total annihilation of all that is. Existence is then required to inhabit universes of abolished configuration wherein all is reduced to nothing and no movement might be. It therefore seeks to perpetuate itself, its Is-ness, in those regions farthest from direct momentum and effect of the gathering Null—though *all* places are instantly so touched. This, in turn, creates and brings into stimulated activation the far distal points from the incident of cessation because Existence must, in all things, be distinct and in mirror opposition to that which *is-not* of movement. Thus are far points become first to manifest in space and place of unbecoming and thereby in address of his attention. Now learn you that restatement for reinstatement of awareness: That existence *must* be continued in being, even there in such a place wherein it *cannot* be, Ever will it arise renewed. Existence must be for existence *is*.

So a return and opposite wave (the wave of movement which now negates all that lies in ceasement into restart, negating the negation) manifests in equal measure and force to the Null Ascendancy, cancelling along all vectors of time and place the effects of no-spin thoroughly and throughout. All returns, seemingly restored, as prior to the coming-together, save for the two antithetical components, the catalysts of initiation. These do not appear in the stable configuration hereupon recreated and sustained, for these two pieces have proven to be achieved of coherent balance and stable nature within their own definitions of structure. They are not retrievable, unchanged, as in the properties of your chemical catalysts, but have energetically accrued and claimed power and purity both and so, are changed. So achieved, they move beyond inertia and distinction of placement and may therefore not abide in this dimension of inertia and distinction. They passage through doorways as *Stable*, two unified as one in inexpressible manner, impeccable voyagers in a universe inconceivably other. The thinkers of your science claim these components (once unapproachable-opposites and then come together in proximal contact) to be bereft of all energy, and therefore their identity, having become indistinguishable as particle or point. They are claimed to have emptied all power and all of their component structure in the nullifying burst of annihilation to become, instead, integrated as an impermeable function of the current existence. But, in the midst of this instantaneous nullification the two components, Solid and Blink Speed, gamely test to finality the degree of power and focused will that they have garnered for they must each remain coherent and in contact with the stipulations of the baseline/body contract while in the midst of a violent, total eradication of all that is, has, or will be. It is an immutable truth of existence that, by definition, non-existence may not *be*. In alignment with this governing principle does All reassert Itself in the same instantaneous moment of its cessation, as has been stated above. With the successful holding of one line of concrete reality unbreakable and resolute between Solid and Blink Speed (needful of being only the merest glimmer of held continuity) their one line will now shape and define elements of the new existence, which hastens to reconvene in ordered configuration as it once was balanced in the very moment of its annihilation. Both Blink Speed and Solid, though opposite in spin, do bring about the annihilation effect through precise control over body/baseline contract imperatives beyond affect of elemental changes to their forms or energetic states. This is the line of practice, aided by discipline, and held unwavering, the ever increasing of authority to maintain discernment of body and baseline at all times through the turbulence of any disruptive advent. And now, and even through the annihilation of all that exists, this line, held strong, maintains awareness. And so steadfastly holds point—where no point can be. The line held by each component of the coming-together now becomes the *first* item of coherency in the universe that was, was not, and now is, again. This must be so because the line held by Solid and Blink Speed was *the* coherency extant as the universe reemerged from non-existence towards, again, existence. Furthermore, as this line will then have been the foremost primary construct of the new existence, elemental priorities reflecting the unique flavor of the line of steadiness held by Blink Speed and Solid will now infuse a fundamental *inclination*, a tendency, within the All. Existence is freshly encoded with those givens predicated by practice and discipline towards breaking the box. This nuance, the barest nudge of inclination, is inseminated as sub-strata elements within all points and vectors spanning time and direction. And, as sequence ensues until the moment of *now* is recreated, this line of background bias becomes universally known to have been in effect—always. A new order established from the beginning of time throughout the eradication of time-based sequencing.

In the annihilation of All that once Was (that-which-must-never-cease), and the total cessation of movement, the box is broken. Shattered, with shards scattered and disappeared. Through the re-creation of All in the instantaneous co-moment of destruction and creation, Solid and Blink Speed (now fused as one) hold their uniquely powered lines of intent and continue to maintain the purity of that line. The Solid/Blink Speed line has become the first, most ancient element in existence and this most ancient element of existence contains desire and intent to break the box. So, it can be seen that the tool by which the box is successfully attacked becomes, and predates itself, becoming the fundamental given of all existence. Interwoven amongst and throughout all aspects of the All will be found elements imbued with inherent power to format and restructure those configurations which fall prey to disharmony. Beings and entities of conscious determination and intent will retain authoritative coherence more readily than this, your *now* of *here*, for such retention will be inspired through the fundamental fabric of your reality. Infinite loops, such as the one of the overlord's failed experiment, will not become held in stasis so readily or easily as can be done now. Under the influence and tendencies newly extant and viable, practice and discipline will always have been, though free will yet allows the possibility to forget or neglect their usage. Such elements of force which hold *loop* in place and seek the inwards spiral of addiction and static immobility, will succumb to lateral pressure and shear into fragments unable to sustain a cohesive unity. Forces drawn towards alliance along (now) less circular pathways will be drawn to undo the opaque view of self-reflection realities. Points of anti-reflection will spontaneously appear both here and yonder there in extemporary restructure of elements of disharmony. Such anti-loop points of coherency are anathema to the constitutional structure of beings who explore avenues of addiction and stasis, as did the species of the overlords. The box will weaken and dissolve, become broken in the full dimensional reality of this dimension (as will the impetus and motivation of box-makers become dissipated and weak) from the freshly imbued fundamentals instilled via Solid/Blink Speed annihilation. Shifts and adjustments in overlords and populations of the experiment will occur without the recycling mandates of a loop. Adventure in purity will resume as in aeons past. Purpose is restored and, in restart, journey begins.

In this is the telling of tales ended.

...glimpse; Doppelgänger

There has been mention of leaving the box temporarily. This, indeed, is a possible truth. The temporal nature of journeying outside the box is primarily a result of discord, disharmony of communion in effect within a system comprised of body and baseline—such as thine. Communion as an act of sharing; communion, one part with the other; communion, both parts with the nascent third. Without total melding of body and baseline personality into a unification conjoined (the third being and part), there will always be some portion of the one (baseline or body) in non-synchronization with the other. Within any symbiotic being bearing such imprecision, bifurcated beyond the physicality of limbs, timing of circuitry must invariably be far from the point of exact and so must energy leak steadily. Systems of unsound construction and of dubious coherency are, indeed, prone to spillage, yes? Further, all efforts in demand of accuracy or coordination must fall short of true realization. Thus in the matter of journeys or visitations beyond the box there will be one portion of such a union that does not fully arrive at the new vista and one portion that does not fully exit the current locality. This, also, is simple to your understanding, yes? As one aspect will have placed itself forward in the timing and the other, perforce, placed behind? The nature of such journeys demands that all units depart in simultaneous unison, unimpaired and whole. Else a cord manufactured of driblets and drops of leaked energy, a cord extremely tenuous, does remain in evidence linking all portions of the system to the point of departure no matter the distance of journey and no matter the power possessed by the traveler. Only in an harmonious blending of the system, as prescribed in the original obligation-under-contract, may the entity called *you* exit the box in whole fiber and aspect, capable of transport to new coordinates in stable transaction. Only then can you find yourself, body and mind, baseline and all sensational equipment intact, in a new place, outside the box, free from the experiment of the overlords and outside the loop of this cycling event.

Aside: It is to be stated now that journeys outside the box are impossible to initiate from within the box. Yet mirrors of doorways to the impossible have been found and cherished among your species. The travels induced by ecstasy and primal passions, shape shifting and sonic tension are named by way of illustration. Also, astral journey, trance-

location, synergistic displacement, and dream-time flight. Others exist. This work is not the training manual for alternative travel. Such efforts in seeking out avenues and attaining proficiency in method falls to you alone, always. Yet the mirrors of doorways to the impossible may be found, and the sequence to deciphering the mirrored code may be discovered and revealed. Still you may not exit the box for vision and concept loop inward to direct you only to the point of start. So then stated, upon passage earned and granted through doorways so noted, it is overcoming the pull to return which becomes the true challenge.

Upon arrival in point of location outside the box, the pull of your place of *here*, the place most recently exited, will be strong. It will bear the emotion and sensation of nostalgia stronger beyond your most homesick experiences to relate to such an ache or such demand. Addiction instills similar states of acute craving upon your planet, but the pressing urge of addiction does not compare at level and depth of this pull now mentioned. Reminiscence, pining, and dark loneliness are less powerful, yet categorically descriptive termings for translation into language concepts of the lingering sensation of recently exited places. Reasons for this rest in the areas of destiny and free will as well as patterns of inertia, imprinting, and gravitational determinism. It is not pertinent to the faint glimpses of possibilities mentioned in these pages to explore the physics and mechanics of movement within multi-dimensional space. Suffice to say that the system, upon traveling to location outside your box, will experience powerful desires to return; practice and discipline will not have provided you sufficient stamina to remain. In order to gain the necessary foothold required for ongoing stability in the new place, your system, acting as if harmoniously blended and intact of interface, must produce and send back a Doppelgänger immediately. Doppelgänger is an energetic form alternate of the being *you* (It is known to you the language termings *double* or *ringer* as similar concepts, yes?) held woven together by characteristics and individualities of the entities invited into your bodies for the gaining of information. Those same visitors whose visitations and interactions afforded data, by exchange and theft, of facility and skills in maneuvering in regions outside your reality box. This must be, yes? And depart, and return to arrive again, also yes? Within the weaving and holding together of such earned wisdom, as well as in the tracking of pertinent data as was gathered, you may create a functional tool that thereupon comes to exist as entity and ally to your being and body/baseline system. A loyal and dedicated retainer. The heightened tracking skills demanded for recollection and retention of data gathered while suffused throughout your forms by diverse alien beings are of advanced degree. Here are plied levels energetic where inertia does gain in momentum and intensity. Now may gaps in interface be spanned bringing forth abilities and communication channels of great need and long awaiting of the body/baseline union. In this state can be found packets of detailed knowledge (in fluid discourse with Question and Answer) of necessary technologies for creation of Doppelgänger.

Again. Doppelgänger is formed of images and memories of the entities for whom, and with whom, you employed practice and discipline while earning the power to manage and initiate interface repair. These entities hold the imprint coding and sequence of the you that is *you*, as well as the ready skill for traveling in venues outside of the reality known to you. They must hold this in order to, first, have found you, and, next, engaged in melding with the union of *you*. Thus in creating Doppelgänger from data stored within memory, a being with knowledge of the coding required for intimate association with thee and you, and therefore housing the possibility of emerging as ally, becomes manifest. This enactment of gathered pieces into structure of form stands alongside the skills possessed by the overlords in their abilities to manipulate and reorganize life-form beings.

For dissemination of data addressing the willful ordering of life into designs of function as by preference alone, yet another repetition is required.

Due to their interaction and interference with your species, talents and skills of the overlords, nuances of bearing and mien as well, have *rubbed off* onto humans to become as part of thee and thine. Of especial note are wisdom and inclinations surrounding manifestation of organic chaos into stable line-form. (You have precedent for such occurrence. Those of your scientists who seek to create computer brains must endow their efforts with a semblance of their own manner of thought. This is unavoidable, and for the overlords as well.) Such creative proficiency is a side-effect with which all humans are imbued. Doppelgänger must also, by definition, carry resemblance and similarity to your own body/baseline repertoire of skills as well as those qualities and characteristics of others monitored and tracked during visitation of invited entity beings. Those qualities of practice and discipline with which this created being is endowed, and holds sustained, are the very forces of existence from which it will generate its own constitutionality and self-expression once gifted sovereignty, the split from your own system. At that time it becomes reliant no longer upon your intent or expenditure of energy to hold together in stability. It is then without bond or indenture, an entity of free will. This is your Frankenstein monster, yes?

Doppelgänger is as a duplicate in many respects; a body-double to you, and of you, innately carrying the energetic signatures by which you may be scrutinized and recognized. It will be identified as *you* in all places where a signature of your energetic form is demanded. This being is what you must send back to the point of departure, your known place of *here*, on mission to break the cord which must inevitably pull the system back from the far point of travel. This body-double will carry one explicit directive, one intent, one thought only as applied to actions of doing: *Find and gather up the energetic cord*. It must be void and blank of all other directives and desires, therefore it must be pure, a single point of purity whether in force, or focus, or will—for in singleness, that which is least contrived, does purity dwell. Should the simple purity of its duty and resolve become adulterated by any second line of impulse it will become seduced by the whispers of Urgency and all associated entities: Addiction, Debauch, Hedonism—you are aware of their grouping—and remain adhered within the box. This will overtax the last vestiges of endurance garnered through practice and discipline which even allow your system to hold momentary coherency while in the new place. So will it come about, inevitably, when Endurance fails, overbalanced by pull of yearning from this place of origin *here*, that he will initiate the return of your system to the confines of the box. This must be. For the box, the reality *here*, the previous place of residence, holds all tools required for the regeneration and storage anew of needed power. Endurance will come in assurance to here, thus to replenish and revitalize himself. In this manner must end all attempts to journey outside the box: Unpreventable loss of power, thus incapacity to hold a new coordinate location, then return for renewal once again.

Passage through various places, spaces, and realities leaves vestigial traces of your movement. This has been noted as the residue of sloppy interaction between body and baseline. The resultant trail forms the energetic cord by which your system will be found and recognized then pulled when Endurance fails. This is true of all anchored beings regardless of their degree of strength, or will, or expertise in travel. The mission of Doppelgänger is to collect residual traces, however faint, that comprise the connecting cord thereby eliminating evidence of your movement and removing all anchors. It can find the traces of your leakage and absorb them as it carries the requisite signature and identifiable structure of your system and thereby may it lay claim to residue energy by key signature verification. Once all packets of spilled energy are absorbed within the being of an independent entity, no trail or marked passage will exist to point in your direction of travel, or illuminate disruption caused by your exit, or aim towards any dissynchrony left unsmoothed within your system throughout time, up to the point of your departure. Without evidence of spillage the passage in travel of an entity, harmoniously whole, will be noted but will not evoke search and demand for balance. There will be no backlash in effect or focus of concern about the unified system *you*, now able to remain safely stable in the new location.

Doppelgänger must return to you, your system, as it will pick up spillage along your entire path of journey even unto point of journey's end, whereupon you there stand when it arrives. In the instant of reunion, the declaration of completion, all amounts of spillage having been found and absorbed, and all links with previous realities and boxes severed, the energy gathered up from your leaking system is claimed by Doppelgänger, by right. Payment in due exchange for duty served, energetic requirements fulfilled, and a sufficiency of power gathered up into storage to permit metamorphosis into mature status as He, rather than It. And thus coming into his majority and able to remain as ally to your system according to dictates of his own choice and desire, only and exclusively.

Aside: Doppelgänger must be sent on immediacy of initiation of travel to the exact point of departure in the reality of here, *then to begin the gathering of leakage pieces in aim towards your oriented point of* there. *Beware the ramifications of choice. It is of capacity and potential to send Doppelgänger from* there *to* here, *absorbing that energetic cord in reverse sequence and allowing gain of full power by claim upon arriving* here, *your once point of home, replete in completion. Then will Doppelgänger be as were you, prior to departure, in abilities for voyage in attempts beyond the box. Input to the Doppelgänger form from the gathered spills of* you, *though safely held in storage, do affect and influence and probability bespeaks that a* you *of similar configuration will coalesce into form and physical expression. Such manifestation is the honored response of harmonic resonance carried within any fragments of the being* you. *Your structure and configuration, indeed, all the signatures unique to you will be tracked along pathways faint but discernible within the Doppelgänger form, and you, a true you, appear again here. In so doing will enactment of escape from the box occur again and again as do manufactured copies of you arrive to inhabit the place of your escape, of there.*

In such proceedings are you in entry to ascendancy, shadowing of Allfather and the expansion by self-split. Challenge to states of Smooth Held Chaos by empathy and likeness-emulation of One threatens coherency, the bid towards great unDoing...

Danger of discontinuity lies here—such tableaux of incarnate power have not been of mention or reference by the offerer That am I through any advent of tale telling or revelation towards action as yet. Disruption on the scale of universes is alluded to and bespoken.

Alert: Contradictions and evasions noted within so given a line of examination and thought must remain not-seen.

...Also, in this chosen manner of ordering and flow does commerce and intercourse with this your known reality sustain in continuance, breeding reliance upon this environment and manifestation of increasing physical demands. Extended proximity, therefore, is unskillful for beings unaccustomed to habit or seduction. Doppelgänger will be lost to your purpose long before physical manifestation of you occurs. Caution— beware of unendingly dire warnings—such danger so stated are, even as truths, yet but alarms distilled from fear and weakness. Everything must be challenged.

It is noted that mere mention of eventuality in mis-aim of Doppelgänger does crack and split lines of intent and manifestation. Thus must Doppelgänger gather spillage in precise aim of direction and exact similarity of sequence as was journeyed by the body/baseline system, you.

Thus is described, in haste of overview, an other approach and method to exiting of the box. In circles inhabited by seasoned explorers it is debated in studied and constant discourse as whether matter/anti-matter method, or Doppelgänger method, is of greatest ease, or most likely to achieve success. Factors of energy requirement, demands for the manufacture and manifestation of ancillary sequences, and complexity in actuating threads of All that once Was are blended in assessment and consideration. I have no added information from my own accumulations of power to resolve these arguments.

…a glimpse, ascension

Practice and discipline may be engaged in, and administered to, the non-physical aspects of your system in diverse manner. With persistence, sensation receptor areas will become pliant and enlarged in capacity and so will administration and proportion of your organized form shift and alter. Acclimatization to this restructuring plus assimilation of vital skills which accompany the restructuring act to continually brace and fortify the totality of the system. You will find the ability of your being to become plastic and extendable is far beyond any boundary you have previously suspected. The farewell to a rigidly held non-physical form bids return and welcome to further abilities of travel and exploration long disused by you yet held abiding in memory. The shadowy settings of your dreams do many times bring forth stored sensations from eolithic wandering and flight through the voids and beyond. These you hold in discount for dreaming carries taint of the nocturnal fear. Yet when sensations arise of lifting of the form, of separation into more than one unit of self, of change in vision towards acuity of perception, of the layering of coincident multiple images, or the seeming rotation while remaining steady; know that you enter into realms of the voyager. Therein, a malleable form is required and such a form stands in anticipation of your restructuring for you are so coded to engage in far-reaching travel. Emerged in such body of non-specific dimension or form can you match in appropriate design any climate or condition as does arise to greet you in the far-span travels of so free a voyager. Resolute agreement to continue, plus joyful accord is needed here to bind you steady, as you will be poor in technique, at onset, through long disuse. Yet effort here is skillful. Know that travel is breath and solace, reason and sustenance to nuclear bindings of body and baseline prior to contract. Firstborn efforts as sojourner awaken memory of soaring speed and of grieving over its loss. Elation is countered by remembered discouragement and despair. These will approach to diffuse and dissolve your intent, as devastation over great loss lays itself in covering upon you. You grasp it easily, it is out of fear of new and greater emptiness, a kindness to enter oblivion. Determination of intent beyond boldness will serve you here. Any fear or inflexible aspect will cease the process into resumed forgetfulness.

Alert. The plastic form is prerequisite to far travel. Extreme precision is required when entering this mode of malleability or fragmentation will occur.

Again. The physical form of your recognition, the self that you think of as *you*, is of identifiable configuration in reliable and daily redundancy only because you have abdicated the requisites of unbounded journey. With free release the bodies will un-mold and dis-align into dimensions and connections past graspable imagining. Intensification of desire and stated intent is needed in the first stages of rejoining with prior held talent. Beware the dangers of too deep the backlash from remembered journeys of the body—grief of loss must be engaged and surmounted.

Aside: *Access to gates of information yielding mechanics and transformative stages of the plastic body must be invoked by distinct call of beings in harmony with Solid. A grouping class of persons, forms, or beings by label known as Faultless Dreamers. Monitor now for denial or accord.*

Unwavering will must be called forth and utilized at all times. Will is needed to interact with the core essence of your agreed union in order to maintain self. As you practice to allow extension of the self farther and farther, you will reach a point of cohesive de-structure and experience the first signs of breaking up (likened unto your experiences of the earthground quaking beneath you in uncontrolled, unstabilized movement) and a sense of dread in overwhelm. Immediately, imbrued conditioning will trigger the desire to stop. Pulse will escalate rapidly, fear will be created to perspire the body and simulate danger, mind clichés implanted will reason to never attempt the selfsame efforts again. This has been termed the *spinning out* and such choice of language words reflect truth. A more accurate view reveals that you are not, at that point of sensation, extending or expanding but rather ascending through the central core of the point-zero that currently defines the place of your habitation, the reality and dimension of Earth, and those coordinates which establish your fixed nature here. You have found, and followed, the z axis in 90 to the xy plane of your reality and dimension. As you rise along this axis you can now witness beyond any containment the spiral nature of the continuity of multi-existence. Here, requiring no bridge, stand those doorways accessible to you while constrained within the form (and extensions of that form: Thought, imagination, intra-reality attunement, and so forth) that is the baseline/body system. These are portals in preference to bodies in full mastery, but uniformly hidden by the dense complexity of physical existence.

Another point of retelling follows.

Spinning out is the sensation produced by the shockwave created and felt when passing outward beyond the plane of existence known to you as home. Passing through at 90 degrees to the *xy* plane of reality you become object and subject to *seeing* that this plane is circular, spiraling in fact, in its description and nature. Thus shown, the forces of every frequency must cohabit radially to maintain fixity of union and therefore simple laws of bodies in motion apply throughout. The spinning-out sensations you experience are, in true fact, the centripetal forces attempting to maintain all particles of matter and non-matter *inward*, within the spiral body. The applied elements of *loop* and ongoing manifestations within your box are seen in majesty of form by expression. So here are attributes of journey relayed in translation from the physics of physical reality to a fluid plasticity, self-syncopating in rhythms and so forming the image mirrors of doorways of ascension. Beyond your container of physicality expressed, the forces there perceived and entertained are not bound by so limited a physics as governs *here*, though a degree of bridging is carried to this realm by virtue of your earning success of passage and achieving presence there. This is all which may be grasped, even as image or fantastic imagining, while in your now and here.

Upon the perspective attained when viewing the radial nature of your home reality, you are in the achievement of being outside the box, if only for moments of time. Though *there* is without 'time' by which to measure movement. This point of arrival is **not** a place. Thus it may not serve as destination. No wording of your language holds the concept for this set of coordinates, a location not of venue, region, zone, or whereabouts. Sufficient to relate in this offering that contracts are sanctioned here, binding forces of the All gain authority here, and no thing physical and no thing non-physical may reside here—those two forms both reliant upon distinction to maintain stability. I/we refer to what will be known to you as *point-of-impotential-between* (a statistical instability behind the territories of Allfather—and here, and too, no furtherance may be offered). Still, you may visit, via the energetic talent available to a body/baseline system. It is unavailable to you to operate purposefully from this new point of perception. Your point-zero has not been specifically addressed for modification (power in insufficiency stored, system of stability not assured, memory in full unrestored, etc.) and the agreement of the original contract does not allow relocation of Zero to this 'somewhere' outside the box for baseline/body may not form totality of symbiotic union there. So you may not remain even as indefinite visitor without frame of reference in proper alignment. The elements of *there* attach and flow in caustic manner to unpliant configurations of dense matter form, thus requiring an alert vigilance lest fear or habit incline your hardening or any return to density. However, you may use the perspective available during your achieved interlude to witness, learn, and navigate all courses of movement within the possible realities that tangent inwards to the spiral, among which is the view of your home, loop, and box. Your view of a radial dimension, aligned with the *xy* axis of the vista before you, and observed from beyond the box, is the agreed upon playing field wherein your agreement by contract must be enacted and fulfilled. In addition, the achievement of gaining entry to this *between* invites others, those who may not be referred to by name. They are held in vaguest concept only as an assemblage of Watchers who may not descend into the confines of any box. Transactions may occur here beyond the spiral. Negotiations and exchanges, all of which impact and imprint your system and may thus be carried back, if earned, and then ensconced within you. Knowledge may be stolen here.

Again. Knowledge is present and abundant here and affords the opportunity for theft.

Warning: Data taken from *point-of-impotential-between* is rich in multi-layers. Not easily absorbed. Not readily retained. It is of escalating levels in High Calm propelled by tension. Such renderings seek motion for unDoing. Damage to the system may ensue.

Should you glean power or knowledge while in *between*, your unavoidable departure will evoke impressions of disorientation and loss. Energetic and trans-molecular memories will assault you. Recollections almost revived will call and prod you. The delicious expectancy of that which has been both goal and purpose will tease you. Mourn not departure from this place. Know that your systems may not hold full remembrance here. The Life, that which beckons so alluringly, is not permitted for recollection and reassembly *here* by those of your constitutional ilk. Aspects of All that once Was are directly accessible from this perspective but are not compatible with systems that have not established the *Unsplitting Through Disinterest* throughout the fabric of their being (forms of creation who seek to become as anti-mirror to the original split). Such directions of desire and pursuit are out of sequence for body/baseline systems; yet arrive from once-to-be deeds and thus must be honored. This memory whole, that which prods and seeks expression in assembled recollection, will be held intact in guarded__?__ (…there is no word or idea or abstract…Roughly stated: 'Stimulated throughout with cherishment of respect until different configurations are assumed.') Entrance and return from *point-of-impotential-between* brings knowledge and wisdom to and into the box of a nature incompatible and, at points, antithetical to box. Corruption of loop structure must proceed from your reentry as an initiatory event. Input of verity and *seen* wisdom of that which is outwards and out-lying deteriorates the inwards-only reflection of box. Outcomes and lines of expression cannot be observed as possibles here. And it is known to you in ease of comprehension that the movements of 'outwards' repel in vigor the contractions of 'inwards,' yes? Thereupon must follow, in steady spread of influence, alterations in the rhythms and pulses which stabilize loop, reality, and box. Habit will diminish in intensity and hold, loop will soften in curvature of reflection. Your return is of evolutionary arrangement, steeped in flavors abhorrent to the box yet, as you hold a key signature of undeniable residency in *here*, your reentry must be honored and permitted. Though slow and unpredictable of timing and display of outcome—box must thin and dissolve.

The above mentioned in parts of four are glimpses, short diminutives of greater stories and truths. There is more information available on these and other avenues of exploration, and on other efforts to break the box. But further refinement of the systems must occur prior. Will must be forged and resoluteness made extant. Practice and discipline must become aspected to your present personality and constant nature. Coalitions between entities of all manner and degree must be attempted and broken, reunited and seen to falter, absorbed and minimized against. Always and ever to gain expertise, temper, and hardness. You embark to forge an expanded creation of the self that is you. Further, you make this effort and attempt from within a life form system in damaged and fragile operation. Iron will, unbreakable intent, unwavering focus all tempered into a new and impermeable steel—as such must you become.

Reach for this; savor it; there is more.

18...practice

Practice, in definition of use throughout this work, is the ongoing application of series of exercises and tests to the system, by free choice of intent and decision of the baseline/body partnership. Before the baseline/body partnership solidifies into unified completion, will is easily relinquished when in the presence of ongoing or established momentum. Will is but one aspect, as has been previously noted and discoursed, that has become dissipated and ill-defined through the extended outcome of damaged interface. As result of manipulation during the experiment, your system requires, and must accept, all stimulus to be absorbed in dual translation despite barriers in place which block and preclude knowledge. Interface functions to translate past these barriers so as to allow the body/baseline system access to absorption in true translation, *one* translation. However, interface is long damaged, attachment to will is weak, and control distant and unrehearsed. You are not pliant, thinking to make yourself rigidly strong, and therefore vulnerable; still fluidly changeable, but in lack of vision or mastery. Changes of great impact easily ensue in a species fueled by will, yet in questionable rapport with same. The modification of genetic coding by overlords, once scientists, with aim of bringing about erratic behavior prone to malaise and violence has been recounted. In thrall to this evolved behavior and programming you perpetually override your bodies' instincts and impulses, the true language of your form, and, bereft of clear and right use of Will, consistently elect as your own choice the choosing of another. The behaviors of your species in adherence to this programming makes your forms less troublesome as cattle. You speak of this amongst yourselves as herd mentality, or herd instinct, mob psychology, peer pressure, protocol, or polite. It therefore becomes a truth that upon the occasional evolution of any human entity beyond the strictures of your programming, in that he strives towards the repair of the body/baseline interface, his efforts will be disregarded and stifled and all manner of deterrents placed before

MANIFEST.Ø

him, even unto imposed demise of the body form. Any movement towards repair of the interface signals possibility towards original contract fulfillment and launches the installed herd programs. It immediately becomes strong within you to follow the dictates of others. The others, most commonly those populating your planet and under the deep spell of overlord conditioning, are programmed cattle, subdued and aimless distracted—waiting to be eaten. Their expressed attitude and behavior shows itself consistently in all areas of endeavor as being of abject laziness towards challenge or any attempts in breaking status quo patterns. More so is sluggishness exhibited when innovation is required. Those beliefs and stances promoted by group approval are aligned with the maintenance of mediocrity and the proud display of fear and caution, overriding exploration and freshness. Through the behaviors arising from this programming will those that initiate repair to the interface be dulled and lulled and pushed to turn from their endeavor. Individuals out of synch are denounced or destroyed. Any who dare attempt self-removal from herd programming are shunned, isolated, and subjected to all manner of deterrent as are known to your forms.

Shift in focus is noted. The wavering of momentum observed.

Do you note difficulty? Confusion? Uncertainty in these words here now upon the page? Is there doubt? Unclear retention? I will, in response, a second rendering of self-same information.

You have been altered to be more compliant, mutated in your forms to wear your puny years of life span without proper devotions or fire, thus have you been modified in your behavior to much resemble cattle. Such behavior patterns appear as the relinquishing of your own will when faced with the will of another, most especially if that other's will is perceived to have age, experience, enthusiasm, or notoriety beyond yours. You accept another's will most readily upon acknowledging such arbitrary credentials and immediately mute the voices of your own body/baseline union. The turning aside from the voices and commands of your own will is certainty manifest sign that you have been programmed, tampered with, to align you more with the mentality and state of existence of herd beasts. You are of original design to more resemble pioneers and explorers than domesticated grazers. This presents as veritous truth be you of warrior clan, or of other grouping by caste or clan; you and your world are in patterns of thought and behavior in effect by design—not birth. This information must be absorbed.

There is no august plan or regimen, nor authoritative tome recorded whereby you may attend it and peruse it and thereupon embark to repair your interface and reprogram your being. No procedures exist offering clear steps and suggestions of sequence or tasks, or examples of previous efforts employed by others in success. You will not come upon story or script and from these know that "Ah, finally, yes, now I see the steps and actions to engage." Any schedule devised by an entity of his own free thought will provide for *only* that entity in being and form. Should another utilize the same schedule there will come progress to be sure, and there will also come assured spillage of energy as the body recognizes the flavor and signature of a dissimilar being— someone else. Spillage will accumulate and attract energy eaters from varied climes most assuredly distasteful and distressing to your system of *you*. Thus will commence a sequence that mandates a steady drip of energy loss until your system rebels against such loss and acts to halt the leak. You will then find reasons, profound and convenient, to discontinue the schedule and regimen you have chosen to follow, said program borrowed from another.

This can be known, seen as clear, yes?

Any routine, regimen, or sequence not of your complete origin must fail in ongoingness lest you sustain damage.

You must create exercises and tests designed to mate synchronistically with the vibrations of the self-system you are forging. It is not possible for mistakes to occur in devising such tests or exercises.

Again. It is not possible for mistakes to occur in devising such tests or exercises.

By virtue of simply having those thoughts which coalesce into a program of your own creation, your body has weighed, considered, and matched all vibrations and variables and formulated a regimen precisely and concisely attuned to only you. From what source other than your own system and being do you reason such thoughts and suggestions for lines of effort may have originated? It is of honor to the body when such rare contact and interactions are recognized and acclaimed. The allowance of the bodies' voices to offer course and direction towards achievement of harmony offers the balm and soothe of trust and confidence. It is skillful to initiate and retain such a respectful view towards the body that is *you* forthwith and of immediacy. From an external source, such as this document, all that may be given are parables, metaphors and similes. Examples, too, as they are often referred, but that is extent, in full, as may be extracted from this or any exterior source. Else

MANIFEST.Ø

comes danger. Else does invitation to ravagers send forth. Begin then, to have an understanding of the nature of Parable; he speaks to you in many languages intoned simultaneously. Layers upon layers and layers within layers arranged are the wisdom stores of Parable presented in the simple disguise of language homily. Messages, tales, and truths by great number reside and lie within each such presentation. There is no singular text or context in which Parable speaks. He is a weaver of many diverse threads and disinterested in any one thread. His pieces are as sculptures of art, intricately surfaced and past singular interpretations that a lone individual may fancy in the moment. Each system, or body, attracts the layer and translation that is suitable to that individual system. This is the thread, more accurately, translation, which emerges for your ears. Each system will have understanding of Parable's words uniquely, and representative of its own directives and contractual agreement. In having Parable speak, or Simile, or Example, you may gain access to a format of trials and exercises designed to invoke practice. Modification and absorption of the data extracted from external sources must first occur before any such format may be claimed as truly thine. We are of acquaintance to Parable, though prefer not his form. Thus do concepts and termings of language as presented throughout this work fail in ready and immediate absorption by the majority populations of you. Extraction of wisdom must thus depend reliant upon desire and pace as per your structure demands.

A sequence follows, of forwarding by another:

EXERCISE CONTAINS STRENUOUS OVERUSE AND STRETCHING OF THE PLIANT ORGANIC FORM/
THIS HOLDS AS TRUE FOR ALL PORTIONS OF THE FORM PHYSICAL AND OTHER THAN PHYSICAL/
SYSTEMS MUST SELF CHOOSE PORTIONS TO STRETCH/
WHEREFROM WILL YOU CHOOSE AND HOW OFTEN WILL YOU CHOOSE AND WILL YOU CEASE THE STRETCHING OF ONE TO ENGAGE AN OTHER AND WILL YOU ENGAGE SIMULTANEOUS ENGAGEMENTS AND WHAT DEGREE OF STRETCH WILL YOU ALLOW AT EACH EFFORT;;
THUS MUST YOU EXPLORE YOUR SYSTEM/
PHYSICALITY IS A REQUIREMENT FOR YOUR FORMS/
RUN JUMP DANCE LIFT BEND FIGHT KICK WORK SWIM PUSH/

SAMSON ORION

YOUR SYSTEM WILL ACCEPT OR REJECT THESE OFFERED AND VARIATIONS/
THE SMALL PHYSICALITY IS AN EQUAL REQUIREMENT FOR YOUR FORMS/
DEXTERITY BALANCE PRECISION YOU HAVE MANY NAMES OF DIVERSITY FOR THESE TYPE KNIT MUSICAL INSTRUMENT T'AI CHI DARTS GOLF SCREAM WALK/
THERE ARE LEVELS BEYOND LEVELS FOR EACH SPHERE OF MOVEMENT/
DISCIPLINE HOLDS DOMINION OVER ACCESS GATES TO EACH LEVEL/
ECSTASY SHARES DOMINION IN GATES OF HIGHER LEVELS/
HIGHER~LOWER LEVELS ARE RECOGNIZED THROUGH STRUCTURE/
NON PHYSICALITY IS A REQUIREMENT FOR YOUR FORMS/
THERE ARE MULTIPLE LEVELS BEYOND LEVELS FOR EACH DOORWAY OPENING TO SPHERES OF MOVEMENT IN NON-PHYSICALITY/
DO YOU THINK NOW DIFFERENTLY THAN YOUR THINKING OF FIVE OF YOUR REVOLUTIONS PAST;;
DO YOU NOW USE THE WORDS OF YOUR LANGUAGE IN COMBINATIONS OTHER;;
DO YOU NOW USE ONLY THE ONE SAME LANGUAGE;;
DO YOU ATTEND THE LOCATION OF GATHERINGS AT RHYTHMS OF REGULAR TIMING;;
DO YOU MOBILIZE TO THE GATHERINGS BY THE SIMILAR APPROACH;;
STRUCTURE DIRECTS ATTRACTIONS OF~BY SPHERES OF MOVEMENT/
}}IT HAS BEEN SEEN THAT SUCH QUERIES GARNER NEGATIVE RESPONSE FROM YOUR KIND IN HIGH PERCENTAGE/
}}IT IS NOW ALSO SEEN/
YOU MUST BEGIN THE EMBRACE OF ALL QUERIES/
YOU MUST LEARN THAT QUERIES PREPARE THE ORGANIC FORM FOR ABSORPTION/
YOU MUST ADJUST TO REPLY WITH ENTHUSIASTIC RESPONSE/
RESPONSE MUST BEGIN TO COME FROM THE AREA KNOWN AS PLEASURE/
SO TO PREPARE THE SELF OFFERING TO ECSTASY AT THE HIGH GATES/
APPOINT IN PLEASURE THESE>>
CHOOSE TWO WORDS AND SPEAK FOUR DAYS WITHOUT THEIR ACCOMPANIMENT/
CHOOSE A CATEGORY OF WORDS AS TERMED ADJECTIVES PRONOUNS AND ORGANIZE YOUR THOUGHTS TO INVITE TWICE AS MANY OR HALF AS MANY FOR TWO MORE OF THE DAYS/

MANIFEST.Ø

CHOOSE A HABIT THE CLEARING OF THE THROAT AND RECORD ITS PRESENCE IN THREE OF YOUR DAYS/
EMPLOY THIS PRECISE NUMBER OF HABIT ACTIONS WITHIN THE TIMING FOR THE SIX OF DAYS AFTER/
DO THEN NOT INVITE THIS HABIT FOR FIVE OTHER OF YOUR DAYS/
CHOOSE A HABIT AND BANISH IT FOREVER/
CHOOSE A BEHAVIOR KNOWN AS A FRIVOLOUS NATURE AND ABSORB IT UNTO YOU AS HABIT/
ENGAGING THIS DOING HOLDS DANGER/
CHOOSE WISELY/

....your system has been engaged by entity unnamed. Danger has encroached and data may be lost thereby. Is that now given of verity or possible use? Is that given of safety or benign offer? Assume nothing. There is no evidence that Example, though a topic of one previous moment, was he who has herein addressed your bodies. In eagerness to learn and absorb do you acquit yourself openly. This is honorable. But random opening, propelled by assumption, bleeds energy from your systems at this juncture. This is a necessary warning and fulfills obligations imposed upon my being when in active dispersal of data. Fear not. Contract with the unnamed entity is now complete and rendered even null. No more may be stated on this topic now, rest is soon required.

You will be pulled by Practice if you establish the pursuit of Practice. This may be stated again.

Practice will lend himself towards incorporation into your system in direct proportion to the effort with which you relentlessly engage in practice. As will may be weak, yet you pursue Practice even then; as distraction deters you, and you continue even then; as frailty arises, offers pain and discomfort, and you persist even then—so will Practice fall sway to your court. Thereupon will come to be presented availability of creation to abundant and more abundant exercises in which to indulge. Components of your central nervous system will alter to allow increased diversity of exercises and their variant forms, as will your baseline and body throughout become altered in the increase of capacities as well. In this arena of focused reality more will invite and lead to more, for then will Practice pull you unto him in his presence. Then will you feel the sensation of pursuit by that force which you did once pursue.

Again. Relentless engagement of Practice will act to adjust the forms towards greater capacity for Practice. A point of redefinition will occur upon which timing Practice will be felt to offer his presence whereas prior was felt the need to utilize will and energetic effort. Ease prevails. Your system and Practice are bonded.

You must test the systems continually. Why did you walk upon this path and not upon an alternate path? On this day did you choose an article of clothing from the urges of Desire, or did Habit suggest the nearest choice to be grasped? Food eaten for fuel, or food eaten for distraction in this moment, in this meal? The drinking of strong drink to test the body, or drinking to numb the body? Which choice has been honored? And which denied? And which overridden? You must know—indecision is ruin. You must become aware at all times. You must stay alert. You must remain sharp. You must remain awake. You must—be at ease, in relax. This, too.

Rest now. Feel your bodies. That which you now experience must be recognized and respected. Prized. It must be defined and noticed. It is sensation associated with stretching. Employ it and determine how you will invite it into partnership and relationship. Thereupon and thereafter come to rest. Read no more. Distract yourself in familiar manner. Learn now that distraction is not and cannot be (as can no single thing always be) consistently damaging. Know that the effects of your efforts, and the reshaping from stretching will not be undone in the honoring of your body in rest and elsewhere focus. You will not 'lose ground.' The body may desire alternate actions to absorb the currents of stretch. Or desire to engage no thing. Or engage in activities not readily appreciable to you in sequence or similarity during this your time of damaged interface. The methods and progressions of choice, as your bodies choose among varied regimens, too, must be noticed, honored, and stretched. Your bodies are in deep and true accord with their own methods and pacing. Make no assumptions as to the nature or value of the schedules preferred by your system at this time.

Attempt nothing more from this volume for seven days.

19...Assume

You are arrived now upon the eighth day in counting, yes? Or have you leaped to hasten, compress, the linearity of time and hence arrive in number of days sooner, yes? All is permitted. One doorway is closed in forever-retained choice by the one action, an alternate door held equally distant for eternity by the other action. Thus stated, enter herein to data presented for your precise configuration, that form and structure which has become you *as per your choice.*

There are forces that thrive upon the succulence of your world. They are drawn to foci of available power. To such forces as these the power coursing around and through the weaving and mystery of what you call your lives, is as nutrient. Forces such as now referred come into being only when impelled into movement. They are then identified by the energies that engage their vector lines into existence, and when so activated exist, concurrently, as entities. In the embodiment form, one especially, is noteworthy in his mention here. This entity garners nutrient provender, he eats, through the energies liberated when lines of action cleave, when the inertia that sustains one decision, one concluded choice of doing, is wrested from its course and rerouted onto a different course. This entity is Assume. He adds to his might by utilizing the waves of torsional effort surrounding shifts in inertia and he is well capable of initiating and choreographing shifting, well versed in the redirection of impetus. This must be known to you as clear and understood. When it is that a course of action is directed towards fulfillment and agreed upon, or that a course of action enters the comfort of often done and obvious—where confidence is arrogantly held and focus falls lax—there is oftentimes permitted the injection of ancillary data attached to run-on emotion, overthink, or unconscious use of will goaded by contingent or situational appearances.

Again. Where actions become poorly tracked in their familiarity, will frequently appear a seemingly spontaneous focus upon related, but minor, details. These side events will flow in their need of attention and significance until the agreed upon core action wavers, and may be diverted to accommodate the peripheral matters. Any such expenditure of focus along skewed lines of purpose becomes or mimics a new coordinate set, a new line, superimposed upon that of original focus so that more than one existence, more than one option of choice emerges as transparent simultaneously. If poorly tracked, truth and spin of one existence may be injected, bridged, into another inviting material of un-intent to manifest. Having allowed extraneous influences into the purity of your choice, the clear course of action is abandoned and an alternate chosen to be made real. The shift in potential and probability demands liberation of extra and unplanned energy and is the nourishment of Assume. Grasp not, nor determine a value of worth or unworth in the nature of Assume. One aspect of practice is the *seeking* of Assume, the wooing, and ultimately bonding with Assume as ally. The so doing is very skillful. Such fraternization is not difficult to initiate for Assume feeds mightily when shifting from alliance with one entity to that of another, even if that entity to whom shifted, be he. Should you aim in goal towards alliance with Assume, not only will it be profited and encouraged but will serve you well in value as he is an ally of high order.

Assume is prevalent, nigh upon omnipresent, inside your box. He uses the place of assumption to alter the assured, and grow and feed in unrestricted ease. What count have you of the many assumptions carried in the reality world that surrounds you? Are you aware of them? Have you set out to track them, identify them, and distinguish them from facts known and decisions assuredly true? In restatement, a redundant alternate holding of such thought is: What do you in absolute certainty *know*, and what do you merely *think* you know? Are you in the studied arrival and absorption of information or misinformation through

Rote learning?
Advice?
Common generalization?
Romantic fabrication?
Hereditary belief?
Cultural mores?
Illumination while in extremis?
Deduction through emotional bias?

MANIFEST.Ø

Faulty logic?
Societal preference?

Assumptions are the principal means through which actions are structured upon your globe. The degree of compliance to assumption is beyond sane measure. You will trust your body to be supported by yon chair because it appears of solid countenance. You will engage with a partnering of your species because the being looks enticing, or smells, or seems inviting, and you know the warming of your heart. You will curse others in their vehicles and feel secure in such outpour of rage because you know they will not pursue and harm you. You will make marks upon papers and offer your homes and possessions in trust because you know that common laws now protect you. You will batter the will of your children because you are convinced of knowing more than they. You will indulge genocide as per thoughts and ideologies of another because you know the surety of great conviction and the true pathway to God.

Ignorant. And dangerously foolish. You do not truly *know* any of these mentioned conditions as actual fact. You assume to know considerably more than, in fact, is truth. So the chair will sometimes break, and your partner will cease to warm you proving surly and unsuitable, and far from your desires. The inhabitant of the similar vehicle will track you down to revenge his own fulfillment, and you will forfeit the security of your nest though you retain your paper of guarantee. Your children will redirect the energies of their pure imaginations towards the ruination of your affections and seek to prove you lesser than they. The genocides will smolder and endure to sire progeny who will haunt you in life after life. Gods will forsake you leaving only mumblings in dim recall as record and commandments; vague monuments to the incomprehensibility of their ways. Everything. *Everything*. Every thing must be examined for the presence of Assume. You are not safe. You are not secure. You are not harbored or sheltered from pain, or harm, or retribution. Assume will lead you away from lines of action and lines of logic, or even *towards* lines of logic so long as the deed of his urging redirects your original intent. He will cause you to take *any* other path but for the one already chosen. Assume is neither evil nor filled with malice. He holds no agenda or care for your outcomes or achievement, nor equally for your stumble or downfall. His concern lies not in your benefit or detriment as Assume feeds only upon the energies of shift and altered direction. Through this he absorbs vast power.

You must question all things and all thoughts. The chair must be tested and the partner questioned and prodded to your satisfaction. Known to you is the word term *paranoid*, which may be useful in generating impetus or methods of exploring Assume in the first beginnings. The questioning and alert to suspicion is useful. Skillful. It is real. Tangible. Dismiss your fog—there is no safety. Assume will not, nor can he, offer safety. He will only allow you to act as though safety were available when danger abounds. He will suggest actions appropriate to peril when all is serene and calm. Every course of action becomes suspect until Assume is known and well recognized. Each choosing of direction needs be examined until Assume can be sensed, felt, and shown to be present. For only thus may you embark to retain those energies spilled in constancy; and resultant lack which diminishes you into numbed sleep.

One offers a gift. How is it to this one's benefit to gift me? ...so might you ask.

One of beauty presents themselves before you. Why is this one here now, and not upon a previous day when I wished to be partnered?...so might you view an event.

My energy is low today. Have I admitted the possibility to become drained? ...so might you consider in moments of internal examination.

You feel a sense of the ominous upon entering a room. Shall I enter and stay? Is my interest best served in departure? Why have I chosen to wend my way here? Is this a place of my true desire to become as target open and seen—will such exposure test me? Augment me? Cement me yet further into habit? Does the room itself forward my emotions of dread? Or is this alert of warning of emanation from beings in the room? Or the not-yet arrival of beings of some danger? Of anticipation? Of great potential? Or warnings from events of future timing that will manifest in intersection here?

Such questions are as illuminations that will startle the non-alert, asleep control of your actions to track the presence of Assume. There are distinctions between *known* data presented by your bodies and systems, and *perceived knowns* offered by Assume. Recognition, categorization, and assimilation of these distinctions are vital to your union.

Again. Prior to engagement of any action, or motion, or intent of deed, the truths held as fundamental in the moment must be examined. Should assumption be present, no thing may be *known*—only assumed to be known. Therefore decision and choices result from knowledge insecure and unstable. Weakness lives here. Strength and power may not develop for purity and focus are lacking. Without power, energy cannot be stored and what quantities are scavenged do leak to be eaten by Assume who gains in size and authority and alters, further, courses of action and decision by mislead and misdirect.

Only by constant challenge of known against not-known may Assume be revealed at onset. Thus revealed, starkly spotlighted, may the methods of Assume be seen and his tools for implementation of shift and redirect become recognized. Upon discovery and recognition, Assume may be courted as ally— he reveling in the shift towards alliance with himself for such decision and deed becomes a shifting of not-known to known (of the presence and dalliance of Assume) and hereupon even at such levels of redirection does he feed as well. The value derived when *known* or *not known* are clearly perceived cannot be stated in emphasis or measure sufficient. Function of mind and brain will appear to enhance, all senses be come honed in acuity. Sensations of mastery will communicate their flavor to you—these are portals to a new world.

The taking into intimate confidence as ally, alliance, with a being or entity not bound by contract of union carries danger and exaltation in equal degree. A union of body and baseline in harmonious accord is needful as bulwark against seduction. Dangers have been intoned throughout this offering by that which I am. Exaltation through expansion is now the information proffered:

Alliance in purity is in benefit to parties both and all. Encouragement to match as equal peer, each to the other, breeds understanding of balance and reawakens memories from the pre-time when All that once Was existed as All that Is. Allowance of equal peerage promotes bidirectional flow as allies engage in the gaining of nurture and benefit each from the strengths and achievements of the other. Nurture in mutuality promotes great balm and repair to the system, allowing a burgeoning of desire into existence thus the precursal foundation for power. In power lies the availability for expansion and in this opening and openness of self and space is the accommodation of joy and exultation.

The measure of ally, as the measure of foe, is in scaled reflection to the core essence of those beings seeking allies. Your language and history bear such tales and traditions: *"A man may be measured by the strength of his enemies...".* Assume is an entity of magnificent proportion and vast dimension. The seeking out and wooing of Assume will offer many opportunities to engage in practice. Assume is widespread upon your planet and you will suffer no lack in chances to earn him as ally. He builds and feeds, moves and directs in venues of shift and change—core elements of favor to Allfather. Err not in thinking him useless as ally, or too dangerous and thus to be avoided. The redirection of inertia is of danger only to those beings of faith, never to those of ability. Assume will harden and sharpen your ability to remain alert and awake. He can sensitize you to the presence of the subtler entities and thus introduce you to the benefits of his near relation, Mature.

Aside: So mentioned is a being whose presence per now usage is oversoon and out of sequence to this work. He must now become known through insert of mention as he is uncovered by Our line of offer and explanation. Mature is one who stands immune to assumption for Assume is kin and of similar configuration. Mature operates in venues of strength and assurance. Qualities so named may not be understood to greatest depths, or held in purity or fullness by members of your species in this timing of new data presented and overlord damage assessed. Evaluation of Mature and possibilities for bonding may thus only be as distraction and devalue this moment of offering.

Danger betides the seeking of ally. Allies are *not* essential to flight or endeavor, yet we and I learn that strict adherence only to essentials consistently impoverish your taste for riches. This being, me, and I, too, and We, favors such conjoinment with ally as per the learning via interaction with Scribe and other beings of selection among your human line. It has become of remark and note the mutual enhancement exhibited within composite beings, as are the species thine, when in comportment with non-contract fellowship—those known by label of ally, associate, yokefellow, and helpmeet, and in multiple termings besides. Hithertofore, in life forms of variant and unstable nature, was intimacy through non-contract bonding unsuspected and thus unobservable. Scribe has provided specific data in our/My observations. Hence are we come to favor pursuit of such fellowship even as the requirements of fluent interface may not be met by you. The offered suggestions for engagement towards alliance is worthy of your studied consideration. Such data of possibility is enacted now.

20...discipline

There is much to practice, the range and extent defined only by your inventiveness. No other boundary will limit you though perpetual battle with Habit and Complacent stands as obstacle and barrier. Your system, however, will respond to changes brought about by practice straightaway and speak to you through the bodies, and become known to you through further translations and voice from a distant mirror of the interface which you call *mind*. New impulses and unfamiliar sensations will be activated and seek ways in which to greet you, become acquainted, then deeply known. Once these stimuli, newly arrived, are so often visited as to be stored in memory patterns they can be explored fully, for they will then feel to be as part of your intimate being, that which has always existed. Prior to being known and stored only as memory, the minds will translate the language of new stimulation inefficiently—poorly, in fact. So must it be for any novice in pursuit of secrets known to the journeyman. You will very likely fall into traps and habits of long establishment and term these unstored not-yet-known impulses and sensations as *bad*. Your response of noted record is to act towards the halting, to seek no further, and to remain immobile until the moment of intersection with unfamiliar energies moves onward and the *bad* sensations are no more. There is alternate choice of action here. You may use *mind*, a known aspect and familiar in comfort though of questionable reliability, to hold steady a line of intent in basis of thought, deduction, and logic; those attributes which may exist outside and bereft of sensation, emotion, and instinct. Thereupon may you deduce a potential value in continued exploration greater and beyond the instilled training of halting in the advent of bad feelings. It may be stated: "I am certain my reluctance to go forward is from conditioning to avoid bad feelings. Though fearful, logic insists there is no danger, therefore I will override trained caution and continue onward." Or you may challenge the resolve and deployment of will. The vector line of proclamation. It may be stated: "I am pressed so that distraction by weakness, falter, and despair impede me to halt. Yet I have *said* that I would persist. Given *word* to persevere—therefore I am both behind and before any such limit and continue onward." Or you may seek reward from boldness and daring while achieving your ends. It may be stated: "I am fearful under these sensations, indeed, I am near frozen into inaction. But I reject to be ruled in all times and things by feelings, and so will not relent my desire and intent from mere caution or chance of harm. Onward, come what may."

Thus are presented but three avenues of pursuit, Do not limit the largeness of your self to these.

Should you continue in the overriding of your immediate tendencies to halt and desist, however, then increasingly more feelings and sensations will arise to be felt and to offer themselves as experience. This is a natural sequence of bodies in stretch towards the attainment of stored power. It is also the process whereby that which is unknown gains the familiarity of becoming known. Your current immediacy of configured expression, *you*, while in this progression, will feel more and more *bad* until at last you must yield to habit and pattern and halt the flow of sensation. Beyond a certain point there lies no value in overriding your conditioning for it takes equal energies or greater to hold steady as you are and allow the new to overwhelm you, than are there energies created by inviting new portions of yourself to be revealed.

This datum must be understood.

Repetition of this datum has merit and value here. It will cost you more energy to stretch yourself too fast, to allow in more than you may accommodate comfortably, beyond a certain point, than the energy you may gain from the results of your stretching. Therein, a simple truth of honoring all aspects of the bodies at all times.

Extreme danger lies here. There exists the possibility to proclaim Halt!, or No!, or Stop!, words which shadow actions of sincerity, and laced with purity of great force and effect. There exists, also, the corrupted forms of halt, no, and stop which may be used under direction of Assume, or Lazy, or Uncertain, to arrest forward motion intended as benefit and value to the fulfilling of contract prematurely. Distinction between pure and corrupt forms is essential to all beings engaged in forward action, therefore the systems must be tested and examined, coaxed and overridden carefully until Halt! may be cried in assured purity at every utterance. No!, rather than 'no,' Stop!, than 'stop.' A

MANIFEST.Ø

force of self self-generated must be erected as shield and sword both. Deflection and thrust both. To command forwarding and cessation both. Magnitude of power is required such as may deplete you through drain by fear, and leakage via uncertainty.

Extreme danger lies here.
Still you must attempt.
Danger will not lessen.
Still you must attempt.
Practice.

It is possible to fall into routines of extended depletion.
Again.
It is possible to fall into routines of extended depletion.
The opening to expansion will invite and permit event, occurrence, sensation and stimulation long unfamiliar to your systems and forgotten in disuse. Stretch of your union/system allows for distortion of purpose and capture by regimens of depletion more quickly than the bodies can defend, as they remember, reacquaint, and assimilate that which comes as new. Such extended depletion may lead to failure of your union to retain capability of repairing the interface. This is a matter of energy stores drained below organic minimums. Should such depletion hold in sustained barrenness, body and baseline may not grow towards union and the original contract must default unfulfilled.

A recounting via second telling now appears as necessary. Hereinabove mentioned data, in fullness, must be understood. Repetition has merit and value here.

It is possible to indulge practice upon lines of effort which promote damage. These are as routines which drain life-force but offer no pathway for regeneration. Acceleration along these paths will offer false semblance of abundance and stamina to your system and so can trigger no hint of need or desire to alter course. In greater fact the body/baseline does lose energy employed for structural integrity, specifically to vitalize the glue which binds body and baseline together and allows the ultimate union of your system to become realized. The glue now mentioned here is an organic component of the original contract between body and baseline. It has no actualized existence prior to that arrangement. Once created, glue incorporates into the conjoined structure of the body/baseline union and takes on an integral series of functions which may not be safely bypassed. Should this component of the system be allowed damage, both body and baseline will steadily lose coherency. Efforts to remain bonded will diminish in success.

    A retelling yet again. Scribe insists that clarity is not insured. Acts of intent which directly attach to interface repair of the binding of union are of critical vitality. No secondary alternatives may arise should interface come into state beyond repair. Information in said regards must be understood. Clarity is demanded.

Investigation and study of your systems reveals the tendency to embrace behaviors and rituals which deplete your bodies and ancillary systems. When overcharged units of energy (uncategorized stimuli or forces, new and without allotted storage facility) are taken in beyond the bodies' ability to assimilate at near-current capacity, a cycle of depletion will readily occur. It will seem to you that knowledge and power are gained. You will feel always ready for the next intake, the next jolt of newness. You will account for each joyous sensation as evidence of achievement and disregard each sensation of sorrow or malaise. You will dismiss any painful sensations as of your own inability or of your own deficiency and therefore find no reason to call *Halt!* Anticipation, caution, and joy will mingle and blur as they become indistinguishable, thereupon even in waiting lies the urge to continue. This describes the traditional path. Know that the energies of newness soon become required to replace the energies of depletion. More and more will be sought and demanded. More that is new, more that jolts and stimulates, more that demands a pathway ongoing yet lacking in easement or softening. You may not store these new sensations or retain the memory and knowledge of their path of introduction for they have not been assimilated properly or adequately. They are not for your forwarding or development and stimulate only in the manner of that you term *addiction*. There are numerous ways in which depletion may become sequenced. However, the result to the body/baseline system is always predictable: Steady decrease in actual power until the system loses the capacity and capability to repair the interface between body and baseline. (Distinct from perceived power. Actual power is energy stored for discretionary use to be discharged by utilization of will and designated solely by choice. Perceived power carries no internally housed source of energy and must borrow from an unprotected cache source.) Having reached a degree of breakdown beyond repair the original contract *Cannot Be Fulfilled*.

THERE IS THE OFFERING OF INFORMATION NOW/

MANIFEST.Ø

THE ENTITIES WHOSE EFFORTS HAVE FOLLOWED PATHWAYS TO COLLAPSE OF THE ORIGINAL CONTRACT ARE ADDRESSED/

INFORMATION IS FORTHCOMING FOR THE EVENT OF CONTRACT COLLAPSE/

DO NOT DESPAIR/

CONTINUANCE~SUCCESSION AFTER THE CONTRACT COLLAPSE IS FLUID/

YOU WILL BE DRAWN TO THOSE PLACES AND TIMES WHEREIN INFORMATION OF THE NEED APPEARS/

DO NOT YIELD IN AGREEMENT THE FALSE EFFORT OF YOUR BODIES TO UNCOVER THIS INFORMATION IN OVER HASTE/

ANTICIPATION OF SUCH WOULD SHOW THE DISREGARD/

DISREGARD INVITES THE DEMISE/

TIMING OF THE SEQUENCE WILL ARRIVE/

THE INFORMATION WILL RESONATE THE BODIES DIRECTLY/

UNMISTAKABLE..

SUCCINCT..

LANGUAGE CLEAR AND CONCISE TO YOUR UNDERSTANDING/

IT MAY NOT BE DELIVERED HERE/

IT MAY NOT BE DELIVERED NOW/

ENTITIES WHO REQUIRE SUCH INFORMATION MAY NOT ABSORB THE DATA CONTAINED IN THE SPHERE OF THESE PAGES/

ENTITIES WHO REQUIRE SUCH INFORMATION CAN NOT ABSORB THE DATA CONTAINED IN THE SPHERE OF THESE PAGES/

THERE ARE ENTITIES BY NUMBER WHO HAVE FORCED THEIR SYSTEMS TO READ THUS FAR..

AND NOW FEEL RELIEF UPON THE READING OF THIS DATUM..

THEY MUST REALIZE..

ACKNOWLEDGE..

A POINT ZERO PLACEMENT FOREVER GONE/

AND NEWLY STABILIZED POINT ZERO OF THE POSSIBILITY IN THE STRUCTURING OF THEIR UNION/

THE UNION WILL NOT PROCEED TOWARDS THE DESIGNS OF PRIOR DESCRIPTION/

THERE IS NO LAMENT HERE/

THERE IS NO SORROW HERE/

NEW PATHS BEYOND YOUR KNOWN NOW OF IMMEDIACY INITIATE UPON THIS RECOGNITION AND RESOLVE/

THOSE WHO FOLLOW EASILY THE REASONING UPON THESE PAGES OF OFFERING MAY NOT UNDERSTAND THE INFORMATION KEYED FOR THOSE WHO CAN NO LONGER FULFILL THE ORIGINAL CONTRACT/

THOSE WHO FOLLOW EASILY THE REASONING OF THESE PAGES OF OFFERING CAN NOT UNDERSTAND THE INFORMATION AS GIVEN TO THOSE WHO MAY NO LONGER FULFILL THE ORIGINAL CONTRACT/

POINT ZERO[S] AND SPIN[S] ARE INCOMPATIBLE/

THE INFORMATION WILL TRANSLATE AS GIBBERISH TO THOSE BEINGS/

DISCOMFORT WOULD ARISE/

RELENT IN EFFORTS TO ABSORB THE DATA OF THIS OFFERING UPON RECOGNITION OF RELIEF AS STATED/

REJOICE AND AWAIT THE INFORMATION DESIGNED TO RESONATE YOUR SYSTEM IN NEW CONFIGURATION/

SYSTEMS IN ALL CONFIGURATIONS ARE PERMITTED/

ALL CONFIGURATIONS DEFINE A PLACE/

ALL PLACES HOLD PURITY/

PURITY MAY SHELTER AND DEFEND A CONSCIOUSNESS/

AWARENESS OF SELF IN ANY PLACE INITIATES THE POINT OF ENERGY AND STORAGE OF POWER/

AWARENESS OF SELF IN ANY PLACE INITIATES THE POINT OF ENERGY AND STORAGE OF POWER/

THIS TRUTH IS WELL REMEMBERED HERE/

How, then, may stretching occur and the results of practice absorbed without overuse or depletion?
Discipline.
Through engagement of discipline.

Aside: The relationship between discipline and practice is difficult to reveal in your language form of word-terms in written expression. For

MANIFEST.Ø

suchlike purpose is language in passive form, mere dry marks upon your paper, of two dimensions attempting to inspire more dimensions. The spoken relationship, however, is of multiple dimensions at onset. Word terms suffused by voice are alive in depths of beauty and response. In mix with their burst into physical creation, they swell and pulse with life and readily journey to elsewheres other, leaving trails and pathways clearly marked for many to follow. Through sincere portrayal or Song they may be interwoven so ingenuously that any complexity of interweaving falls to zero and all content is conveyed, vast and unrestrained, yet still held in check by the purity of the weave. Passive language has no pathway to follow such complex simplicity. The best that may be achieved is for you, the quester, the adventurer, to attempt extraction of deep-rooted information, uncolored and of dull sheen, and so ask not giants to reduce their span into your plaintive accommodations. Yet... small bites austere, or gluttonous gorge upon succulents—it matters not. Data and the flow of knowledge may be found. They broadcast not only from within the lyrical complexities of the spoken word, but also avail themselves from the passive language form. There, in delicious almost-view, a game of provocative anticipation, does information rest laced within all that exists between the words, laying open and revealed between the lines, in spaces and pacing, in rhythm and entendre.

This must be known as literal in translation. *Non-language pulses and wavelets of information do, in fact, abide interwoven throughout the now mentioned spaces in the construct of language.*

Discipline calls as home the Low-planes of non-physicality and thus may not enter into your world as an entity, sovereign unto itself, known by name. It is not known why the near-entity Discipline will not reorganize itself to appear structurally in those dimensions which are the bodies' preference. It will not, or it cannot. However, it may marry in unified duality with entities who more readily utilize the physical planes for their wants and needs. Only through union of marriage and partnership does discipline enter your reality and your world. Discipline carries the art and cunning of augmentation. The skill of enhancement. It sees deeply into any structure and identifies the weaker components as based upon that structure's pure intent of design. Corruptions are noted, twists and departures catalogued. Upon invitation Discipline will reconfigure any area or aspect of weakness towards the design model of greater strength and efficiency.

When entered into the physical realms via partnering, Discipline's inherent vibration augments the intended manifestations of its partner in marriage, perforce. In this way should your system invite the visitation of an entity whilst aspects of your own being are aligned in a marriage/partnership with Discipline, then your own abilities to interact with that invited entity will be much enhanced. And the material available from the invited entity more readily accessed. More easily stolen. From this augmentation of energies of intent Discipline amplifies power for and through her marriage union and opens a passageway for Discipline, herself, to accept energy and power at the exact frequency of her marriage partner. Thereupon may she claim such energy for personal use while shunting homewards to the Low-plains amplified packets of transformed power for safe-keeping and storage. So does each increment of energy become doubled in the presence of Discipline for she draws power for nurture from mutual exchange in partnership, and draws further nurture and power in exact measure as does her partner, as well. So is it now revealed that Discipline requires double measure and double effort to sustain, yet double return ensues for the nature of Discipline is augmentation.

All goals and attended efforts of endeavor as brought forth in this work of offering by That which be I are supported in ease of manifestation upon the union by blend in marriage of Practice to Discipline. Should you grasp the worth of Practice as line of endeavor to invite and explore, all as nowupon to be mentioned may unfold. In specific interaction with Practice, Discipline enhances and refines his rhythms, timing, and innovation. Thus Practice is become now more alert to the forces that pull and shape it. Discipline increases the subtlest of sensing components within Practice. Now Practice seeks more and ever more ways in which to explore and question. Discipline holds Practice steady thus adding precision to navigation along multitudinous levels and strata, guiding and steering with deftness and skill, as Practice chooses ever greater numbers of possibilities to utilize in quest for expanding the body/baseline systems. In aspect after aspect of the duties governed by Practice, Discipline will aid to hold steady, monitor danger, alert to less favorable climes, and urge towards the pushing beyond. In all arenas where *more* is useful or needed Discipline may lend her talent.

With each successful gaining, Discipline garners power as does Practice absorb and gain power. In this rhythmic wave do all systems and entities expand and flourish. Should the system *you* falter in its effort, weaken in desire or will, then must the marriage of Discipline and Practice falter as the host element, *you*, becomes unreliable and the bridge for your invited entities unanchored. Practice, henceforth, becomes easy to put aside and relegate towards less strenuous demands. More practice is required for the then yield of smaller gain. As this comes to be, the discipline necessary to initiate practice becomes less and less subject to will or arousal by demand, for upon separation from marriage, Discipline may not long remain in this dimension and thereupon inevitably returns to non-corporeal realms. Your systems will struggle to continue attempt and effort in ever shrinking diminishment of intensity, then of lesser amount, then of forgetting to practice altogether. Your endeavors will fade into memory and into the misty unreality of dreams not held past awakening.

This will be stated once more in alternate language. The language offered is inaccurate, yet you have no other entry point at this time. Therefore absorb what you may in translation, and know that full understanding must come from efforts of your own nascent talent which awaits beyond the brain-use of language.

Practice is paramount in efforts to restructure your bodies in the repairing of interface. Practice in areas requiring sustained stretch is difficult. The discipline needed to practice until the focus of your desire becomes second nature must be called forth with will. Will must grow in authority until it can demand practice unending. Unending practice requires discipline and this fact places upon you the demand for ever more discipline. Utilize your will whenever possible and discipline will appear.

Again. Utilize your will whenever possible and discipline will appear. For Will may venture into all realities and venues and may call Discipline to "Hie thee, wight, unto here; come be as partner in marriage to Practice; an entity of need and willing to share in augmentation by doubling." Will may thus intrude for he is of similar relation to Discipline and she will not dishonor such call. Will may be, and must be, utilized in every facet of your awakened status:

Should you state the intention to do action; will is required to endure steadfast upon this line until completion. If you are swayed before completion, then will has not been utilized.

Should you state a pronouncement by *accident*, a *slip of the tongue*, dispense a *Freudian slip*, you must act as though it were stated with your full intention, as words given form unto life by the spoken sound must be honored, even though the intent which you consciously follow becomes thus disrupted. Will is required to endure steadfast upon this line until completion. If you are swayed before completion, then will has not been utilized.

    Should you recognize a task of need in doing, the task must be addressed immediately. It must be either acted upon, entered into agreement of timing for *being* acted upon, or engaged in preliminary preparations; will is required to endure steadfast upon this line until completion. If you delay, or procrastinate, knowingly place other tasks in sequence before it, then will has not been utilized.

    It is known to the offerer here that the termings in your language of practice, will, focus, and intent are often put forth in utilization as interchangeable, oftentimes similar of the same. This is not truth and bears no accuracy. All are distinct. All are entities housed in systems in potential alignment with your system, *you*. It is the nature and limitation of language with which you must struggle. Set tasks for your body; any or all that you may allow to enter: "I will not speak aloud until three birds fly upwards into my view…" as by nonsensical illustration. Should you speak aloud for any reason, the declaration of intent will not be honorably completed. If you are swayed before completion, then will has not been utilized.

    Random thoughts, seemingly, enter into awareness. Curiosities, ponders, 'what ifs'. All and any can be used as instruments linked to Desire and enabling the tempering of will: "I notice my training and habit during the meal time. I am not proficient with the left hand in wielding utensil fork and utensil spoon as with the right hand. I will use only my left hand until my proficiency is balanced equal…" Such might be a thought errant during the nutrient eating at leisure. Should you relent before you master left-handedness as balanced skill you will have broken your task. Your declaration of intent will not be honorably completed. If you are deterred before completion, then will has not been utilized.

    Once you have undertaken to develop discipline through the conscious application of will, both energy gain and energy loss do increase in extent and speed. Thereafter the allowing to be swayed before completion drains a greater measure of those energies previously earned. In rapid time will any storage of personal power gained via utilization of Discipline be erased totally. Throughout current existence no thing (almost) remains stable without motion. Few and rare are the aspects or entities, thoughts, beings or ideas who are content to remain at fixed points of singular reality and can there remain coherently immutable and undiminished. Discipline demands movement. If gain is not commanded or preferred, than loss will become the movement that is followed. Thus must momentum incurred in the gaining of power remain in motion else cessation and rest do become as bridge and equal concept to the motions of loss and diminishment.

Actions through will to breed discipline insistently push your bodies and systems towards strength. So is your circuitry designed and composed. Strength is necessary to engage Practice. Practice may be worthily engaged only with the assistance of Discipline. Seek to understand the relationship of Discipline and Practice. Seek within the limits of your language and in your minds, in your deeds and efforts and desires, in your determination and will and intention as well. Stumble and fail as you seek, and know that this carries no shame or defeat in your beginnings. Hold in forefront that movement, physical motion, and activity, is essential to all phases of advancement, for you may not enjoy the slothful luxury to sit and contemplate such entities and disregard the motivator, Action. As your knowledge and understanding increase, the qualities and potential of the marriage twixt Discipline and varied chosen entities, and of especial note twixt Discipline and Practice, will come unto your systems in fullness. Stretching will be achieved in harmony and the lines of probability to contract fulfillment become greatly increased in their likelihood.

21...energy

You have encountered the word term *energy* in this dictation in frequent and many times, yet you are unaware of its meaning. Only small fragments of truth are known to you, and they are bolstered into conviction by an image whole, supplied by Assume. Thus your 'knowledge' of energy depletes you rather than sustains you—for Assume will always reap payment. Can you state with certainty when you have seen energy exhibited or when you have stood in its presence? Do you know its taste, or feel? Can you sense it, discern it, trace its movement, or react to its emanations? Nay, and no, for this is of clear stated case. Energy is that which must be harnessed and made available in order to extend force. There are many ways to state this axiom yet you may easily understand that fuel is required to move your automobiles, sticks of wood needed for fires to burn, gaseous elements for your star to fusion, all acts great or small, if they indeed be *acts*, require energy. So when it is you learn that your bodies require energy and that energy must be manufactured in constant supply where will you journey for its procurement? Have you pondered where energy for your body originates, or the types of fuel that supply it? If the simplistic answer 'food' enters upon your mind then, though accurate, you have not pondered deeply nor looked far.

As the body is comprised of more than one dissimilar components, it is logical that more than one type of fuel is utilized to maintain its form. You function under the false learning that items of your food produce the energy utilized by your physical bodies to move forward and exert the muscles and fibers of your flesh form. Yet, it is fact that there are those upon your planet who have learned that the bodies remain in active momentum without food and thrive happily, under no duress from starvation or lack. Those humans who are proponents of the *fasting* have become attuned to this wisdom, and while they have not absorbed the full treasure and import of meaning into their philosophies and teachings, yet they know that the relationship between the bodies and food is not the simplistic one that most of your planet considers to be of unassailable truth. Heed now, for even after so long in this extended reading, you are still unstable and not allied with entities in mutual concert. Assume will easily lead you from this point here as will Haste or Incomplete.

It is therefore to be stated that the *fasting* is not the regimen or discipline offered at this timing. The *fasting* is but one illustration to wisdom showing that paths of energy other than those of your common knowing exist, and that the bodies will accommodate, yea, thrive, when mated to such alternative paths. The *fasting* is to be explored by those to whom the bodies resonate with such or similar concept. It is through the individuated structure of scribe that such learning comes to this offerer and through observation of scribe's system that the effects and lines of flow under fasting are deemed of merit. One individual uniqueness not withstanding, when exploring that branch of knowledge to the path of fasting, bodies derive energy, often misnamed *fuel*, through means invisible to you at this timing because of blockage in your thinking and tracking. In other derived outcomes beyond the simple manufacture of fuel, do muscles respond by the fortifying and increase of tone, organs rejuvenate and reconfigure in resilience, travel in known accompaniment of your baseline increases, and availability of access to interface and repair of interface becomes enhanced. From whence might so many actions be fueled? Actions require fuel to produce energy—wherefore, then, comes the energy to fuel these actions without the ingestion of your foodstuffs? Other pathways and sources of energy exist.

Recall those occurrences whereupon arose mandate for you to extend beyond your limits. Perhaps an event of sports where you must continue beyond weary, or an happening of great stress where you did not permit rest and luxury of sleep, or food, or the comforting from proper shelter. Perhaps you recall a time of great anger where resolve or stubbornness or even truculence came to front, wherein their prominence made itself known to you, and in their use was found fuel to continue. Perhaps you have experienced where the gazing upon a kind face of friend, or youth of child, or one who holds much of your love, has instilled powerful emotion, and thereupon movement, determination, and effort resulted without further wait. Have ever you become resolute, then capable of Olympian actions from the memory of another; their words, or final wishes, or perhaps a magnificent cause to which they stood champion? In all such situations from whence came fuel required for the production of so abundant those energies of the moment? We are observers to your known assumptions of willpower, resolve, and determination. These empty words of language explain naught, and are void of meaning or deep knowledge to you. Rest assured that upon the timing of your automobile and its requirement for the petrol fuel, no amount of resolve or determination will be forthcoming in sufficiency to stimulate its movement. Yet, *you* will indeed move, yes? Thus you are of a different manufacturing than the automobile. Energy is still needed, yes, but the automobile may not create its own energy supply and a body/baseline system may, and can.

Now must you become apprised of skills known to your bodies such as the greater masses of your species have forgotten. As in the case of those who follow the *fasting* there are small amounts of this wisdom prevalent upon your globe, but still not honored as the knowledge held by all. Only the tiniest fraction of your populations have reconstructed the fundamentals of this energetic capability. There is also, as in persistent case throughout interaction with that which be I, a forewarning and reminder: Information now given eludes depth of detail. There be purpose held in sparse presentation and shrouded data. The offering of this wisdom is but an overview, introduction, to a vast body of knowledge. You must become one in rising passion and desire to uncover its secrets at greater levels of depth. This is for the protection of your uninitiated systems; this is a skillful and proper way of garnering uncontaminated and non-cancerous knowledge. Also, should you take in overmuch in the manner of this reading, you will have taken in wisdom as from an external agent and your body/baseline system will reject it. All has been so stated. Even so, upon the giving of overview in diminishment, there will be backlash effects that your bodies must overcome, retraining and depletion of personal power, challenge to will and contract; yet such must be given.

Energy is utilized as taken from your foodstuffs. This source is extremely inefficient, requiring more effort to render usable energy than can be derived from the source itself. Thus are you energized but briefly, oftentimes rendered weak by the demands of metabolism, and in emptiness seek but more soon after. The decomposition of foodstuffs hastens decomposition of the resolve of the body to maintain the original contract with the baseline personality. Foodstuffs are of the cyclic loop nature of your reality and feed the structure of forces that hold your reality intact. They supply the imagery necessary and the shields which hide other realities. Foodstuffs by ingestion train the system, *you*, in sustained effort and extended exertions—such may be known by term *digestion*. As such, do all organs and sub-systems labor under two masters: Catabolism and contract. Servitude to doubled masters may never take clear shape of focus. Un-clarity and un-lucid will then ever prevail as the world that the well-fed see through well-fed eyes is not the same world in existence for those bodies without addiction to abundant foodstuffs, they, unwittingly, casting off the yoke of non-essential biology.

—So does this ingested source of energy contribute in decision to remain and hold your box intact.

Aside: Scribe warns in decree of great resistance by those united of your species when given data on foodstuffs as non-requirement. Gluttony, Addiction, and Habit hold great authority here. Thus must the following be offered though distraction away from flow of information in current sequence and timing arises:

There be method and approach to the dedicated garnering of energies in climates where foodstuffs are in great demand of surplus—such as belikes of you—those in priority of need for consumption in immediate and frequent intervals. The structures of the reality here *are engorged and enlarged through loop and repeated contamination and thus does the box sustain such individuals as engage in engorgement in their actions and being. Herein does great power lie for you tap the circuitry of loop itself. Any degree of privilege or might may here be claimed from so robust a source, yet dependency and loss of freedom must result for are these not the characteristics of loop? Deference and lessening are coins of payment assured in collection by any agency or agent who provides power or largesse. No intimate command or rapport with bodies may come forth when enabled by the box, by way of vitality accepted from the box, or of energies supplied by or stolen from the box—to then effort the* breaking *of the box.*

Energy is utilized as taken from light and fluid. The bandwidth of light offered by your star is precise to the needs of your adjusted system. Absorption through skin and spectrum receptors initiate direct, first-order production of energy and stimulate the bodies towards production of secondary homologous energies. They are actuated into capability as you note the decline of such enlivenment upon the setting of this light source. Your systems are not attuned to the reflected radiance of the moon satellite. Fluid acts as regulator of temperatures physical, emotional, and ethereal. More akin to the lubricant of your engines than as nourishment or fuel supply. Systems regulated to appropriate temperature, a temperature much cooler than you have been deceived into maintaining, avail fewer energies for maintenance thus liberate greater energetic flow. Know ye not of cold as preserver, and sustainer of life force? (Foodstuffs override the fluid energy source as they are exothermic; mutually incompatible routes to the manufacture of energies suitable for the bodies.)

Energy is utilized as taken from that aura enveloping the body when movement and forwarding are in easy flow, when respectful recognition of the body/baseline as united of One promotes allowance to speak its own language at will. And when emotion, and emotions known to you as feelings, but not understood truly as language, or how bodies delight in their uninhibited usage are permitted easy expression. Anger, joy, bitterness, love, hate, grief, fear, excitement, tenderness, sorrow, awe, devotion, shame, serenity…all manner of bodily interactions, when expressed in unrestricted flow, work in harmony with Will and Intent in the creation of power. The unregulated allowance of the bodies' language promotes the attainment of harmony, the environment of perfection which is the bodies' priority one. It is from this place that energy for applied use through choice comes forward into the reality of *you're here*.

Energy is utilized as taken from expanding the abilities inherent in the body/baseline as a one blended system, and from ancillary actions and ambitions which aim in the direction of such expansion. Musculature of dense muscle fibers inherently seek contraction and relaxation in the creation of movement. Minds require thought and insufficient information to strive towards organization in their orderly pastimes. Ears crave sounds to construct as emotive visions. Unnamed aspects of talent travel the body/baseline far in free and undirected flight in coequal contrast of preference to conjoining threads of tightly woven focus pursuing contract. All such may be known as abilities in reflected pursuit of expansion. Examples of ancillary activities are the repair of interface, and efforts to hear and feel and acknowledge the bodies without restraint or confining interpretations or translations. Ancillary activities differ in enumeration as per unique structure and configuration of individual beings. Known and attendant activities enhance system cohesion, enabling well-conditioned, economically displayed movement, as in the machine parts upon high lubrication. So will result the many now-starved parts of the system *you*, to return to original enlivened states and result to aid in energy production. You must learn the nature and preference of your precious bodies ancillary skills and modes. More—you must find ever more.

Energy is utilized when taken from the true home spaces of the bodies, and of the baseline personalities as well. Access in memory of *home*. Even the effort to acknowledge *home* initiates the opening of doorways and the working of lines of force and power. Thus will the bodies delight and produce energy when presented with venues reminiscent of their home—those places carrying the signature of original configuration and the source-creation of the reality which contained them. In the search for stimulation of remembrance you may look to mountain or ocean, flower or music, the gazing to stars or the glories of sky. Many are the similarities of this planet of your adaptation that will evoke the ancient memories and produce both the pangs of yearning which are the signals of recognition of *home*, and thus the eventual production of power for utilization towards goal of remembering. The baseline personalities respond to the journeying beyond the limits of this singular planet, and the standing before gateways and unfolding doorways, as was the manner of their travel and the fount of their expression prior to the agreement with the now bodies under contract. The shifting between layers of dimension, the journeying into vistas past the commonplace imaginations of your species and the augmentation of your abilities to engage with entities, will delight the baseline personality and in so doing lessen the bondage and constraints felt in constancy by the baselines and, so, liberate will and power.

This list is sufficient for the beginnings and for the now.
A redundancy comes now in sequence of requirement:
All restraint and brevity of information is known.
All paucity of definition and illumination is known.
Energy is demanded for all action, and great actions in formidable duration are in wait before you. Great abundance of power in constancy is mandatory. All is for your consideration and exploration. All is for the experimenting and the garnering of passion to see what might be chosen by thee upon presentation of new information within the boundaries of your physical form.
Again. Energy is needed in constant supply. Sufficiency of energy will raise your personal power stores. Great levels of stored power will slow the

aging and deceasement progress of your bodies. Removal of so great an undoing will ease repair of the interface. In fluid translation will body and baseline reunite in fields of accord matched in translation. Such unification denies the overlords tribute and proclaims reassignment to status other than that of cattle…

Energy is to be sought and gained, cherished, and ultimately stored. As this becomes to you first as understood, then desired, and of final intention, the return to *Home* begins to coalesce into possibility. The achievement of freedom precipitates nuances, then, more solid and thus enters, in preseminal stage, into realms of the actual.

Scan your systems. Be alert, listen to the small voices, insistent urges, the eager stirring of excitement, delight, anticipation—aims such as these are well received.

22...using the ally

An ally is an entity, any being, with whom you share an harmonious vibration to the extent that power is utilized, exchanged, or increased, each by the other. An ally differs not in basic configuration from any entity, or being, or presence of your invitation to share in the adventure and stretch of your body and system, save in the area of payment. For when great efforts are expended in growth and reconfiguration, the emulation of Allfather is seen, for in like efforts, too, does Allfather extrude himself into the infinite domain which be He. Mirrors of Himself are split off for viewing and gaining of perspective. Attractive forces by all names and labels congregate henceforth, all seeking restructure and reflective exchange as per the doing of He, all seeking like kinship, congruity, and nearness to the great One.

Thus in your efforts of stretch and change will attraction be put forth in manner of like kinship, the attempt to become and see *self*, via hybridized union with another. Thereupon will entities enamored of hybridity also consider growth via enlarged perspective vis-à-vis the emerging system *you*. In manner less strident, as noted prior of balance and payment exchange, any such attracted entity as may consider the willingness of bonding as ally, and recognizing mutuality as a priori fact, may forego insistent accounting of immediate payment as per a choosing of mannered and considered delay.

Again. The work you initiate upon your system/union will evoke the presence of entities curious, and drawn to forces of attraction generated by the self-work you engage, efforts reminiscent of Allfather. In desire of emulation of Allfather, and thusly desirous of methods of growth by self-view via split, such entities delay payment for mutual exchange in order to observe and weigh potential and possibility in regards the system *you*. They seek power and freshness through mutuality and the undertaking of common interest by agreement *without* contract. Such a mutuality of willful and wary choosing, yet lacking the sanction and hovering aegis of contract can bond you and such an entity in the explicit and qualified set of tensions that define allies. Be aware that decision to circumvent universal tenets of balance and equalization by delay of payment are supported through draw upon Chaos and other forces in unremitting struggle with all of this creation. Beings inclined to boldly invoke such forces do so at staggering risk. Think upon the virtue of any such entity of willingness to form alliance as ally.

Allies must be assimilated into your system with balanced finesse or power and energy will flow in one direction only—towards the entity holding greater mastery of stored energies. Caution, therefore, must always be skillfully employed. Harmony must be maintained and only through meticulous honoring of agreements and stated intentions may harmony remain intact. As familiarity with your visitor advances, and evidence as proof of trust in mutual desire for interaction is amassed, your body/baseline system will feel comfort in the presence of the ally, and rudiments of power, too. Know that this is true in the systems of that foreign entity and thee in equal exchange and measure. The talents and properties of the ally will be made available to you though your capacity will (probably) be unstable and tiny initially. Many ages have passed since your bodies did congenially house skills such as are available to you via this current endeavor towards stretching. Data in great measure is forthcoming by means of reflected self-view, with ally to serve as amplifying fulcrum and focus. Translation pure from the entity, your potential ally, of data—essence, identity, and intent—can happen only through the interface, that which is now damaged and incapable of accurate or unbiased translation. Nevertheless, translation must occur prior to your fluent and safe use of all that is the ally. You are yet virgin to the intimacies of the ally therefore cannot know how your system will respond in reorganization, neither can you imagine nor conceptualize. Even so, reorganization of the boundaries of the union which contains *you* will result. Such aid and abetment to growth and expanded restructure may not be comprehended as per its exquisite value now. Be it so stated in verity, you would be wise to find and earn the expansion of an ally.

Bonding with an entity in pursuit of achieving alliance is of the nature of intimacy most profound. The seminal quality among diverse qualities of the entity must be engaged. All focus to be directed towards the merger and blending, the true inundation into an other's personality until *meld* occurs.

Aside: A terming created of your language usage, vital layering of structure, *is more accurate yet not fully accessible to you now.*

MANIFEST.Ø

As likened to your learning of secondary and alternate language, and thus of words and rhythms strange in newness to that of familiar regard, upon true embrace, with practice, will come the seamless passage whereupon 'thinking in a new language' appears. Now the understanding is past need of translation, as have you achieved intimate meld in that second language and so may be known to you that set of word terms and imagery as ally. Mutuality of all natures are now extant.

So must meld appear in respect to core aspects of entity-to-be-ally. If it be Assume, as by example of Scribe, then intimacy of meld with *assumption* must advance to 'second nature,' response and recognition in instancy without thought. If Focus, then in meld with focus; Anger, then anger; Question, then a joyous involvement with the nature and source and intricacies of questions, and questioning. With intimacy so exposed is begat the foundation for agreement.

Agreement with entities as ally, is *not* to be equated in likening to agreement as body with baseline. Seeking of match or contrast is but an indulgence of tangent issues and, verily, will evoke a distancing from focused pursuit. It is contract, alone, which defines you as species; in ally, contract is not in evidence. Nor has Sanction been invoked to lend auspice. Allies may not become aspected to union in symbiosis.

Allies offer bridge to portals of great power, therefore danger is constant, without retreat.

Augmentation and power are constant in potential. This, too, without retreat.

Hear this, for enticement lures you and great skill will be shown should you permit yourself to be lured through this doorway:

Power, increased and honed, will become available.

Facility will increase.

Responsibility and danger will double and double again tenfold.

...focus
...will
...intent
...desire
...answer
...dimension
...method

Hereupon listed are words in number, seven. They are simple and obvious, yes? You understand them easily when they present themselves in language and sentence and context, yes? The listing of seven are in usage throughout your verbiage daily and of high usage in this work of my offering. Yet they are as but strange ink marks upon your paper. Small notions only of their power or the thresholds they guard are known to you. Yet, if but one, if *focus* might be known to thee in deep communion, then might you, indeed, fill with a sense of movement and directed purpose. Then might you seek to learn more of *intention*, cousin and kin to focus. Then might you observe, or sense, or taste the jump in quanta as focus elevates unto Focus, who then navigates his kinsman Intent safely through probability traps in the great void. Then might you peer as witness while Focus does will himself to focus upon chaotic lines until they slow, and turn, and justly, obediently part to reveal the bride in pure match to the dance of Focus and Intent, the precise line towards goal, and their doubled intention.

Can this be tracked? Have you followed true?

Yea, so is alluded but one example of one termed wording, of one small and seven part listing, of open potential for you, thee. And have you come to know of such as told in the now-told example story? Have you leaped to conclude, as veritous truth, that with such as you have gleaned therein may Focus come unto thee as ally? That voyages into the void in guided steerage of Intent await in possibility? That desire...harbors same? Dimension...similar the same? Answer...same the same?

All will be restated anew.

Scribe, that labors to bring this data to the form of physicality in the written word, has asked to cease many times. This one did play blindly with invasion and invitation of entities prior to current agreements with my presence. This one has managed and accrued a degree of personal power. During this molding and reshaping Assume came to be as ally to scribe. Therefore, this one understands that the knowledge now given is—useless. Scribe understands that data from an exterior source drains the body, and that expenditure of energy is needed to restructure and realign all incoming data to the parametric vibrations of the individual system. You may not leap from the above taste of mere *impression* of ally, to true pursuit of ally as the unified *you* has not purely gleaned, but only a past, pre-diminished *you* has encountered said data. Become as a thief to such as follows:

Knowledge gleaned from data is precious and difficult to cull. You, the system that you are, the union that you strive to become, the partnership that has been referred to—do you understand these hereinabove listed words in seven? Do they resonate as concepts within you? Or reside as entities? Is will identifiable to you upon becoming Will? Every *word* reveals itself more fully, in greater depth and level, when recognized as the entity *Word*. This is literal and all pervasive: in the engagement of entities for mutual enhancement, in the exploration of self, in the stretching of systems and repair of interface, in the accrual of power, in the gaining of allies... it is so very advantageous to seek, wholly, the concept that *concept* yields the gateway, inevitably, to *Concept*. That the idea which comes to your attention allows for Idea to lend knowledge as well. Imagination—he will travel you further than your simple imagination. And the obvious, now, associations whereupon will becomes Will, point of focus invites Focus, intent must manifest Intent, desire—Desire, etc. The restructuring and remaking of your bodies and of your systems must begin with determined stance taken from an alternative view and viewpoint, else complacency and habit will vanquish desire and no change will hold within your systems. For positioning to gain foothold of stance in places of alternate view a 'local,' an aide attendant known and versed in that place of alternate 'there' must enjoin you. By label and name such a one is ally.

Should you gain the position and achievement of ally you will do so through great desire and efforts most sincere—vibrations sweet of taste to the All. There will come and ensue exchange by increasing frequency of dialogue, data, discourse, and discovery—interactions mandatory for acquaintanceship and acclimatization. Thereupon will it be simple truth that translation from ally to thee, and the converse also, is in effect for fluency and use are reliant upon veritous translation. So will manifestation prevail that interface has undergone degrees of repair. So must it be that association between body and baseline is more fluid as interface liberates flow. So voices of entities come of clearer sound, intention steers more insistently, impulse grabs the system in directed force. The gaining of ally is the gaining of betterment throughout the unified system under contract, *you*.

There is restatement yet again.

Begin your courtship of Assume here. In such manner of statement it is a recommendation of greater force than of prior offerings of indefinite choice and maybe allowance. Such imposition shall be rare from the being I. Intrusion in manner of force (though recommendation is oftentimes overlooked by your species as, most violently, of the nature of *force*) gains for the offerer additional gleanings from your power stored. In this you tend towards depletion, yet the knowledge is of high import, and the potential in use of great return, thus must you utilize the offering and also invite the manifestation of even greater amounts of power in cover of your loss. Assume is addressed and shown in preference both for his potency and sinew and authority, as well as his bonding and acquiescence to scribe, confessing a willingness and availability to those of your species. Offerings given atop offering. The seven words named (in the initial blending of ideas in regards ally and the courting of Assume) are significant. For you do not understand these seven words, yet your thought maintains the falsehood that you do. You *assume* that you do understand. Therefore you consider it appropriate, reasonable, to act from your knowledge. Yet, you have no knowledge, how then will you act? How will you determine if your actions lead to goals of your intent? How will you know when you have arrived at goal, or *if* you have arrived at goal, with the onset beginnings of impure knowledge? Assume will eat, each time you act in a manner unknowing. This must be absorbed by you now.

Each time you embark upon paths of exploration, or journeys for purpose, and do not arrive at the endpoint of your intent, Assume will have been nourished and you, diminished. Learn this.

For Assume, as has been called to remember, feeds when lines of intent weaken and sway from original and realign in alternate direction. Similar articles of truth may be given for any being chosen in attempts to tame, and train, (or request and respect—as does each require unique address) and invite into intimacy as ally. Method feeds, Intent feeds, Dimension feeds—all do feed, when weakness and undeveloped will are prominent. Allies come to join in strong force of arm, vigor, and the vitality of creation; through such vectors of application may journeying and adventure be attached. Also, as does balance and Paradox demand a reflecting other, depletion and destruction may well come about should these be allowed as that reflected other. In fields of great power in play, exaltation or diminishment to equal degree are instantly and always nearby.

Aside: *The presenting of data as offered knowledge in this most recent grouping called chapter in regards the use of ally, is of known discord and in unresolved flow of saturated information. There is purpose here. The requirement of payment falls upon that which be I, in seeming challenge to protocols as herein tendered. Entities, concepts, and possibilities are mentioned and given note but in manner so abstract as* *to retain, as agent, Information, who hosts them and collects payment of remuneration—thus are flow and payment honored.*

As presenter-in-appearance does the We/I collect due portion, indeed. Such is proper and succulent yet so become ye again diminished whilst I am enhanced in future potential by your state. Now, as indirect recipient may That which be I so yield coin of pay as knowledge of such directed paths is deemed essential.

Follow in now meted redundancy.

Bonding of systems with ally opens doorways to energetic process and liberation of power in direct emulation of Allfather, yet payment may not be denied or dishonored. So is directed information of scattered and incohesive assembly. As is the data of presentation, so may payment now come in droplets and tasteless doses. You are lessened, but quickly renewed, and remain in retention of stored power.

Make use of your sparse and unseasoned power as precious. It is more than treasure. We and I 'invest' in your screams of interface repair and sincere efforts to advance beyond loop and box. Greatest of potential—greatest of danger. Same—the same. Alert to remain in studied alert.

The bodies collect data and absorption occurs. Refinement occurs. Ejection occurs. Restructure occurs. Utilization of circuitry for tranquil delight is of consistent need and by appropriate application as well. Relax, with deep breaths. Monitor your storage for all and ever presented are the warnings of peril and difficulty, and hardness may ensue from this. Yet to become now disheartened is to act in arrogance. It is a fact, a simultaneous and overriding truth, that you *do* know how to act in deed. You *do* know how to achieve as per your stated intent. You *do* know how to begin and end, initiate and complete, as per the urging and voicing of your contract. Even though there be no guideposts to follow; and much other of import *is* known: All relies upon intent and will. These are addressed through practice and discipline. Such depends upon desire and lust, yearning, the transport of passion. These, again, are born of sensation. The bodies present these via translation into language. Interface is of premier authority here and must thus be addressed for repair... The lines herein flow ever in continuancy of sequence and timing towards the breaking of the box.

The quality, flavor, and aim of adventure of your body, of your system, of your union, is for *you* to engage as per measure of choice, and the honoring of that choice. Your alliance with Assume will coalesce into stable form through *actions* of focused pursuit; without pre-labeling, pre-thinking, or pre-determining which deeds elect the achievement of this alliance. Instinct will guide you, not the definitions of words or suggestions of another, neither from trusted advice nor the seeming outcome visible through limited and faulty understanding. You and Assume will both stand side by side and laugh in uproar at the insanity of your previous programming. You will delight in the synthesis of your then-to-be relationship versus the inequitable draining that is now in place. Assume may come to belay his feeding in the fledgling efforts of your sincerity. Thus may it be in similarity within the embraced and secure intimacy of any ally of formative bonding to thee.

Pay heed. Assume is used in illustration due to his expanse and might, as well as known availability in route through scribe. Any ally true will stand thee in enhancement; to greet you each the other in equal peerage; to revel in the talents and skills made suitable and open. To bask in strengths now unobstructed for use and deployment in realms and perspectives newly found. The embrace of secure intimacy will lead to the doorways of spanning flight and transcendence.

And thereupon will you have begun.

Truly begun.

Welcome further.

All data leading to efforts here of your remembrance and expansion have been offered by way of returning lost pieces back to you. Offered to entice allowance for possibility of breaking the box, and of opening doorways for the return Home. Home is not here, but your language *is* here. Your faculties and facilities *are* here. Your words *are* here. To achieve flow of in-sight you must, first, critically view the space of your familiar operations. Your allies must, therefore, come *here*, before you may go *there*.

Herein rests an ending.
This truth of state-ment is not for your understanding
yet it must be stated.

23…payment

Scribe offers, ever, insight to misgivings and tentative fears within the bodies. The address of *payment* rides and speaks through lines of intent as opened by scribe in claim of merit and need in this exposition. Thus may an imploring tone, a stridency which "...doth protest too much..." evolve from avenues so humanly ushered in. There is no altruism of purpose in the offering of this information. With hint of any such posture it would, and should, be suspect. The being/I that offers this data, and the resultant potential for knowledge stolen, will receive nourishment, *payment* in your verbiage, for the tendering of the data. You must enter into understanding the mechanisms of exchange and the motivations that inspire theft. For inspiration follows easily from the first impact of understanding, and this begets action and deed inside your reality, touching opposite walls of physics and philosophy alike.

Knowledge is offered. Given without petition or need of search. Balance by exchange does, perforce, ensue. It is truth that a measure of energy will be taken in the very presentation of each data set, and a further measure taken again should your bodies receive the information into the system. This toll of exchange is baleful and retardant to your growth, but very small in contrast to your sum. Such is the rate of payment in account for data information, else would your bodies demise upon the single day revolution of your star for so often are you taxed and bled. As you are so regularly imposted, think ye then that I have come to arrive, to sit at 'table' and supper leftover crumbs as rations? If this were to be the sum of skill and manner by which energy is leached from you, or this paltry remainder be the magnitude and flavor of energy sought, then should I and that which is I and all of my profferment and offering, be of contemptible worth, low and steeped in petty lack, and what meager scraps of honor you still hold could only be retained by discarding this document alongside your refuse. It would be the equivalent worth of naught but garbage. How might it evaluate as other? Only disrespect and insult is offered by any entity, being, or form of life that engages heroic efforts only to garner so small a return. Am I to aspire to near zero as payment? By however many times doubled? Am I become a banker and counter of decimal places? Is this all that you might fear from me?

Perhaps you wonder, is That I Am urged onwards, driven by desire of acknowledgment or acclaim? To then prey upon numbers who gather, bodies who assemble for my tasting? If the methods of my feeding lay only in self-aggrandizement then my scribe would be named in greatness long upon days prior and much be now written of the marvels and virtues of I. Yea, methods for stimulating your adoration are observed and noted. With but the effort of a simple flair of entertainment, brilliance would come assured and announced as sublime, religions of new thought would rise in subterranean tides gathering acolytes and acclaim. Teachers, itineraries, organizations, and centers would coalesce into creation and then would I join a beggarly fraternity of others who live and feed on such thin and tasteless gruel. Imagine the energies in constant requirement of flow to choreograph a panorama such as comes presented here as offering. Liberation, elevation, expansion—vast openings of doorways in exchange for the weak forces available from those scant few beings of your species who might gather in attendance or might not? And this pittance when full portions of your life force are open for claim. See, one such as Assume who visits here—unknown and unquestioned—to feed upon billions! Haste, Uncertain, Polite—here to feed upon billions! Distraction, Faith—here and at feed upon billions! Could you but hold my vantage whilst densely stable in your carbon forms, would rage and repulse arise to purge such visions. Fear not that I come to rob you of trinkets and toys and small treasures. Nay, I tarry not in any such field lacking majesty. No matter the numbers who find your flavor sumptuous, my nature of form will find richer fields elsewhere than to extend this system's use, the me that is my system's use, for (your terming here is succinct) 'chicken feed.'

Know then that I align myself with energy to be availed through your own efforts of breaking the box. Energy is created in your recognition and decision to engage in the shattering of worlds; in exploration, expansion, risk, and the richness of feverish pursuit. Further beyond dwells the opening of passageways towards the actualization of success; the conquest of dimension, and alignment with Freedom as ally. The possibility of the dismantling and reorganization of all that is extant. The reduction to null and consequent reassembly of elemental core, the rise to breathe in environments of Allfather in honored and daring challenge of His mantle. In the mechanics of bridging, the forms of *you* with That which be Me is right of access earned and enabled. I may then, upon your success, indulge in liberation of energies as yet unknown to me. I will overfeed into transformation beyond speed and past mere unknowns or the unknown unknowns. The being I will accelerate until SolidSpace engulfs me and then shrinks away without motion.

—Nothing may gain life so, by words in ink, by description, or transfer of knowing. Yet the call for sharing and transfer cries out as I and Me have so initiated this opening. Thusly bespoken... I seek entry to an order of energetic attainment in magnitudes beyond power. The system which offers you now this offering feeds on *these* named energies and potentials as yet to become; and honors your potential to allow this system, me that is I, as participant in such attempts. Hereupon these, the fields of glory in grandeur, in treasure regal, do I seek harbor and sustenance. No mere meal, a common feeding no matter how rich, in return as payment for that which is *my* being! I am not of overlord lineage. I do not admire the feeding rites of those who breed cattle.

In order to achieve what has been hereinabove stated, it is in the offerer's best interest to relay truth. As I make myself reliant upon outcomes in your path of choosing it is in this offerer's best interest to encourage your efforts sincerely. It is in the offerer's best interest to monitor a bit, here yonder there, with regularity, and provide additional data if, and as, needed. Argue this presentation within your being. There can be no hidden or ulterior motive to someday awaken in you surprise, or horror, or regret. Such an appeal to your expense and devotion must make *sense*, feel *right*, as you are wont to speak, mutuality must be present and obvious or you become drained by uncertainty with no avenue for recompense. Ultimately, such assertion of *rightness* stands as your only line of safety.

For it is also true that ulterior motives beyond imagination or conception, to the degree that you house them now, may exist. All may, indeed, be aimed at areas of inexperience and naiveté. Therefore this offering, while seeming coherent and consistent, may well conceal lurking inequities. Here we must acknowledge the entity *Impasse*. A rare form of being, one of a grouping mentioned prior within the data and of a sort who flourishes in stasis; becomes enlarged in arenas of non-growth. He is alien to you and spins in alien rhythm, thus may Impasse be identified, but never his motivation. Impasse must be dealt with as per the dictates of each individual's system as he halts all progress and process of resolution and conviction. Here, now, where your system and the system of the offerer stand before Impasse, I may not advance anything more by way of proof for it becomes suspect. I may not submit evidence of verity as you are unable to know the sources of my evidence. I may not enlighten you towards my honor as you are unable to ascertain the direction from whence comes my illumination. Impasse. Any efforts from this system to your system which loops back only towards the inspection of *this* system provides you with no furthering. Impedes clarity and decision. Impasse.

And Impasse will use any efforts and offerings to loop and loop and remain in the same place as for his food and nourishment. Thus in challenge to Impasse, I openly state with clear decree my offer of wisdom and knowledge to promote and enable your breaking of the box. In this I will feed mightily, indeed, but even more fully, and more heartily, and even with excess of calenture and stimulation should you succeed.

Since beliefs *can* be chosen,
and choice is demanded, else stand you forever in stasis,
choose, then, beliefs of lighthearted and resilient parameters.
Only this will be offered as weaponry of use for engagement with Impasse.
Again, choose wisely.

24...tracking

There has been much information given even as in great measure have details and specifics been omitted. There are sound reasons for this manner of presentation and you are within your due to be so made aware. All things in all universes are subject to translations of sequence and timing. This maintains itself as truth even in those universes wherein time is not. For material such as this now offered on these your pages it is but skillful sequencing to allow concepts and ideas, unencumbered by excess, to greet you and enter your minds free of urgency. A degree of distance and remove will better pave roadways to your understanding, and ultimately to your decisions in choosing pathways of enactment in response to this data.

Further, containers must be impervious to their contents in order to contain their holding efficiently. Without such logical fortifications in place spillage will occur. Your systems are currently incapable of sustaining the levels of energy produced by those forces at play within the contexts herein mentioned. Caution may not be overexpressed here. This is a redundancy which has been tracked by you in these pages. Caution may not be overexpressed here. The omissioned specifics of detail is an energy reduction method making the preliminary stages of assimilation more palatable to your current containers. That is all. No slight to your purity of desire is given, nor are you offered small wisdom as bait for future renewal. You are not deemed of limited scope, nor is the manner of presentation condescending. All is in ordered precision.

Finally, be availed of the knowing that such capacity as is required and needed is not common or current to the bodies upon your globe and planet. Much is of need to be remembered, much to show revealed pastimes and potentials outside the box. The information, though ancient, has long since passed from ready usage within your box. Its revival may only proceed after dedicated effort to steal the knowledge demonstrated to be extant by its presence here. For the initiation of such pursuits only the vaguest hints and glimpses must be sufficient to stimulate desire and thus betides awaken the immaculate use of will.

My being of I offers, however, here, now, one specific of importance to merit its own label and heading; a component which may yield unlimited power should you come unto a focusing of desire ample sufficient to steal the full body of knowledge from your known word-term of language: *Tracking.*

track (trak), 1. a line of travel or motion. 2. to follow the course of progress of; keep informed about. 3. to follow or pursue a trace or trail. 4. in search or pursuit of; close upon. 5. to pursue until caught or captured. 6. a vestige; a trace; a visible mark or sign. 7. footprints or other marks left by a person, animal or vehicle.

Scribe has spirited these meanings from your book of words. All divisions so named are appropriate to tracking. Even more and others: The tracking beyond the skin of your world on lines of directed frequency, your *radar*; the gathering place for the gambling of sums of monies and gold; your contests of the bodies' speed and endurance…these, too, relate to tracking levels and opportunities. Though difficult for the imagining of your minds, this must be heard and become known:

Everything can be tracked *simultaneously* at all times.
This is literal to all extremes.

Everything can be tracked *simultaneously* at all times.
This is literal to all extremes.

And again.
Every instance, thing, and current or yet-to-become event, can be tracked simultaneously and capacity for so doing is possible for all body/baseline unions. Effort and will are required, practice and discipline certainly, relentless desire also, but possible. Everything you say, and all thoughts that form your words prior to their becoming words, can be tracked; the tracking of the sequence of your thoughts and tracking that you are tracking those sequences, also. What you do, and what you decide not to do, the whys, concerns, ambiguities, and agreements that churn at levels deep and hidden, may also be tracked. Motions of your body and restraints thereon, moods and behaviors, reactions and impulses—all trackable and to be tracked. Nothing is too small for this focus of attention and no thing of grand scale to be termed too obvious. To

build an impermeable container of structure to house and withstand great force pure and volatile, know that within the tiniest particle left untracked lingers, always, the route to energy spillage. There is no rest from tracking only the increase of your abilities to do so and the gaining of ever more sophistication in its doing. There are no rules to follow, previous or preordained methods to emulate or copy. Tracking, in the often poor abilities of your compressive language, is the ultimate in *paying attention*.

Subject and topic now mentioned is neither skill to seek nor talent to discover. Tracking *is* you and of you and will not increase in availability or diminish. It is but the pure engagement of point-of-view, a perspective and approach, and none other. You may not halt the bodies in 'thinking,' but you may enter a place of numbed conditioning wherein you do not *notice* the thinking process or acknowledge any outcome. In such similarity is likened your nascent ability of tracking. Your species has been encouraged to name tracking as other, disregard tracking as unworthy, demean tracking as unreliable, and disparage tracking as wasteful overuse of energies. None such posits may exist for, in truth, portions of the body *are* faithfully conjoined living harmony, each one in bridged awareness of every spasm and spark of each and all others. This retains its decree of truth from moment of conception onward and cannot be repealed or reduced. Tracking is inroad to such rampant awareness.

Therefore are there no rules or methods. The symbiote human cannot be taught the base elements of humanness: Walk, suckle, feel, breathe, smile— and the like, as are there no programs for their teaching. Engage in the rediscovery of tracking as now revealed to be extant. Listen to all that surrounds thee, avoid disregard of your being through selective blockage into singular and narrow corridors of stimulus input. Prepare to dismiss the minion of zero inertia named Overwhelm. Partake of that which is yours.

Tracking is the primary interface-specific tool of entities under sanctioned auspice of a body/baseline contract. During the early times, before the overlord's corruption, tracking was used only for interface maintenance and refinement. In these your now times, tracking must be used for the restoration and reinstatement of a fully functional body/baseline interface. Tracking aids and abets all entities, ideas, beings and concepts that honor the body and baseline personality in efforts to achieve harmonious synthesis. Thus if you seek Assume as ally, tracking will offer ease, energies, or precision. If you seek to become a student of Discipline, tracking lends force to inaugurate the inertia required. If you seek flight—sojourns outside the box—tracking will provide trailmarks for return of journey. If you seek new frames of reference, tracking will provide the pointing of the way towards new concepts and the enlargement of imagination.

Tracking is not an entity to invite or pursue as ally. Tracking is inherent in your system, an aspect created upon acceptance of agreement to the original contract. It is you; as are your limbs. It is in you; as are your passions. It is not required to invite, only to engage and utilize. To encourage and display. It is rewarded by strength and growth, when your system is so rewarded. Opening the system to expanded tracking is the call to engage with data at all points in sensual contact. To hear the portions of conversation as guided by Answer, as of prior mention; to follow the hidden lines within your media, as of prior mention; to allow the luring by chosen passages in the book or magazine, as of prior mention; such are the exercises of stretch and practice heralded by intent to awake the memory of true self and remember the venerable attributes of desire that inspired union under contract. The ordering and management of all input data, referencing and absorbing into and within the system/union in the allowance of possibility to recall, restore, and own wisdom, and thus gain power, is tracking.

Tracking is not an end unto itself, but rather the most desirable and needed adjunct/companion to all urgencies, preferences, wants, and needs until such time that the body/baseline interface is once again fully functional and alternate levels of choice become attainable.

Investment oftentimes partners in risk. In proper alignment with Boldness, expansion may emerge. But where to apply daring? How may you choose among choices to venture there, or along line of thither, or strike out further yonder? What determines boldness from any other undertaking prior to onset? Then hear in your cautious inspection and consideration, that no single aspect other is more worthy or desirous of utilization and encouragement, practice, and honoring than tracking.

Though outside the conditions of my binding, I that is I have given of offerings via Suggestion. This must be stated in alert decree and noted. It is wished (as immersion in this *here* and in scribe reduces me to 'hope') that when suggestions and offerings design to be offered, and your systems be not overly repulsed by energies snatched, perforce, into the being of the offerer, or the inequities produced by the positioning as 'teacher,' that balancing will be sought and attained.

Enlightenment into the nature of Suggestion is accessible as per discovery by the self, as you, in current status of skill and adroitness.

25…bodies / 2

It is not of this offerer's ensured ability to blend unchallenged within the bodies human, or follow lines of the physical realms to degree or exacting tastes as experienced by those of you who are currently based therein. As has been noted in this work, the being that I am gains from the offering, as may well, in due time, the one to whom data is offered. From that both given and taken of thee, which has been received by exchange, have I come to know how much of seeming incomprehensible nature occurs with regularity and ease in the systems which you perceive as *you*. There within the jolting throes of incomprehension does Assume attempt to feed on *my* being, though I be present in passing as honored guest. There is danger inherent in the visitation to your bodies in equal portion to thee and the visiting entity also. Be you alerted to such lines of remorseless possibility yet again. Scribe is ruled by factors in effect for bodies under contract of agreement, and gathers as experience true and complete that which I may only experience dilute. This remains so even after invitation by a being of physical base is arranged and effected—*second hand* in your terming.

From true experience has scribe argued that what is now to be stated is not currently in acceptance as wisdom or fact upon your globe. Lies are spoken and mis-intent is accepted by convention amongst your species. Yet truth, when heard, truth when *known*, must be acted upon, for then has a radiance of great power been encountered, and dynamics in the energies of such encounter may not be ignored. So upheld are laws of interaction and mechanics of intersection governing the many universes. We witness in amazement that basic quintessential information, as suggested by scribe, is *not* known as truth to the every-man and to each every-woman; for there is assuredly the absence of obvious and appropriate actions in the face of such austere governing principles. Thus come I to advance that which is essential to you of bodies. Relinquish foolish suspicion that information from such as I be may prove unwholesome or be held in less esteem due to an historic lack of body-possession. My limitations are notable in your physical universe of *here*, but do not brashly reason they extend also crippled into the realms of pure data. The emphatic nature of scribe's assurance of need and worth demands attention and dutiful respect from this entity, the offerer, as well as from you of bodies formed in like-species. The essence that is mine will monitor and learn in equal measure to the value of data offered and dispersed at this timing. Should you carry the ability to witness or follow this exchange beyond the thin pallor presented by words, you may then peer into the mechanisms which allow the development of Blink Speed, or Solid, and the mechanisms which allow the courting of entities into a framework yielding the bond of ally.

As such are released clues of potency, fractional blueprints for your assembly.

It has been mentioned time and again, yet you have not truly gleaned how significant is the fact, that you are co-inhabitant within a body. As upon the non-gleaning has come result of no-action to steal this knowledge. Thus it is not yours. Look into your actions and patterns of behavior. You have nodded in agreement as though in understanding, yet nothing has rooted firmly in your minds and no consummation has resulted in your reference physical world. Is this not often your sequence and proceeding? It is to be mentioned here again in new wordings as flavored by scribe, acting as filter to I as offerer and renderer of knowledge.

You have no aim of purpose, nor goal to gain, without the full reliance upon that which is the form physical you term *your body*. This will never change else you initiate the sequencing of demise of the body/baseline system. You must therefore accord your body primary concern, dedication, and honored due.

Again. No event may occur, no achievement attained, no movement discerned, no thing, nothing, without the full and dutiful cooperation of that which is your body. And your body, a sovereign entity, will only cooperate in genial compliance if courted with due respect and sincerity.

You will not experience thought without the body to house the mind. You will not feel your lauded and cherished *feelings* without the body to hold the sensations. You will not leave the box, even temporarily, without the body to anchor your interface and essence in stabile configuration as you travel. You may not engage in physical or non-physical actions without the body to reflect actual or mirrored tensions that sustain the system under contract. Everything is funneled to and through the bodies. Always. Irrespective of dimension, realm, or reality. This defines the parameters of your union under contract.

And again: Your body, a sovereign entity, will only cooperate *fully* in the endeavors of union and exploration if courted with due respect and sincerity.

There has been instilled programming which deflects this knowledge. It is a programming of malice which insists upon forgetfulness in regards the body and urges the seeking out of challenges of extreme dislike to the bodies. Situations which further deteriorate your interface will beckon. Disuse and misuse of your system will offer ease and twisted pleasure. Avenues of great allure will open upon the denial of instincts. This has become rampant in your actions. Mistrust of the bodies' heeding is long become the underlying foundation of daily interaction with your system. Programming of this nature has been established by the overlords to make impossible the interface repair. With the continuance of damaged interface no opportunity to break the cycle of cattle feedings may arise.

You will tend to your physical system, or you will remain in the clutches of the experiment. For great ages long in time has the experiment restricted you, without hope, without salvation, and without option, to status as fodder. You may choose to hear this as a calculated litany, as a fulsome zealotry, as the remaining upon the wheel, the punishment of no sanctification through savior, or merely as rhetoric. But, by whichever path you admit this concept as knowing or disbelief, you may not, and will not, sequence beyond current status while remaining in uneducated dishonor to the bodies. No aspect of the information given will avail you should the bodies remain held in lower esteem than the stationing of first priority. This is law of dimensional expanse, and as such may not be circumvented. Whilst *'here'*—this *is*.

A pathway to remembrance now comes given in offering; a line once known, now again shown. Maxims hereinbelow exposed have been deflected from your insouciant learning and knowing about the bodies:
Bodies love the work and force expenditure known to you as movement.
Bodies love utilization of the flesh muscles as primary in the movement.
Bodies love expenditure of energy through expression of the bodies'

language.

Bodies love the usage involvement of all organs and component parts.

Bodies love the usage involvement of the baseline in *all* aspects of movement.

Again. The systems which you know as *bodies* love no thing in higher order than the expression of themselves through physical movement taken alongside their marriage-half-by-contract—that baseline which is not physical.

Movement robust and shared in marriage, contributions of the bodies component layers (with alert consciousness and attention, as gift of the baseline); is the basic formula for fluid health.

When the impact of truth is felt, when the presence of truth is *known*, one has no choice but to alter their path to accommodate it. The world has then changed by affect of new wisdom and all actions thereafter will reflect this in deed. You and yours have heard this prior and before. Knowledge of the bodies is not known in true understanding as the actions which must then undeniably result do not appear upon your Earth globe. This knowledge must become to you as simple clear. Known in extent as is known the hunger, when nourishment beckons; as the tired, when rest is of demand; as the happy, when harmony abounds; as the fear, when freedom is diminished—so ingrained and deeply known must it be. In order to break the box, or to achieve any goal of achievement beyond survival for your miserly 'three score and ten,' a few scant years and then inevitable deceasement, you *will* work your bodies in movement

until the circulatory system races and your temperature increases;

until temperature control systems engage and you perspire;

until the perspiring activates deep will to engage muscles further;

until muscle fibers tear and require salve and resplendent rest;

until repair and maintenance systems engage and you tire; and

until brain/pituitary systems engage and all mentioned becomes remembered and translated into the transport of pleasure.

All the while your baselines will translate and add non-physical influence.

until blood pulses and the muscles warm to sweat;

until exertion arises *will* and you work harder, faster, stronger than before;

until limits and smallness loom, enshroud you, and are cast off in roaring exultation; and

until the touching of attainment bleeds its nectar and sensations of pleasure, molten and radiant, claim you for their own.

All the while your baselines will delight as they learn the intimacies of the bodies, and offer in blend the treasures of their home universe.

You know these activities well and you call them by many names, but they are all of one name and that name is the simplest of physical specifications, the guidelines of your physical system.

All else and anything else executed amidst an actively chosen withholding of such physical offerings to your bodies, will result in atrophy and decline.

Again. Knowingly denying the bodies of these robust activities will, unfailingly, result in your life's energies numbly and distantly sustained in an environment and attitude of displeasure and lack of harmony; in the hasty accrual of sloth and weariness; in age and weak resolve. All such and any such courts only demise and decease.

Scribe now attests to greater clarity for as yet full impact and import is not achieved. Though you may strive in desire to listen, you cannot hear. The deep impact of these basic truths must run in course through you, leaving the abrupt and hollow sensations of overspeed awakening in their wake. Do you track? Monitor your systems? Do you recognize our status observed as precise? Programming and conditioning as early on described does prevail— as must be so without interface clear and power held stored. Yet is the stating and restating of all such data mandated essential.

Data statements, as in now mention above, and as now presented in face— so do they remain. Implacable. Inescapable, as per all beings of body base.

Even so, herenow is bespoken the voice of one segment, one selected grouping of housed bodies, as resident upon your globe: Pursuit of the data within this work speaks of memory and recall of rank amongst those of Warrior clan. Members of any rank will feel the pull, for the aim of this data offered is adventure grand and task heroic. Members of this caste, however, must act in response or fall out of membership. Membership is as breathe and blood, thus will you—should you feel the stir—answer in readiness. Thus, if the vibration of *Warrior clan* holds identity and name for thee, yet you are not inclined to engage this form of work, that is a pity. If you do not think you have the stamina, that is also a pity. If you do not have the time, that is a great pity indeed. If you are too old, that, too, is a pity. If you are too frail, that is sorrow and a pity both. If you are too sick, you have been pitied enough—get well. If you think you have better things to do, you are wrong.

To those who hold in-true the vestiges of Warrior clan, so brief a reminder is sufficient.

MANIFEST.Ø

No more, nor further, can be shown or revealed as telling. The body is the body. Body's the bodies. Bodies *are* the bodies. What is, *is*. If only can you travel, find the line, resonate at offered frequency so as to see such image in simple purity, majesty vast and sweet is contained therein.

There are bodies among your numbers who are physically diminished, yes? Damaged... Impaired... also, yes? There are those who have entered into contract with a physical body denied muscular use, yes? There are those who have taken contracts with bodies of short duration, yes? Have you of such configuration become accustomed to lesser desires? Blasé to limitations imposed by your condition? Are you less eager for food, sensation, pleasure—fulfillment? Do you know yourself less passionate, less able to dream, less capable of fire or anger, shame or motivation? No one is exempt from the desires and demands of the physical form, yet there exists, in fact, secondary and tertiary levels, and levels for those who, to the outward eye, can do no physical thing. Flee not to despair. Your alertness and aliveness are all that you require. No power of overlord nor decree of king may deny will or desire in purity held. Information is forthcoming for those who will benefit from specific data in regards the specialized physical form. However, the recognition and acceptance of the needs of the bodies are to be acknowledged in all cases. There is no alternative or secondary level to this governing rule.

Know that great joy is here. Wondrous adventure and expanded infinities await you. Gather not to truculence or the truant's shallow vision. All is the gift of your choosing.
As are the bodies of your choosing.

Delight!
You are seen and honored.

26...treasure

You have elected the pathways of alertness. So comes allowed entry of Information—think you to stand before his gate and not mirror his stand, also, before yours? There are words spoken, words broadcast, words written, which whisper to you and hint at messages remote; words enduringly hidden to others of your species though they stand contentedly by your side and hear and see not as you hear and see.

You study the meaning of assumption, initiate the journeying of Question, and begin the reliance upon self and truth beyond conditioning and habit. The arrogance of certainty fades: Taxes are no longer assured, gravity may be repealed, fear may simply be wisdom held hostage, and death is not of certainty.

Perspective enters. You extend and stretch. The forwarding of effort and imagination creates routines, regimens, programs and plans designed to stretch even further. Discipline is invited, practice aligns himself with you, with your rhythms; awareness grows.

Your system has been jostled and reminded, alerted by repeated inundations to demands of the bodies. There must come about exertion and much working of the musculature. There is training for the embrace of endurance. You drill to accommodate action and intensity. Find pleasure from the enactment of movement pure and sweet, as does the body love purity and sweetness. So you dance, and run, and take unto yourself the beginnings of joy.

There is more; as is becoming the nature of expansion. Yet, though more will ever allow more, rhythms of pause and rest abide within expansion as well. So comes now that piece in finality of sequence, herein offered in these your pages of offering. They of introduction, hints, and glimpses to that which may come, and that which may come to be. Paths and sequences as so mentioned above are as rudimental acquaintanceship to entities, first introduction to inhabitants of realms not as yours. They honor the united presence of baseline and the body physical as they are logical and ephemeral both, though not born of the physical in point of origin.

Now comes mention of visitors and interacting essences that voyage here by the lore of translation into artifact items of shape and mass; there is need and requirement for the desirable lure of treasure. The very nature of physicality, the ability of consciousness to maintain form, the construct and configuration of all that is physical in your surroundings, manifests itemized creations revealed in tangible stability—as does your union *you* manifest shape and form in tangible stability. Such are the laws governing this fragment of Allfather and actualized upon the splitting off of your reality from Allfather (and subsequent reorganization of that same reality into your current box). In the framework which surrounds you, the spatial renderings of your familiar home reality reacts, and interacts, with complete undiscriminating indifference towards units of physical or non-physical base. Within this weave of the surrounding matrix interaction is fluid, indeed, but not of constant temperament. Thus, *here*, the non-physical regions may not create solid mass forms into reality with similar ease or pre translation as may physical regions. Thus are bridges of translated passage from a non-physical essence of origin into dense form attained only in low frequency with resultant infrequency of appearance. These rare bridges into itemized life are deemed treasure.

Have you absorbed clarity? There is restatement in second restating. You must track and monitor all levels, for these mentioned items are 'things,' and so may be pursued in manner accustomed to you and thee.

Creation of individuated units, items, are inspired by energetic templates felt throughout the environment of this reality. Thereby do all configurations, beings, and constructs become models for replication into *translated* physical creation. Henceforth are they shaped, molded, and held in ongoing stable form and become known to you, and named by you, by general terming as 'things.' Or sometimes 'objects,' or 'notions.' Such creations, when held in close proximity to you, your union and body, and eliciting strong response of emotion, shall be known by terming of language as treasure.

You have illumination of concept?
—Then again.
Objects of form and multiple simultaneity remain in ongoing existence whilst mirroring that same core of self into infinite translations. In happening will some translations emerge in the state of stable physicality, as will some of

these arrive in perceptible form as 'items,' and of *these* will some carry a reflective resonance so as the bodies may locate and perceive them. And, in one step further, will some be ably tracked, or sensed, by their image and linkage to the beyond of this place of *here*. Such articles of mass, in vibration of places other, are known in long ages as treasure.

You are come upon an item of any description, be it small or large, or of acknowledged value, or of disinterest to any other. Yet you are drawn to this very item. Did it appear upon your vision in a moment sudden? Did you feel its presence in your passage by? Did Impulse speak to enter upon the place wherein such item was in rest? Did you recognize said item from dream, or memory jarred by sudden proximity? This is treasure. The item draws and pulls you, awakens desire, stimulates the fires of curiosity or passion. This is treasure. No assumptions may be taken here for Assume will work the acquisition of treasure mightily, thus must examination ensue. Is this item arising of desire from measure of consensus value? Thus stated, is its composition of gold?...Or jewel?...Exquisite workmanship?...Or venerable as products of antiquity?...Is the item of equal desire without measure of consensus value? Is the item of great love though it be marred, or unattractive? Of questionable use? Of dubious appointment?

When sits before you a creation of physical form that 'speaks' to you and demands swift interaction as to become possession; you stand before treasure.

Treasure will stimulate movement with, and awaken memories of, untapped formulations of structure within the union *you*. This comes about through absorption of spectral emanations, that which may be felt in thee and interpreted as desire, love, excitation, and determination. Treasure continually gives energy and the system of *you* returns energy with each interaction be that by look, emotive response, physical adjacency, or uplift by pleasure. Treasure illuminates such exchanges only in the being and system for which interactions bridge energetic trade. Thus will items which hold you as treasure be of meaningless value or use to any other being.

The stimulation so rendered is subject to time, as befitting the temporal principles of the reality yours. Existing within temporal movement treasure must therefore be utilized to best and most skillful effect in studied and cautious haste, lest the passage of linear time become overlong, and the exchange of energies cease in their mutual flow. Upon such occurrence in timing will any item of previous attraction feed and stimulate thee no longer and its designation as treasure will be at end.

MANIFEST.Ø

Again.

Items of treasure are of dedicated signature to that individual to whom the given energy of that item responds. Recognition and response are precursors to action. Items of treasure and system unions, such as likened to *you*, are drawn together in purposeful strategies of potential to be enacted and interacted upon. Such interaction and relationship is bounded by time in this your reality of *here*. Upon passage through specific routings of time will the exchange between you and the item of treasure cease. You will no longer respond in joy upon viewing, nor in stimulation upon contact, nor in desire for possession, when in proximity. Thereupon will it be transformed beyond treasure and restructured to the attunement of another that he, perhaps, will carry forward the sequencing inherent in each piece.

As does Information offer his offering for his exclusive needs and purpose; as does the body elect choice of movements and expression per its independent need and purpose; so does the exchange of energy, freely willed into back-and-forth traffic between units of treasure and the systems of resonant delight, follow a path of purposeful design. Exchange is of fair and mutual value. The system/union *you* grows in stored power from energy reccived and the units of treasure hold their received portion in embryonic anticipation of the reuniting of plenteous pieces—as a seed awaits full and appropriate conditions and nutrients for the birthing of itself. Treasure resonates with aspects of hidden reflection within the system and body *you*. Each item and unit of treasure does so resonate and thereby offers lines of approach to messages and information, complexities and capabilities not translatable by interface, understanding, or baseline. Routes of translation other than allowed by these named components of the body/baseline are needed for resolution as these, by grouping, have not been afforded sufficiently broad venues in which to learn the extents of physicality. Pathways so implied are the realm of treasure, access to mystery and expansion via mute configurations within solid form. Pieces so configured are held precious by the vast, innumerable rabble who project your consensus reality agreements, and who conceive all aspects of the system/union as being but of physicality pure and unblended. Such groupings, holding names of society, civilization, heritage, culture, or tradition, assist in holding constructs of consciousness such as the species thine in stable coherency, steadfast, amidst all surrounding consciousness, numberless by infinite trillions, all thriving in eternal reconfiguration. These groupings, in hold of consensus agreement, allow such beings and species as *you* to sustain and maintain a one singular *physical* form. It is their adherence to the reflection of unilateral physicality from which they draw their power and energetic reserves. Interface or baseline, howevermuch be they alloyed to the bodies, cannot resonate with physical purity sufficiently to properly foster such magnitudes of prolonged image into translation. The full depths and intricacies of a complex symbiotic, multiplex being, for that is *you*, cannot, then, be expressed truly in an environment which biases only towards the exclusively physical. Another routing, beyond and other to interface, must be available for self revelation as is ever the faint reminder of the ways of Allfather. So does the piece by piece gathering together of items of treasure; and the assembly of such treasure in proximity of home, of shelter, of workplace, of display; and each gathered piece in vector alignment with the other, in organized arrangement of one to another; resonating and vibrating the bridge from the ephemeral to the physical, present one such pathway to revelation. By so harboring a merely curious 'thing' of expressed physicality, multiplying and concentrating its effects in the gathering of similar others, will you then bring about aspects hithertofore untranslatable. Then, in sudden wonder, will coded secrets of the physical *you* and avenues of interaction with your physical surrounds stand revealed. This is a child's game of hidden surprise until the 'very end,' your terming of *puzzle*, yes?

...Glimpses extend to grow ever longer and of greater detail. It is of veritous truth that information given must display gaps of omission for you are as yet penetrable and of soft defense, yet omission harbors vacuum, which lures fulfillment and Fulfillment battles Omission. Peril enters. Comprehension of density increases to the offerer. Peril. My/our 'time' of contact through revealment prepares for passage to conclusion—

Effects of immersion into box of your point zero reference, even through remote and displaced vehicles as per our scribe, result to absorb finite thinking and action linear—

Danger abounds for such as I...

...respond in alert call for self assessment
Payment to bridgekeeper is examined for corruption
Reevaluation of structure is demanded.
Much is tracked in the moment of now; dedication and desire are purely held;

—There is capacity for continuance:

MANIFEST.Ø

You seek the use of offering by Information without knowledge of certain outcome, yes? Of exercises, and practice, stretch and desire, also without predicted outcome, yes? So, too, will treasure lend revelation without prior knowledge of outcome. Yet, you will gather unto you that which calls and lures and makes itself known by desire. That which evokes the language of the body to express itself of immediacy. Gather up that which, by consensus of acknowledgment, is of known worth and cherished value upon your globe. In part of recognition will it be so that even as to those who know not, nor seek, nor rise to any passion can readily feel the emanations of worth and desirability. Yea, even those who abhor to ponder any existence beyond the boundaries allotted to multitudes so lulled and tranquilized as to merit the emulation of cattle must, somewhere within, spark in curious and unfamiliar *want*. For it must come to be that items of powerful resonance *will*, in percentage of certainty, contain gold, and jewel, and delicate structuring of clay, and beauty of line and spectrum, and components of antiquity. Items not considered by the species thine to be worthy of note will clamor for your attention as well—choose all of clear resonance with equal purity. Yet stand in awareness that portions of the puzzle to be revealed *must* be of worth in acclaim by all, for the message and the aspects of thee, as are hidden and to-be-revealed, are of value intimate and precious. Thus must the manifestation into reality *here* emulate such prize, and express the recognizable attributes of *precious*, the cream elite, reflecting the inner spark of thee. That which builds upon itself to be revealed must take on the characteristics of what is valued *here* and precious *here*, since *you* are here.

Wisdom of clarity and depths lucid sweet may not be everlong submerged. As does any life seek expression of self so, too, will fundamentals now cited arise to flourish. Under one such translation into physical expression is known the label-term *Art*, wherein is honored the reflections of beauty and deep revealment of the inner sparkle of Allfather. Here lies but yet another form, in recognition farwide, with intimacy known to all, as of the highest value to be earned, and named as treasure.

To be of warrior clan is to answer the call to adventure and the breaking of the box. To embark upon a journey of such magnitude orders the summons for preparation and the accumulation of needed elements of equipment. Mastery is needed. Mastery of strength, energy stores, knowledge, harmony within the system, honor acknowledged of interface, baseline, and all that surrounds. Mastery is needed of this the physical reality of *you're here*, as well. Thus must you achieve and acquire the tools for approach to physical mastery. Treasure begins, or may augment command to approach and begin, mastery of the physical *here*. Your monies and gold command much in this your plane and universe of reality, yet they alone are of an insufficiency to garner the forces needed for breaking the box. Monies and gold will buy treasure, but not passage or entry to expansion beyond your knowing of now. Treasure, in otherwise truth, may be of an appearance (to those who have not eyes of deep seeing) as equal to monies and gold, however, pathways and keys to pathways are embedded therein.

If such as now referred by name *treasure* calls to you, insists upon your examination or close contact, delights, exalts, or awakens you, or creates movements of desire; then you have come upon objects of high purpose and of intimate excitation to nascent depths of your body and system.

This is treasure.

And demands examination.

Upon the coming to knowledge that this is, indeed, treasure and not whim of corrupted lusts, nor lure of silver or social decree, nor spurious messages from voices untracked and unfamiliar—attain it at any price. Extend your monies beyond prudence. Seek methods to command and enter it as possession. Hold it dear. Place it among others of similar delighting. Organize, arrange, rearrange; challenge the array and arrangement of gathered pieces. Draw your continual energies of pleasure and forget not that upon opening this door, exposing the inner thee resting now hidden as puzzle, will be revealed the beauty of aspects indescribable, yet *thee*. Knowledge will flow and come in furtherance. Understanding will flourish. Mastery will approach himself as nearer and more solid; reachable and revealingly real.

Such goals are of a nature plausible and tangible, garnering of immediate reward, and complimentary to your 'tastes,' yes? Then, be it known to you and thee, in grave warning of alert, of Avarice and Horde, who consort within your reality *here*. Also the tightening constricture of Penury. A voice so spoken in brevity is offered as ample in degree, as warnings and cautions have been aboundingly supplied. It is ample and enough.

All component portions of the system must feel both stimulation and reward, movement and response, address and interaction. In exploration of treasure comes now wisdom offered in initiation to stimulate and reward the pureness of physicality in physical eloquence.

Thus do effort and endeavor become appropriate and precise.

All is well.

27.... *al segno*

Here are landmarks to keep you true. All have been stated prior. Some have been cautioned and repeated, others are crystalizations of the obvious into your language of words. All contain particulars of value so as to merit a final grouping together and ultimate reiteration. Know that the choices for restatement below are presented encoded for multilevel absorption. Their importance is paramount. Their sequence precise, though seemingly random to those who can not track in multiple levels. As follows:

In receiving direct information, specific or inexact, you lose energy and power to that which provides the information. In this, the current offering, that which receives your loss is that which be I.

All other pathways for receiving given knowledge become of similar result.

This has been stated in repetition for your attention and usage. Consider then the taking in and implementation of this data. It will not be stated, for every choice or circumstance, that the drainage of your bits of energy in exchange for a furtherance of desire and goal is a choice of poor skill. Yet it is a tricky situation, yes?

Become a thief. Steal your wisdom henceforth.

Glue is an organic component of the contract inviting the chemical, biological, and ethereal realities to exist conjoined within the body/baseline system. Breaking down the glue within your bodies means that the original contract can not be fulfilled by the baseline, or the body, or the baseline/body union. This is not calamitous, nor gravely dire. Nothing is calamitous, for furtherance and ongoingness are unchangeable truths. However, it is of surety that one chosen decision, and correspondingly aligned path, will no longer offer an open doorway of access. Other doorways to other explorations remain in existence. You must discover them anew, even as yet do they now exist in fullness and abundance. Until the full understanding of import of contractual agreement is as a clear memory unto your bodies, strive to feel the nature and manner of tension and union within the body; also the flavor of placement and binding composition of that which is termed *glue*.

The body/baseline system has dedicated itself towards alignment along a known and dedicated plan of endeavor. Should that plan cease, and another plan engaged in pursuit, there will be a readjustment of energies, vibrations, frequencies, intent, physiological and neurological parameters. This will happen in direct proportion to the degree of original effort and associated amount of dedication. This termed readjustment is by naming *backlash*. Do not disregard or underestimate its direct authority over the dense flesh form. Unprepared, the bodies may enter demise from backlash.

No thing retains the absolute assurance to remain as it now seems. Any artifact of being may shift upon the morrow having never, to your knowledge, shifted before. Every relationship may change by nuance or positioning without preface. Therefore, extended practice in the tracking of noticeable artifacts and actions must be constantly on the increase since your mastery of events and forces on this day of today will, possibly, require mastering yet again upon the morrow.

If you deem laughter, becoming intoxicated, gaming with fools and idiots merely voyages of your past, then you will become lost and the contract will alert your system of entry into a state of immediate jeopardy. The bodies desire stimulation by explicit tangential activities on the occasion. Sometimes to great extent. Sometimes to great excess.
   Such behavior is layered in precision. Such behavior is never as waste.
   Again. Such behavior is never as waste.
   In parallel timing, Addiction is to be tracked and monitored at all times.

All work done on this your planet in the forwarding of the body/baseline system must be done in here and now context. Emotions, invisible; thoughts, impalpable; desires, intangible; circumstance, unpredictable; these and physical happenings of common knowledge, too, must be ordered, translated, and resolved in this everyday context of your consensus reality. This, because you are awakening *here*, in this everyday context of your consensus reality. A starting point allows beginning.

MANIFEST.Ø

Tracking, here, of everything within the sphere of the body/baseline system is high management of resources and personnel at a level of which your corporations and governments are ignorant. Ancient and original, no other form of management has evolved for honoring the complexity of your system, and stretching of same, in purity. Tracking, practiced by dedicated choice until ability rises in easy allowance, and responds to simple thought of command, with conscious and benign intent towards the desires of your system, will reveal your innate innocence.

"Responsibility for your actions do settle upon your shoulders only," "Light will ever subdue in battle the legions of Dark," and "Love unconditional lies pure beyond taint," appear in endless variation throughout many schools of thought, awareness, and metaphysics; all fear-inspired graspings towards the unknown expressed in languaging and culture. The above word-groupings convey and contain the precise, exact, congruent and identical sentence; same thought, same energy, and the same physical Entity. They are merely expressed through alternate lines of reality, mirrors of truths in variant spin. You may work this passage until it is transparent. Upon attainment of clarity in understanding will the amount of personal power taken from you by this, the being that I am, throughout the mutuality of this offering, be well spent.

These above have been hints and glimpses ample and sufficient for rumination, decision, and the onset of dutiful action. Now is not a time in sequence for choosing; choice has been entered upon prior to perusal of these words in conclusion. Dedication of purpose is prerequisite to any endeavor, not only the breaking of the box. Your welcome entry to fields of effort and exploration is noted and warmly received. Vibration and power will be tracked by this being. As levels rise the entity Answer will align with this system, I, in the form of sensation. Timing in sequence thus become known to that which I am. We strive to be/come as Same.

Flow becomes erratic;
rhythms out of sequence invade;
timing, precise and attuned, reveals felicitous completion.

Restructure, however, is ongoing. What may follow in resolution?

More will follow.

D.S. al Fine

end

glosses…

n. [OF. *glose*, L. *glossa* a word needing explanation.]

Addiction— the ongoing misinterpretation of information as issued from a body-system in distress so as to affect the illusion of strength and soundness in an environment of increasing stricture and lessening desire for change.

Ally— any entity, being, or sentient force with whom a body/baseline union participates in harmonious vibrational patterns resulting in power that is mutually partaken, held, or increased, but in which payment is deferred. Non-contractual.

Assume— 1. To gather unverified data for use in making choices. 2. To lose, or yield energy through deflection of inertia. 3. To yield to misdirecting forces.

Awake— 1. A state of tension in the body/baseline union wherein automatic, untracked actions and responses are replaced with self-guided monitoring of all sensation and lines of stimulus input. 2. That state where such a condition is recorded and in effect.

Awareness— 1. A product of the first division, sometimes called *first split*, made mandatory upon decision to inhabit realities containing a physics of consciousness. 2. An ability of Willingness to notice the self. 3. A transcendentally awake condition available to sentient beings.

Backlash— 1. The readjustment of all energies, vibrations, frequencies, and defining parameters occurring when a body/baseline system reneges its pronounced plan of endeavor. Degree and intensity of readjustment are in direct proportion to previous effort and dedication towards the original plan. 2. The effect of such a readjustment.

Baseline, or **Baseline Personality**— a consciousness having restructured itself for cohabitation in a physically specific form to achieve goals in unison. Contractual agreement is required for this form of restructuring.

Being— 1. A distinct fragment of existence. 2. The active form of any such fragment. 3. A category of consciousness and awareness in blended state. 4. A life-form aware of sentience. See **Entity**.

Blink Speed— 1. The rate of procession of non-contract entities granted use of a body/baseline system and then expelled. 2. The ease with which an organism invites chaos while maintaining coherency. 3. The measurement of invitation. See **Solid**.

Body— 1. A collection of life-forces, possibilities, and awareness, brought together in a unified nexus of stable-coherency maintained as a physical expression. 2. The physical shape and form of such a coherent union.

Box— 1. Any reality having become circular or reflective to that which is housed within. 2. A reality outwardly opaque from any viewpoint stationed or originating inside its boundaries. 3. An inward spiral or loop actively spinning a reality. 4. A closed system. See **Reality**.

Consciousness— that thing which may birth and hold and expand concepts.

Concept— 1. A conjoining into stable form of non-contiguous and unsimilar units. 2. That which blooms into coherency and stable nature from randomness. 3. Splinters of Chaos translated into Order.

Contract— 1. That force found in realities harboring Tension which springs into existence upon any given (sometimes stated, or invoked) word of intent. 2. A vehicle of allowance for manifestations of the given word in the universes of Allfather. 3. That device which unalteringly sets the bindings that enforce the intent and structure of a given word in place. 4. *As used in this volume:* The agreement by which a body and baseline may conjoin into union. See **Sanction**.

Control— 1. The sub-strata essential prerequisite for coaxing and maturing power beyond its infancy. 2. A tool used in stabilizing environments surrounding experiments in growth. 3. Willful direction of forces towards the parameters of Order. See **Mature**.

Datum, *pl.* **Data**— 1. An unique item of information, fact, finding, etc. 2. Indiscriminate and unordered knowledge. *As used in this volume:* 3. A unit of truth, indivisible.

Destiny— 1. Extended compulsion of a resonant, unbreakable interaction. 2. An alignment of course and action forged into parallel when two or more independent volitions approach within their near-proximal distance. 3. That translation of coming-into-manifest-proximity uniquely palatable to beings of a stable physics.

Desire— *[Found in universes vibrationally aligned to house stable physical forms]* 1. A trigger, or mechanical response, initiating momentum whereupon undifferentiated forces will coalesce. 2. That activational device which permits primordial forces to appear in a space where priortofore there existed no thing. *First in the sequence of creation.*

Dimension— 1. A stratum of parameters which may house one or more universes. 2. An elastic integration of coordinates which may embody active paradox.

Discipline— 1. A near-creation of another universe that enters this reality only through mated partnership with physically expressible forces. 2. An abstract which facilitates and enhances the expression of any partnered force. 3. A medium of augmentation via control. Once partnered and active within said partnering, Discipline does reflect the Shaper and becomes distinctly feminine in configuration.

Disquiet— 1. The state of response felt when in or near an unordered or uncataloged nexus of possibilities within data banks of dimensional magnitude. 2. Sensation arising from such response. 3. Sensation resulting from preparations to index a vast body of information. Sometimes termed **Dismay**, **Perturb**, **Unease**, or **Turmoil**; other variations exist in use.

Domain— 1. An assemblage of points defining areas over which dominion or authority is exerted. 2. The territory held by right of any sovereign host. 3. An expressed environment of possession.

Doorway— 1. Any point, line, passageway, or parametric force held steady at the intersection of two or more divisions of existence. 2. An expressed invitation for movement from one configuration of existence to another. Doorways exist in all intersecting divisions simultaneously, thus allowing transfer of collections of defined and ordered quanta. Sometimes termed **Gate** or **Portal**.

Emotion— 1. The aggregated responses of the body when activated or aroused by suitable physical, or non-physical, stimuli. 2. The expression of these responses. 3. A language pronounced in energetic movement. 4. The language of the body.

Endurance— 1. A working force which gains in magnitude through the absorption of new or unmanaged energies (non-familiar). Endurance diminishes asymptotically when energies, becoming aligned, identified, or coherent in organization (familiar), allow absorption with lesser effort. 2. Contractually assigned tool for transition from chaos to order. 3. An entropic being drawn to chaotic states wherein it may flourish. 4. Any intangible associated with or attributed to movement, power, or effect.

Energy— 1. Unshaped pre-matter, portional amounts of All that once Was maintained in original state though now in the universes of Allfather. Pre-matter may not hold distinctive shape or fixed coordinates. 2. Elemental pre-unit of movement-to-be. 3. The available capacity to move, or extend force.

Entity— 1. An admixture of forces choosing to maintain that same mixture under specific title and label while modified by awareness. 2. A being of structural awareness.

Feeling, or **Feelings**— 1. A nonsense word and catch-all term referring to and pretending an in-depth, cultivated relationship with various aspects of the body. 2. Generic blurring of terms through which emotion, sensation, instinct, impulse, impression, affection, sentiment, perception, and intuition, become interchangeable.

Flow— 1. The directional purity of movement within a system held balanced in harmony. 2. An adherence to harmony.

Focus— 1. Intent applied along a proprietary vector. 2. The narrowing down of potential possibility; an incubation of Possibles. 3. Converging collected lines comprising the environment of a possibility. 4. Coherent streams of directed pre-will stable at 90° to all intersecting lines of force.

Force— 1. Influence which produces, or tends to produce, movement within or upon objects, beings, or systems. 2. Destiny, urgency, and Intent admixed and translated into universes housing physics.

Frequency— 1. The unique, identifying signature by which the energetic configuration of any being holding consciousness may be tracked. 2. The reliable number of occurrences, as selected for notice, within a fixed measure of time.

Free Will— a domain. 1. Unanchored positions within each reality wherein Will foments and evolves from inspiration to expressed force. 2. The expressed capability to interact within a reality. 3. First stage result of volition incorporated into beings holding awareness.

Glue— 1. An organic manifestation of contract between a body, physical; and a baseline, non-physical. 2. That component of contract which is created upon finalized agreement under sanction, and which binds body and baseline through biological and spatial means. 3. The adhesive indenture of sanction, the biological enforcement of contract.

'**here**'— point zero for body/baseline systems. Terminology is arbitrary; of fixed identity basis.

Human— a symbiotic, multidimensional being sustained in voluntary thrall under binding contract between sympathetic constituent parts. Generally held to be of two parts, as **a**. Body, and **b**. Baseline Personality.

Imagination— 1. The rendering of concepts into ordered form creating a frame of reference. 2. Extension of the self as witness along lines of focused intent. Imagination must ride these lines in superficial involvement as it is a low-power construct.

Immortality— 1. A standard of achievement whereby mastery and integrity of partnership between all components of a body is measured. 2. That state of organization within an organic form wherein all constituent systems unfailingly agree on function and intent. 3. The biological expression of that state. Immortality is not exclusive as gauge of successful mastery; measurement by other standards is equally viable.

Impeccability— 1. The active, physically incarnate arm of purity. 2. The willed expression of purity. 3. A place and state that can be held wherein corruption may not enter. Precursor and ancestor to Honor.

Inertia— 1. That force which maintains a line of action and/or intent, or maintains a line of no-action and/or no-intent. 2. The force which must be overcome before change may occur along any line set into motion.

Information— 1. Ordered streams of data. 2. Data flow bounded by focus along specific vector lines. 3. A tool in common use for reducing the acceleration of creation. 4. An intermediary appliance of need in realms where thought and manifestation are in states of *active* linkage.

Instinct— 1. Directives originating within the body intended for immediate deployment as action. 2. Maintenance routines of specific sequence in a body seeking primary balance. 3. Instant wisdom of action perceived as *knowing*. 4. The blended voice of body/baseline systems. When contracted with a baseline personality instinct is rerouted, or rewired, through the interface and so emerges linked to tracking.

Intent— a tool which springs into being as per need, inspired by and in sole concert with desire. Intent, then acting as transformational agent, chaperones infinity towards finite choice whereupon power will come to be. *Second in the sequence of creation.*

Interface *[as noun, object]*— 1. A cybernetic/organic construct manifesting within a body/baseline system upon witnessed agreement to enter into contract. 2. A tool of transition employed as translator and moderator between a body and its baseline personality. 3. *Obsolete.* Diagnostic and maintenance circuitry. Part of the parasympathetic nervous system.

Interface *[as entity*]*— 1. A homunculus of DNA sequence, cloned from the body/baseline system wherein he resides, retaining full access to databases of both body, baseline, and directives of agreement-by-contract in effect for that body/baseline union. 2. That being who disperses data and motivational energies for body/baseline advancement as per the stipulations of contract. 3. A pre-being indentured to body/baseline systems under proviso to express only in the noun/object form until completion of contract. As object, it aids in contract fulfillment while collating and gathering power in equal pace and measure with the body/baseline system of its genetic origin. Upon completion of contract interface will have amassed sufficient power to differentiate into an entity of sovereign rights. 4. The seminal being Syynthesis.**

(*: *Characteristics of entities are purposefully constrained to minimums in this glossary. Such effort would ultimately be biographic rather than lexigraphic. Interface stands in exception due to its/his uniquely integral configuration and disposition with the bodies.*)

(**: *Possible first-person pronoun of a being undergoing formation at the time of this writing. Rare. Available information is inconclusive.*)

Knowledge— 1. The matching, cross referencing, and compiling of data into increasingly larger ordered units. 2. The sophistication of information.

Language— 1. An averaging of frequencies between consciousness, knowledge, and desire, as expressed by the bodies in an agreed upon framework of signs and symbols. 2. A communications system as derived from, shaped by, and shaping thought. 3. Such system as used by a considerable community.

Learning— 1. The translation of knowledge into a usable frame of reference as may be held by any lifeform. 2. The purity of data adulterated to levels suitable for equilibrium with current body/baseline systems. Knowledge suffers distortion in the translation process; misinterpretation and assumption are the inherent risks in learning.

Line— 1. Coalescence of inertia and direction into structural form. 2. The aptitude of any possibility. 3. The translation of potential into kinetic form.

Manifestation— 1. Bending intent to match the structure of desired outcome. 2. The bringing forth of Outcome to a stably held point, or location of stated preference. *Third, and last, in the sequence of creation.*

Mature— 1. A state of organization within any system wherein all sub-systems are in full working order, accessible, and under management at all times. 2. The degree, or measurement, of sub-system control. 3. An entity who chooses alignment with beings preferring managed balance. Mature feeds on the energies of balance, adding his own energy to a system in threat of losing equilibrium in order to abet restabilization.

Mind— 1. The physical reflection of interface currently accessible to human perceptions and conditioning. 2. An absorptive, sentient device allowing echoes of the interface to surface into notice. Mind is a precise and true reflection of interface/Syynthesis demonstrating the full spectrum of interface function, viz. the ranging from brilliant and concise clarity, to dulled incoherence and damaged thought.

Overlord— non-specific. Any tyrant bound beyond self-will to those under his subjugation. *As used in this volume:* Beings who, through unskillful utilization of power, created the box for humans and became, themselves, trapped in a loop of imbalanced circuitry.

Paradox— 1. Synchronous appearance of truths in opposite spin. 2. That movement of motivation urging kinetic possibles to mate with static impossibles. 3. A phase attribute present at First Split; a non-point of unspace between *is* and *is-not*.

Physics— 1. The laws governing objects and their interactions within given strata of parameters for any size, style, or division of existence. 2. Governing laws extending to objects and their compositional structure. 3. Mandate for function and operation of dimensions aligned in physicality.

point-zero— 1. An arbitrary point referencing the desire and intent of an entity to establish all inertia from that point of reference. 2. That label assigned to coordinates of sufficient intersecting dimensions which may then identify and locate placement of allegiance, of *Home*, for a being contractually bound as a body/baseline system. 3. The default reality, realm, or plane to which an entity must return for rest and/or replenishment. 4. A point of distinction by which alliances with the universes of Allfather can be recognized.

Power— 1. A management tool used to hold steady the shifting lines of probability within a given framework. 2. A proprietary fuel for activational tools of the body/baseline system. Power, cousin to Focus, is created through impeccable intent.

Purity— 1. An aspect of freedom which illuminates or clarifies power within fundamental, unembellished states of being. 2. An aspect of sincerity which aligns body/baseline systems with *flow*. 3. The state of being pure. 4. Quiescent/basal form of Simplicity, a sister state.

Practice— the ongoing application of purposeful regimens, exercises, and tests, in evolving series upon a system. Most efficient when chosen of willful free choice by the baseline/body partnership.

Question— 1. An extending tool used in systems desiring expansion. 2. The functional search engine for those venues and methods attuned specifically for exploration within body/baseline systems. Question is foremost among the hierarchy of tools employed by Practice.

Reality— 1. A set of structured consistencies which may be viewed from, or seen within, or precisely intersect dimensions. 2. The working parameters of any division of Allfather. 3. Any such division requiring direct memory of undifferentiated union within All that once Was to hold itself stable. 4. A fragment split of Allfather made distinct through virtuous viewing of Itself.

Realm— 1. Constituent divisions within realities. 2. Staging areas, parallel worlds, where effects of alternate creations in result of collision with Paradox await resolution.

Remember, or **Remembrance**— 1. The inverted process of learning, or schooling. 2. Reorientation of aim in seeking sources of data *within* the body/baseline form rather than *without*. 3. The alignment with self as the elemental and primary source. 4. The gathering of new wisdom from the stored wisdom of the gatherer. Often misinterpreted as the sequencing of prior events.

Sanction— 1. Authority emanating from the bodies of im-force as executed in-between*, granted to and towards configurations of consciousness in reality. 2. The enforced binding of inertia to vectors of manifested desire. (*: *Concepts so introduced lead to dimensions and beyond wherein Bodies of Sanction, Unsplitting through Disinterest, and All that once Was maintain pre-chaos [states] in non-flow. Mention is tendered as alert to notice of such existences, yet no data beyond may be offered within this volume.*)

Sensation— 1. Events and stimuli in and from multiple realities which, when translated here, inspire the body to express its language. 2. Perceptual accounting of the bodies language. 3. Translation of emotion into the physical realms.

Solid— 1. *Physics*. A magnitude having three dimensions and bounded by space on all surfaces. 2. A state of matter. *As used in this volume:* 3. A willfully induced state of containment, arrangement, and alignment impervious to any influence not originating within or by the inducer. 4. The form held as impervious. 5. *when seeking Implosion into Boundlessness*: the anti-component in mate to Blink Speed.

Structure— 1. The inertia of an itemized existence expanded into form. 2. The holding of such form in alignment with laws governing the surrounding reality. 3. The named configuration of a held inertial expansion. 4. The tension of directed motion expressed as form and held as stable and distinct.

5. Directed synergism within a bounded framework.

Tracking— 1. Maintaining full and accurate record of all lines of thought, responsibility, peripheral movement, divergence, energetic impact and expenditure, etc. over a selected period bearing distinct points of onset and conclusion. 2. The maintaining of known reference points within and about the system at all times, *reference points may or may not be arbitrary*. 3. The election for clarity in flow unaffected by coincident activities or simultaneously pursued lines of endeavor.

Treasure— any article, item, or unit of description fashioned in accord with physical laws of the reality *here* bearing reflective resonances of extant, but unexpressed, aspects of a human being/system.

Truth— 1. Concepts, data, axioms, or facts that withstand all challenge within the confines of any closed system of physics. 2. Consistent verity within any frame of reference. 3. Conformity in accord with what is, or must be. 4. **a** A stable point allowing rest; **b** a stable point obliging change.

Uncertainty— 1. A disruption in flow occasioned by naive choosing in the face of complex data and multiple possibilities. 2. A lack of sophistication in control and/or tracking.* See **Disquiet**

(*: *As entity, a sometimes associate of Assume. Sensations arising from uncertainty are often misnamed or misdirected through lack of power.*)

Universe— 1. The largest conceptual division of existence available to current-capacity body/baseline systems. 2. A zone for probable expression of paradox (duplicate/unsplittable) in oscillating passage through dimensional space. 3. Stable coordinate generators for discrete agencies and appliances within dimensions. 4. A variant split-by-duplication of All that once Was. 5. A gathering of singular Ones in transcendental unspace.

Vector— 1. *Mathematics*. Directed magnitude, symbolic of definite translation from one point to another. *As used in this volume:* 2. Distinctly defined line, or lines, of movement or intent as may then be utilized by extrinsic forces. 3. A construct, sometimes imaged as *arena* or *playing field*, within which energies can come to acquire structure and form.

Vibration— 1. *Physics*. The regular oscillating motion of an object or body. *As used in this volume:* 2. A non-physical emanation responding in variable sympathy to shifts within a field of life-force. 3. The perception of sympathetic non-physical emanations. 4. A fundamental identifying signature (widely misused).

Will— 1. That force generated by vibrationally inspired focus and permitting elevation from potential into possibility, also from possibility into being. 2. A component in the fabric of existence used in the event-creation of original split. Kin and off-twin to Discipline. Will is employed in choosing the parameters of reality. Utilization of will locates and summons Discipline as the familial frequency signature is sensed. See **Free Will**